Hiking
North Carolina's
State Parks

Hiking
North Carolina's
State Parks

The Best Trail Adventures from the
Appalachians to the Atlantic

JOHNNY MOLLOY

The University of North Carolina Press

Chapel Hill

A SOUTHERN GATEWAYS GUIDE

This book was published with the assistance of the
Blythe Family Fund of the University of North Carolina Press.

Designed by Jamison Cockerham
Set in Scala, Scala Sans, Alegreya Sans, and Officina Sans
by Kristina Kachele Design, llc

Manufactured in the United States of America

The University of North Carolina Press has been a member
of the Green Press Initiative since 2003.

Cover illustration: Widow Falls in Stone Mountain State Park in North
Carolina © iStock/gsagi. Page i: Fort Macon State Park. Page ii–iii: High
Shoals Falls, South Mountains State Park. Page vi: Triple-trunked tree offers
a hiker respite at Eno River State Park. Page xvi: The falls just above High
Shoals Falls, South Mountains State Park. Page xxiii: Shorts Lake reflects
autumn glory at Crowders Mountain State Park. Page xxiv: Squeezing past
the Panthers Den at Occoneechee Mountain State Natural Area.

LIBRARY OF CONGRESS CATALOGING-IN-PUBLICATION DATA
Names: Molloy, Johnny, 1961– author.
Title: Hiking North Carolina's state parks : the best trail adventures
from the Appalachians to the Atlantic Ocean / Johnny Molloy.
Other titles: Southern gateways guide.
Description: Chapel Hill : The University of North Carolina Press, [2022] |
Series: A Southern gateways guide
Identifiers: LCCN 2021041602 | ISBN 9781469668239 (pbk; alk. paper) |
ISBN 9781469668246 (ebook)
Subjects: LCSH: Hiking—North Carolina—Guidebooks. | Trails—North
Carolina—Guidebooks. | Natural areas—North Carolina—Guidebooks. |
Parks—North Carolina—Guidebooks. | North Carolina—Guidebooks.
Classification: LCC GV199.42.N66 M654 2022 |
DDC 796.5109756—dc23/eng/20211020
LC record available at https://lccn.loc.gov/2021041602

FOR THE

FOUNDERS, MAINTAINERS, AND SUPPORTERS

OF

NORTH CAROLINA'S STATE PARKS

Contents

Piedmont

Coast and Coastal Plain

Mountains
Hike Summary Chart

	Hike	State Park	Distance (miles)
1	Rainbow Falls Hike	Gorges State Park	3.8
2	Canebrake Trail	Gorges State Park	10.6
3	Mount Mitchell Circuit	Mount Mitchell State Park	5.6
4	Lake James Hike	Lake James State Park	5.1
5	Views from the South Mountains	South Mountains State Park	8.6
6	High Shoals Falls Hike	South Mountains State Park	4.9
7	Profile Trail	Grandfather Mountain State Park	8.2
8	Cragway Hike	Grandfather Mountain State Park	3.7
9	Elk Knob Hike	Elk Knob State Park	3.8
10	Views from Mount Jefferson	Mount Jefferson State Natural Area	4.7
11	Riverbend Trail	New River State Park	7.7
12	River Run Hike	New River State Park	2.5
13	Stone Mountain Loop	Stone Mountain State Park	8.2

Time (hours)	Difficulty	Highlights
2.5	Moderate	Hidden Falls, Rainbow Falls, Turtleback Falls, Stairway Falls
5.3	Difficult	Giant swinging bridge over scenic lake, river, and creek
3.3	Moderate to difficult	Highest point in the East, views, spruce-fir forests
2.4	Moderate	Lake views, pre-park history, additional park activities
4.2	Moderate to difficult	Remote ridges, multiple views, backpacking possibilities
2.3	Moderate	High Shoals Falls, other cascades, extensive interpretive information
5.1	Difficult	Iconic trail to multiple vista points amid spruce-fir forest
2.0	Moderate	Multiple views from outcrops on Grandfather Mountain, spruce woods
2.1	Moderate	Mountaintop vistas, high-country forest
2.3	Moderate	Panoramas galore
3.8	Moderate	River views, backcountry camping
1.2	Easy to moderate	River views, Stump homesite
4.4	Moderate to difficult	Granite domes, vistas, historic farm, waterfalls

Piedmont
Hike Summary Chart

Hike	State Park	Distance (miles)
14 Crowders Mountain Circuit	Crowders Mountain State Park	5.4
15 The Pinnacle Hike	Crowders Mountain State Park	5.5
16 Lake Shore Trail	Lake Norman State Park	5.4
17 Views from Pilot Mountain	Pilot Mountain State Park	2.7
18 Mountain Trail at Pilot Mountain	Pilot Mountain State Park	5.4
19 Yadkin River Hike	Pilot Mountain State Park	5.3
20 Hanging Rock Highlight Hike	Hanging Rock State Park	4.6
21 Cook's Wall Loop	Hanging Rock State Park	5.8
22 Moore's Knob Tower Hike	Hanging Rock State Park	4.7
23 Haw River Boardwalk	Haw River State Park	1.9
24 Three Rivers / Fall Mountain Hike	Morrow Mountain State Park	5.0
25 Morrow Mountain Hike	Morrow Mountain State Park	5.6
26 Occoneechee Mountain Hike	Occoneechee Mountain State Natural Area	2.8
27 Buckquarter Creek Loop	Eno River State Park	4.9
28 Fannys Ford Loop	Eno River State Park	4.5
29 Eno Quarry / Cabelands Hike	Eno River State Park	5.1
30 Bobbitt Hole Loop	Eno River State Park	2.7
31 Pump Station Walk	Eno River State Park	1.7
32 Sals Branch Trail	William B. Umstead State Park	2.6
33 Sycamore Loop	William B. Umstead State Park	7.2
34 Company Mill Trail	William B. Umstead State Park	5.8
35 Vista Point Hike	Jordan Lake State Recreation Area	4.8
36 New Hope Circuit	Jordan Lake State Recreation Area	5.1
37 Campbell Creek Loop	Raven Rock State Park	5.1
38 Raven Rock Loop	Raven Rock State Park	5.2
39 Weymouth Woods Sandhills Loop	Weymouth Woods Sandhills Nature Preserve	3.8
40 Medoc Mountain Circuit	Medoc Mountain State Park	4.6

Time (hours)	Difficulty	Highlights
3.0	Moderate	Grand views, geology
3.0	Moderate	Multiple vistas, geology, lake
2.5	Moderate	Lake views
1.5	Easy to moderate	Views, bluffs, rock climbers, biodiversity
2.7	Moderate	Vistas, trail around Pilot Mountain
2.4	Moderate	Old canal works and islands on the big Yadkin River
2.8	Moderate	Three waterfalls and outcrop with stellar views
3.2	Moderate	Panoramic vistas along stream and lake
2.6	Moderate	360-degree views from historic tower
1.1	Easy	Lake-viewing deck, wetland boardwalk
2.5	Moderate	Aquatic and land views, history
3.0	Moderate to difficult	Mountaintop views, high point in state park
1.3	Easy to moderate	Loop to distant views, bluffs, quarry
2.6	Moderate	Interesting geology, historic mill, home ruins
2.4	Moderate	Iconic swinging bridge, riverside rapids, backpack camping
2.5	Moderate	Eno River, Eno Quarry, Cabe Mill site
1.4	Easy	Trail along Eno River to Bobbitt Hole, backcountry campground
1.0	Easy	Pump station ruins, dam ruins, Eno River
1.2	Easy	Sals Branch, Big Lake, good exercise trail
3.8	Moderate to difficult	Streamside hiking, homesites
3.0	Moderate	Mill site, Crabtree Creek, less-visited woods
2.2	Easy to moderate	Vistas of Jordan Lake, old tobacco barn
2.7	Moderate	Jordan Lake views, walk-in camping
2.7	Moderate	Loop to Lanier Falls via Campbell Creek
2.8	Moderate	Highlight reel hike to Little Creek, Raven Rock, overlook, lock remains
2.1	Easy to moderate	Old-growth pines, swamp thickets, red-cockaded woodpecker habitat
2.2	Moderate	Trail over Medoc Mountain and along creek bottoms

Coast and Coastal Plain
Hike Summary Chart

Hike	State Park	Distance (miles)
41 Merchants Millpond Loop	Merchants Millpond State Park	5.7
42 Bennetts Creek Hike	Merchants Millpond State Park	5.6
43 Jockeys Ridge Hike	Jockeys Ridge State Park	2.1
44 Pettigrew Double Hike	Pettigrew State Park	10.0
45 Tar Kiln Loop	Goose Creek State Park	7.2
46 Cliffs of the Neuse Hike	Cliffs of the Neuse State Park	3.9
47 Fort Macon Hike	Fort Macon State Park	3.5
48 Jones Lake Loop	Jones Lake State Park	4.4
49 Lake Waccamaw Loop	Lake Waccamaw State Park	4.5
50 Carolina Beach Hike	Carolina Beach State Park	5.6
51 The Hermit Hike	Fort Fisher State Recreation Area	3.0

Time (hours)	Difficulty	Highlights
2.9	Moderate	Merchants Millpond, Lassiter Swamp, alluring woods
2.8	Moderate	Swamp scenes, Bennetts Creek, pond spillway
1.6	Moderate	Giant dunes, beach views
5.0	Moderate to difficult	Phelps Lake views, historic Somerset Place, big trees
3.8	Moderate	Tidal waters, deep woods, wetlands, historic tar kilns
1.8	Easy to moderate	Park lake, Neuse River, cliff views above Neuse River
1.8	Moderate	Live oak forest, Atlantic Ocean beachcombing, restored Civil War fort
2.2	Easy to moderate	Mysterious bay lake with watery views
2.3	Moderate	Lake views amid varied ecosystems
3.1	Moderate	Beaches, huge dunes with views in coastal woods
1.5	Easy	Hermit home, trail along Atlantic Ocean

Recommended Hikes by Category

Best Hikes for Scenery

Best Hikes for Lake Lovers

Best Hikes for Stream/Waterfall Lovers

Best Hikes for Kids

Best Hikes for Dogs

Best Hikes for Human History

Best Hikes for Views

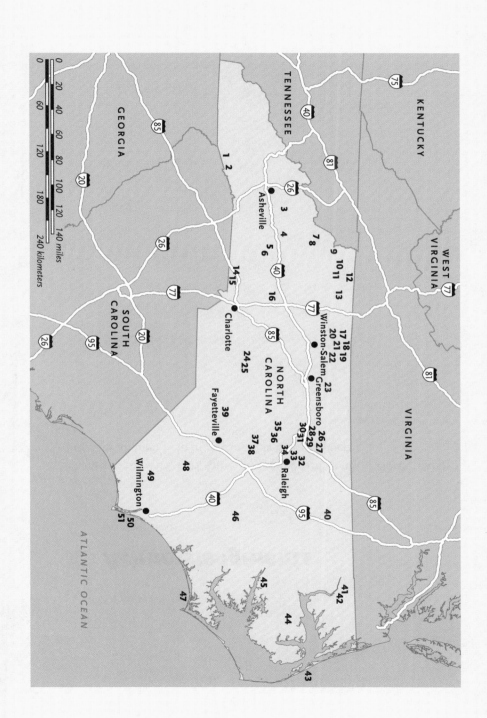

Scale

0 20 40 60 80 100 120 140 miles

0 20 40 60 80 100 120 180 240 kilometers

GEORGIA

TENNESSEE

KENTUCKY

WEST VIRGINIA

VIRGINIA

SOUTH CAROLINA

NORTH CAROLINA

ATLANTIC OCEAN

Asheville

Charlotte

Winston-Salem

Greensboro

Fayetteville

Raleigh

Wilmington

1 2
3
4
5 6
7 8
9
10 11
12
13
14 15
16
17 18
20 21 22
19
23
24 25
26 27
28 29
30 31
32
33
34
35 36
37 38
39
40
41 42
43
44
45
46
47
48
49
50
51

85
20
26
26
77
20
95
26
40
81
26
40
77
75
77
81
85
95
85
40

Acknowledgments

Thanks to my wife, Keri Anne, and to the University of North Carolina Press for all their help in making this guide happen.

Preface

It has been a humbling privilege and a challenging task to write a guide detailing the can't-miss hikes in North Carolina's state parks. May you use this compendium to enjoy North Carolina state parks as much as I have while undertaking this project. The Tar Heel State is blessed with a thriving state park system ranging from the state's highest point at Mount Mitchell in the Southern Appalachians to sea level along the mighty Atlantic Ocean, and a lot of special places in between. Hiking trails thread through these preserves and are our conduit to experience the wonders found within, whether they are the spruce-fir forests of the western highlands or the noteworthy crags of places like Pilot Mountain and Crowders Mountain or the massive dunes found at Jockeys Ridge. Other parks harbor North Carolina history within their bounds, from the bastion at Fort Macon State Park to the Hutchinson Farm at Stone Mountain State Park.

I have been exploring North Carolina's state parks for decades and looked forward to systematically combing the system for the best trail adventures for this book. Immediately coming to mind are certain scenes. On the coast I can see the turkey oak and pine forests rising over blinding white sands at Carolina Beach State Park, also home to the strange Venus flytrap. I can see the American flag waving in the breeze of Fort Macon while walking Atlantic Ocean beachfront. I can still look out on the endless waters of Lake Waccamaw. On the Piedmont, I remember spring rising with dogwoods blooming white at Eno River State Park, and the old mill sites of William B. Umstead State Park, which recall a slower time in Carolina. In the mountains I can see the Blue Ridge forming a backdrop above Lake James, the kaleidoscope of autumn colors while looking out from Mount Jefferson, as well as High Shoals Falls crashing in white froth. I recall a menagerie of superlative scenery that can be found along the hiking trails of these North Carolina state parks.

And what a rewarding task it was to capture the best scenes along the best hikes that together paint a mosaic of ecosystems within state park lands stretching literally from the mountains to the sea.

Throughout the process I kept looking for the best of the best and found some new sights that pleased this grizzled veteran—panoramas of the Pamlico River basin from trailside beaches at Goose Creek State Park, the wooded swamps of Merchants Millpond State Park where alligators lurk, and the waterfalls at Hanging Rock State Park. After completing the task of writing this book I came away with an even more profound respect for the preserved parcels that are North Carolina's state parks. I hope you will, too. Happy hiking!

Introduction

North Carolina's state parks reflect the natural abundance and variety within the Tar Heel State. These state preserves are located within each of the major physical provinces of North Carolina—the mountains, the Piedmont, and the coastal plain. Elevations of these state parks range from 6,684 feet atop Mount Mitchell to sea level along the Atlantic Ocean. All forty-one units actively managed as part of the state park system offer hiking trails of some length and description. The state park system boasts 19 million annual visitors, and its mission is "to inspire all its citizens and visitors through conservation, recreation and education." These three components are further broken down thus: "Conservation: To conserve and protect representative examples of North Carolina's natural beauty, ecological features, recreational and cultural resources within the state parks system; Recreation: To provide and promote safe, healthy and enjoyable outdoor recreational opportunities throughout the state; and Education: To provide educational opportunities that promote stewardship of the state's natural and cultural heritage."

So you can expect to see special natural components of North Carolina's landscape while engaging in outdoor activities from hiking, paddling, and camping, all the while learning about these special places that in turn will inspire you to preserve them for future generations.

North Carolina's state park system came to be when local citizens became alarmed that poor logging practices on Mount Mitchell were causing extensive erosion and unsightly scarring and reducing water quality around the famed peak. Governor Locke Craig went to see for himself, and on March 3, 1915, monies were appointed to purchase the lands of Mount Mitchell. Thus the state park system was born. Interestingly, the next park North Carolina acquired was clear across the state, astride the

Atlantic Ocean: Fort Macon, which it bought from the federal government for $1. Things sped up during the Great Depression of the 1930s, when several parks were added and developed by the Civilian Conservation Corps, including Morrow Mountain and Hanging Rock State Parks. And starting in 1935, the North Carolina state parks system had its own superintendent rather than being managed by other government entities. Later in the decade came Jones Lake State Park, which protects one of the unique Carolina bay lakes that dot the eastern part of the state. The state park system acquired more lands through donation and purchase. The establishment of Eno River State Park in a fast-growing corridor near the Raleigh, Durham, and Chapel Hill area displayed incredible foresight, and by preserving the massive dunes of Jockeys Ridge, the state saved the largest sand mountains remaining on the Atlantic coast. In the 1980s, waterside parks were established at Kerr Lake, Lake James, and Jordan Lake. More recently, iconic mountains were added to the system, with the establishment of Grandfather Mountain State Park and the formerly private attraction that is now Chimney Rock State Park.

Today the North Carolina state park system continues to shine and hold true to its conservation, education, and recreation mission. On the recreation front, Tar Heel state parks are an increasingly important getaway for state residents and visitors alike. And well they should be. We hikers can trek trails, as can mountain bikers and equestrians. Campers can spend the night at a multitude of campgrounds scattered throughout the state parks. Boaters can tackle scenic rivers and lakes. Anglers can vie for fish on mountain streams, Piedmont lakes, and the salty sea. Birders can explore high and low for their favorite species. The state parks are truly a recreation haven for all.

The North Carolina state parks have a rich history, magnificent beauty, and a wealth of trails, so I urge you to make the most of your trail experiences there. That is where this guide comes into play: I have assembled a mosaic of wide-ranging hikes that reflect the biodiversity of nature and the multiplicity of hiking experiences in North Carolina's state parks.

This guide is written to spare you hours of mind-numbing internet surfing, trying to find the best hikes at North Carolina's state parks. Your time is important, and I want you to experience rewarding hikes with family and friends. With that in mind, I mean to get you to the trailhead and on the path, where you can let the surroundings soak in, and then get you back to the trailhead in one piece, with a greater appreciation of nature's bounty, some rewarding exercise, and increased knowledge about the outdoor paradise found in North Carolina's state parks.

The best way to enjoy these lands is on foot. When you hike in Tar Heel state parks, the rewards increase with every footfall whether you are scaling highland crags, trekking along dancing streams to misty water-falls, or tramping the shores of coastal seas.

There is much to see and little time to see it all in our digital, hur-ried era, where phone, television, and computer screens rule the day. A respite in the natural world of North Carolina state parks will revitalize both mind and spirit. To smell the autumn leaves on a crisp afternoon at Umstead State Park, to climb to a lookout on Elk Knob, to view a historic plantation at Pettigrew State Park will add perspective to our lives.

That is where this book comes into play. It will help you make every moment and every step count, whether you are leading the family on a brief day hike or undertaking a challenging hike into wild woodlands. It will give you the knowledge to make the most of your precious time, so you can realize your outdoor experience to its fullest.

This book presents fifty-one hikes from which to choose. Included are classics such as High Shoals Falls at Stone Mountain State Park and the Profile Trail at Grandfather Mountain State Park. However, many hikes are off the beaten path, offering more solitude on the way to lesser-known yet equally scenic sights, such as Medoc Mountain and the tar kilns at Goose Creek.

Two types of day hikes are offered: out-and-back and loop hikes. Out-and-back hikes lead to a particular rewarding destination, returning via the same trail. The return trip allows you to see everything from the opposite vantage point. You may notice different trailside features on the second go-round, and returning at a different time of day may give the same path a surprisingly different character. Loop hikes deliver fresh scenery throughout the trek.

Day hiking is the most popular way to hike North Carolina state parks, but for those who want to see the cycle of the land go from day to night and back again, this guide offers hikes that can be backpacked. At North Carolina state parks, backpackers must preregister and pay a camping fee before overnighting.

To explore the lovely and varied lands of North Carolina state parks, to savor nature's wonder Tar Heel style, is a special experience. Here you can relax, find peace and quiet. Here you can also grasp beauty and splendor: the views from Pilot Mountain, the bluffs of Raven Rock, or the forests along Lake Waccamaw. In these preserved lands you can let your thoughts roam free in eye-pleasing settings, without being hemmed in by our fast-paced existence. The state parks of North Carolina are treasures of the Tar Heel State—so get out and enjoy them.

Planning Your Hike

Try to avoid crowded state parks during predictably busy times—Saturday afternoons, holiday weekends, or days with idyllic weather. Shoot for less popular times if possible, or get started early in the morning. Many state parks limit crowds and shut down entry when the crowd limit is reached.

A hike at a North Carolina state park should be a rewarding experience, especially if you are prepared. One of the first rules of hiking is to be ready for anything. Always consider worst-case scenarios like broken gear, a brutal thunderstorm, getting lost, hiking in the dark, or twisting an ankle.

The items listed below don't cost much money, don't take up much room in a pack, and don't weigh much, but they might just save your life.

Water The easiest way to stay hydrated is to bring treated water from home. Use durable bottles that don't leak. Consider bringing a water treatment system too, either iodine tablets or a filter.

Map Get a map over the internet or at visitor centers before you embark, and take pictures of the posted trail maps with your phone. Learn to read the GPS function on your phone, usually within a maps app. A map program will give you your position, and one loaded with the right maps can be invaluable.

First-aid kit A good-quality kit, including first-aid instructions, can help with a deep cut or simple sprains.

Knife A multitool device with pliers is best. You can pull out a splinter or repair a daypack. It is amazing how useful these can be.

Light A headlamp with extra batteries can save you from stumbling your way back to the trailhead. I wish I had a dime for every story someone has told me about their hike taking longer than expected.

Fire A lighter is one of the best inventions for outdoor enthusiasts.

Bring a lighter and perhaps something to start a fire with if you become chilled, lost, stranded overnight, or all of the above.

Extra food You should always have food in your pack when you've finished hiking. Keep wrapped, nonperishable foods such as nutrition bars in your pack in addition to what you add for each outing.

Extra clothes Bring rain protection and, depending on the weather, warm layers, gloves, and a warm hat. Which clothes are the most appropriate will change with the seasons, but you should always carry a rain jacket to keep you dry and warm enough to make it back to the trailhead.

Sun protection Don't forget sunglasses, lip balm, sunblock, and a sun hat if you are hiking before spring leaf-out or traversing open area such as Jockeys Ridge State Park.

With the above essentials you can focus on the beauty around you and have a safe, happy hike.

Finally, bring along your brain. A cool, calculating mind is the single most important piece of equipment you'll ever need on the trail. Think before you act. Watch your step. Plan ahead. Avoiding accidents before they happen is the best recipe for a rewarding and relaxing hike at North Carolina state parks.

How to Use This Guide

Each hike has its own unique description. A one-paragraph hike summary is located at the beginning of each hike. It gives an overview of what the hike is like—a general sketch of the terrain and what you might see along the way. Following the hike summary is an information box that allows the hiker quick access to pertinent information: hike distance, time, difficulty, highlights, cautions, best seasons, other trail users, hours, and trail contacts. Below is an example of a box included with a hike:

From the information box we can learn the details of each hike. This hike is 3.0 miles long and is an out-and-back. **Hiking time** is the average time it will take to cover the route. Hiking time factors in total distance, elevation gain, and trail conditions. Your own fitness level may make that hiking time longer or shorter, of course. **Difficulty** gives you an idea of how challenging the hike will be: easy, moderate, or difficult. This rating is subjective, but for each one I factored in the same elements as when I calculated hiking time—distance, elevation gain, and trail conditions. A long-distance walk with considerable elevation change on a remote wilderness trail deserves the "difficult" label, whereas a level walk on a graveled nature trail is called "easy." **Highlights** describes the can't-miss part of the trek. **Cautions** reviews any potential hiking hazards, so you can be aware on the front end. Obviously, this doesn't cover every potential pitfall of a given hike, but it does keep you apprised of any hike-specific hazards with which to contend, such as excessive sun (as in this example). **Best seasons** lets you know the time of year when this hike is most rewarding. **Other trail users** informs as to whether the path is hiker only or whether you will be sharing it with mountain bikers or equestrians. **Hours** keeps you apprised of park opening and closing times throughout the year. **Trail contacts** details ways to reach the particular state park of

41 MERCHANTS MILLPOND LOOP
Merchants Millpond State Park

Make a loop at stellar Merchants Millpond State Park, exploring the richly wooded hills and waters. The hike takes you along Merchants Millpond over knolls and into scenic vales before coming along Lassiter Swamp. Stop by a backcountry camp and cruise flatwoods before rolling through more hills that will challenge your perceptions of eastern North Carolina.

Distance 5.7-mile balloon loop

Hiking time 2.9 hours

Difficulty Moderate

Highlights Merchants Millpond, Lassiter Swamp, alluring woods

Cautions None

Best seasons Early fall through early summer

Other trail users None

Hours November–February, 8 a.m.–6 p.m.; March, October, 8 a.m.–8 p.m.; April–May, September, 8 a.m.–8 p.m.; June–August, 8 a.m.–9 p.m.; closed Christmas Day

Trail contact Merchants Millpond State Park, 176 Millpond Road, Gatesville, NC 27938, 252-357-1191, www.ncparks.gov/merchants-millpond-state-park

Finding the trailhead From the intersection of US 158 and NC 32 in Sunbury, head west on US 158 for 5.1 miles to turn left on Millpond Road. Drive southbound on Millpond Road for .9 mile, then turn left into the park. Pass the visitor center / park office and continue to where the road ends, at the park picnic area at .5 mile.

GPS trailhead coordinates 36.438118, –76.694288

Although it's two centuries old, Merchants Millpond is not natural. Formed when Bennetts Creek was dammed to provide waterpower for a sawmill, the unintended result is a gorgeous wooded wetland and lake. Now we have 760 watery acres scattered with regal bald cypress and

the given hike, including mailing address, phone number, and website. **Finding the trailhead** gives specific directions from a commonly known location to the hike's starting point. And the **GPS trailhead coordinates** enable you to find the trailhead by using your navigational aid.

Following each box is a narrative of the hike. This detailed account notes trail junctions, stream crossings, and trailside features, along with

▨	State-owned land	𝘬	Trailhead	🅿	Parking
▨	Water	↔	Gate	⌣	Pass
▪▪▪▪▪▪	Featured trail	⫽	Waterfall	🏠	Ranger station
——	Stream	▲	Campsite	○	Spring
--------	Other trails	▲	Peak	→	Trail direction
⊂⊃	Main road	●	POI	🛡85	Interstate highway
⊏⊐	Minor road	▲	Viewpoint	(221)	U.S. highway
⊢┼┼┤	Railroad	⅋	Picnic area/shelter	(126)	State highway

Map legend.

their distance from the trailhead. This both helps keep you apprised of your whereabouts and makes sure you don't miss the special features. A summary of trail mileage is given at the narrative's end, so you can quickly scan the distance to major trail intersections or highlights. All of the above information should help you make the most of these can't-miss hikes in North Carolina's state parks. Now get out there and hit the trail!

Grandfather Mountain State Park stands tall in the Southern Appalachians.

■ *Mountains*

A rainbow graces roaring Rainbow Falls.

1 RAINBOW FALLS HIKE
Gorges State Park

*This popular hike leads you to not one but four stellar falls.
Start at gorgeous Gorges State Park, and work your way down
to the Horsepasture River and the Nantahala National Forest.
From there, walk up a mountain defile to reach Hidden Falls,
then Rainbow Falls, a powerful river-wide cataract, the mist of
which truly does make a rainbow. Hike a bit farther to view wide
Turtleback Falls. On your return, take the user-created trail to
Stairway Falls.*

Distance 3.8-mile out-and-back, including spur to Stairway Falls

Hiking time 2.5 hours

Difficulty Moderate

Highlights Hidden Falls, Rainbow Falls, Turtleback Falls, Stairway Falls

Cautions Be careful around falls

Best seasons Year-round; avoid warm-weather weekends

Other trail users None

Hours January–December, 7 a.m.–9 p.m.; closed Christmas Day

Trail contact Gorges State Park, 976 Grassy Ridge Road, Sapphire,
NC 28774, 828-966-9099, www.ncparks.gov/gorges-state-park

Finding the trailhead From Brevard, take US 64 West for 18 miles,
then turn left on NC 281 South and follow it for .9 mile to enter
Gorges State Park. Follow the main park road for 1.7 miles to the
Rainbow Falls parking area, beyond the park visitor center.

GPS trailhead coordinates 35.088750, –82.951882

Set fast against the South Carolina State line along the Blue Ridge Escarpment, Gorges State Park is ideally situated to capture the beauty of the
Carolina mountains, including mountaintops, waterfalls, and streams.
The ecology of the 7,500-acre preserve creates a nationally recognized
melding of plant and animal life, protected as part of the state Natural

Heritage Program. We hikers have a large wild area with trails aplenty to explore.

Rainbow Falls is the star of the park, though there are many other jewels in the crown. Our hike leaves the Rainbow Falls parking area on a wide, well-maintained gravel path. The Horsepasture River sings 500 feet below, and at higher flows you can already hear it. Join a pine-dominated ridge. At .3 mile, come to a trail intersection. Here the Raymond Fisher Trail leads left a short distance to backpack campsites. Stay right with the Rainbow Falls Trail, working down the chasm slope to cross a tributary of the Horsepasture River at .7 mile. At .8 mile, a sign denotes your departure from Gorges State Park and entrance into the Nantahala National Forest. The trail is no longer graveled.

At 1.0 mile, a well-trod but unsigned trail leads left to Stairway Falls. You can—and should—visit this smaller waterfall on your return trip. For now, stay with the well-marked and well-maintained Rainbow Falls Trail. Continue hiking and cross a decent-sized unnamed stream flowing off Grassy Ridge. You are now riverside near a well-used campsite. Now head upstream on the right bank of the Horsepasture River, a showstopper of a river that truly deserves its "wild and scenic" status.

Wood and earth steps help you make your way up the rugged gorge, while the untamed river cavorts below. Return to the river at 1.4 miles. A short spur trail leads to a massive deep pool fed by a wide, low cataract known as Hidden Falls. Climb a bit, and then at 1.5 miles you come to roaring Rainbow Falls and the official viewing area, bordered by a wooden fence, rising above mist-covered brush. It is this mist that, when struck by morning sunbeams, forms a rainbow. You can also view the 200-foot cataract from a lower platform, accessed by a trail splitting left from the main path. Rainbow Falls is truly a mighty rumbler, thundering into boulders below.

Continuing uptrail toward Turtleback Falls, keep right beyond the spur to the lower overlook of Rainbow Falls. Be careful where the path nears the top of Rainbow Falls. At 1.7 miles, come to 20-foot-high, sloped Turtleback Falls. This spiller attracts swimmers and those who want to slide down the granite back of the turtle. When the water is high, however, do not slide down the turtle: several people have been pushed downstream and swept over Rainbow Falls to their death.

The official trail ends at the top of Turtleback Falls. The national forest boundary is not much farther ahead, at the base of an upstream cataract. I recommend backtracking .7 mile from Turtleback Falls to the

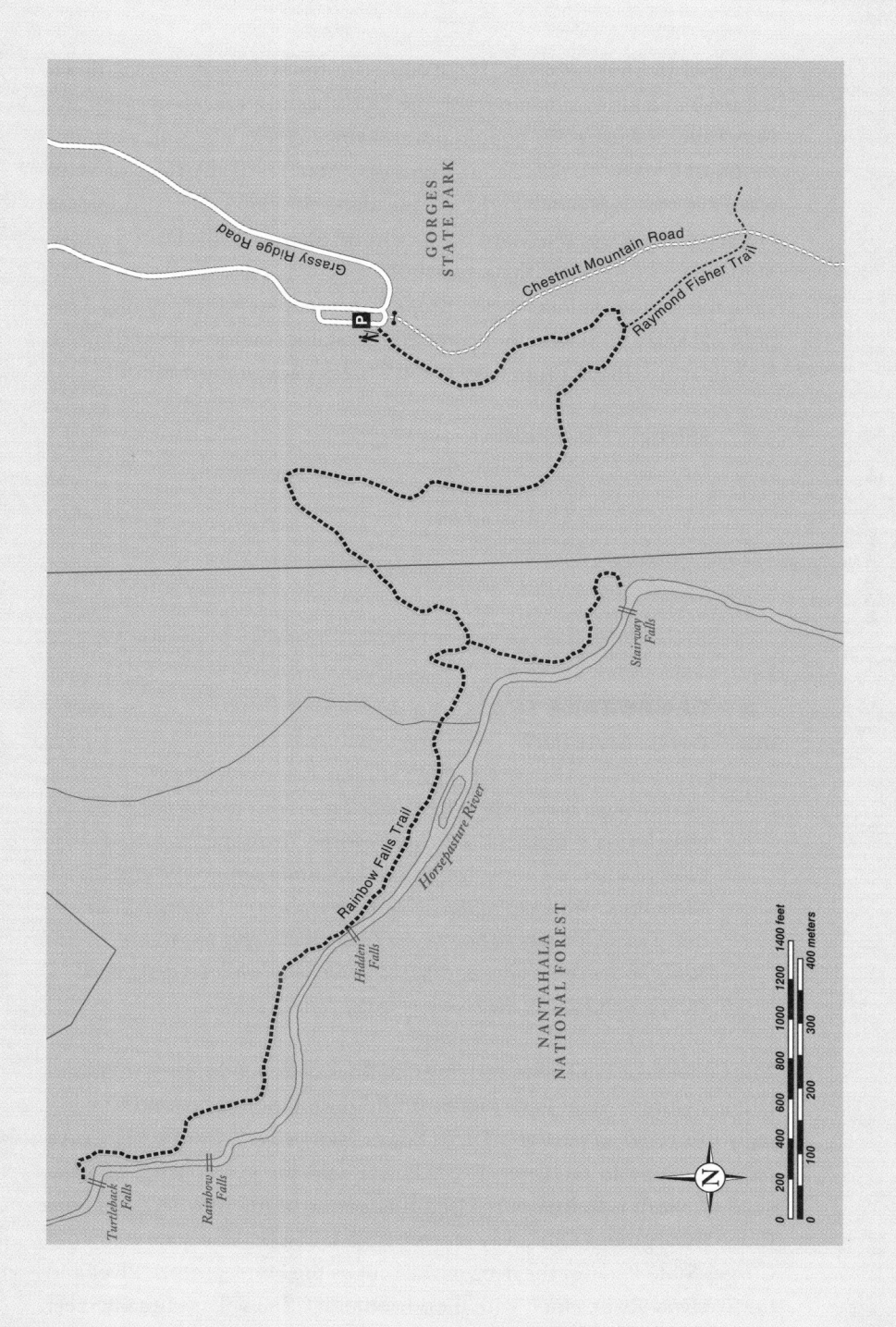

GORGES
STATE PARK

Grassy Ridge Road

Chestnut Mountain Road

Raymond Fisher Trail

P

Stairway
Falls

Rainbow Falls Trail

Horsepasture River

Hidden
Falls

NANTAHALA
NATIONAL FOREST

Turtleback
Falls

Rainbow
Falls

N

0   200   400   600   800   1000   1200   1400 feet
0   100   200   300   400 meters

spur trail to Stairway Falls. Head south on the well-beaten track down the nose of a piney ridge to reach the Horsepasture River at a campsite. Now head downstream, hopping over a small creek. The well-worn but rough trail leaves the flat for a steep slope. You'll hear the steps of Stairway Falls roaring to your right. Persist along the slope, then drop to the Horsepasture River at a sharp bend. Admire Stairway Falls from the base of the lowermost tier of the cataract. Rocks provide a seat where you can view the 50-foot spiller, which drops in 10-foot step increments. This pour-over creates yet another contrasting cataract on the wild and scenic Horsepasture River. From here it is 1.2 miles back to the trailhead.

Mileages		
	0.0	Trailhead
	1.6	Rainbow Falls
	1.7	Turtleback Falls
	2.6	Stairway Falls
	3.8	Trailhead

2 CANEBRAKE TRAIL
Gorges State Park

Hike along a mountain ridge to reach the scenic confluence of three bodies of water—the Toxaway River, Toxaway Creek, and Lake Jocassee, all in the "gorge-ous" mountain setting of Gorges State Park. Walk out to the swinging bridges over Toxaway River and Toxaway Creek. The trek may seem a bit long, but it can easily be done in a day. Backpackers can overnight at a designated campground where the bodies of water come together.

The Canebrake Trail takes you through thick backwoods forest in mountainous Gorges State Park to a beautiful destination. The land was initially protected as part of a Duke Power lake project, from which Lake Jocassee came to be. Later, Duke Power sold the excess land, and the state of North Carolina purchased this scenic segment where the Blue Ridge Escarpment falls away toward Lake Jocassee. The state named it Gorges State Park for the deep gashes cut by the Horsepasture River and the Toxaway River, along with their tributaries. You will eventually meet the Foothills Trail, a 77-mile long-distance path that cuts across the river

Distance 10.6-mile out-and-back

Hiking time 5.3 hours

Difficulty Difficult due to distance

Highlights Swinging bridges over streams, Lake Jocassee

Cautions None

Best seasons Mid-September through mid-May

Other trail users None

Hours January–December, 7 a.m.–9 p.m.; closed Christmas Day

Trail contact Gorges State Park, 976 Grassy Ridge Road, Sapphire,
NC 28774, 828-966-9099, www.ncparks.gov/gorges-state-park

Finding the trailhead From Brevard, take US 64 West for 9.5
miles, then turn left on Frozen Creek Road and follow it for
3.1 miles to the Frozen Creek access on your right.

GPS trailhead coordinates 35.108378, –82.883068

gorges and through the park. The huge swinging bridge over the Toxaway
River is your ultimate destination and presents stellar views of where the
Toxaway River empties into Lake Jocassee, along with Toxaway Creek.
Nearby lies a multisite camping area, a stopping point where you can
enjoy the melding of the waters.

A few notes: If you aren't backpacking, allow a couple of hours at the
destination if possible. If you are backpacking, the camping area has several designated first-come, first-served sites, each with a tent pad, picnic
table, fire ring, and lantern post, in the flats along Toxaway Creek. You
must fill out a camping permit at the Frozen Creek trailhead if you leave
a vehicle there overnight. Be apprised that other campers may be coming from the lake. That is why I recommend this hike from fall through
spring—Lake Jocassee can be busy with boaters during the summer
season.

The Canebrake Trail is not difficult at all. The foot-friendly path traces
an old doubletrack winding along a ridge, aiming for Lake Jocassee. It
gradually descends around 1,000 feet over the last 3 miles, so count that
into your return trip. The Frozen Creek trailhead presents a large parking
area, shaded picnic tables, and the gurgling waters of Frozen Creek as
you prepare for your hike.

Join the Auger Hole Trail and bridge Frozen Creek. The path soon

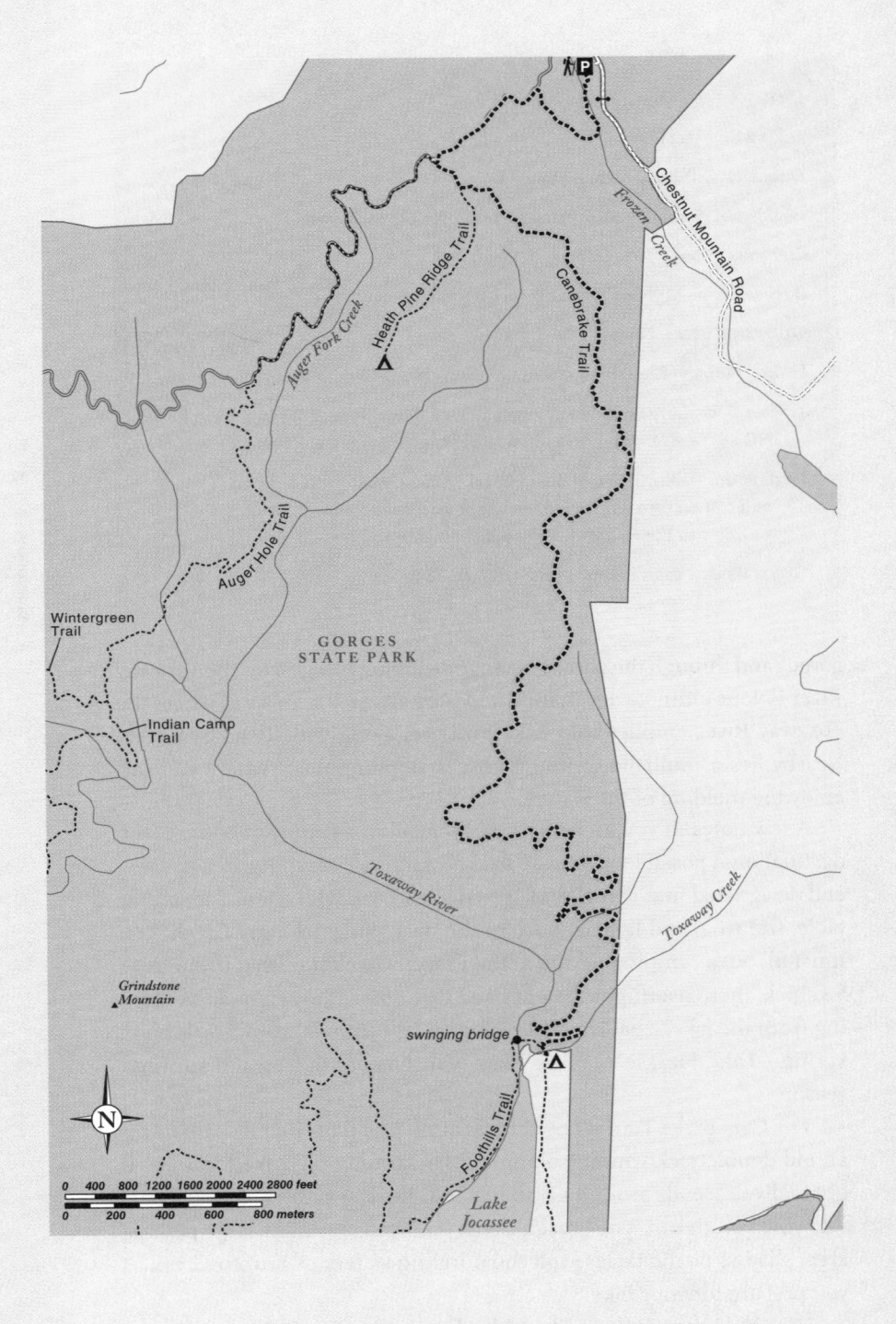

Looking out from the long swinging bridge above the Toxaway River.

picks up an old doubletrack with easy footing. At .6 mile, cross a creek by culvert, then the Auger Hole Trail climbs from the Frozen Creek valley to make a trail intersection at .8 mile. Here head left on the Canebrake Trail, a wide path coursing through pines and mountain laurel. At .9 mile the Heath Pine Ridge Trail splits right, and along its length there are hike-in campsites, which must be reserved in advance through the state park. Now the Canebrake Trail begins a long ridge run that curves south toward the Toxaway River. The pathway undulates through an attractive forest of maple, oak, and pine, along with black gum and sourwood. Old roads spur away from the main track, but the official trail is clear and well-marked. Parts of the path are open to the sun overhead.

At 2.3 miles, cross a small stream branch by culvert. The Canebrake Trail is one of the more isolated pathways in the North Carolina state park system. Now begin the prolonged but gentle downgrade toward Lake Jocassee. The grade is a little over 300 feet per mile, a gentle descent for mountain trails. (Most pathways in the Southern Appalachians have a grade around 600 feet per mile.) At 3.3 miles, the path drops off the ridge and begins winding in and out of small watersheds flowing down to the Toxaway River. You will repeatedly cross these little branches while coming ever nearer your destination.

Come to a trail intersection at 4.8 miles. Here a road heads left toward private property, but we stay right, running a ridge dividing Toxaway Creek from the Toxaway River. Switchbacks ease the descent. Come alongside Toxaway Creek before finding another intersection at 5.2 miles. Here, at a trail signboard, you meet the Foothills Trail, your conduit for exploring the waters that converge here. To your left, over a smaller swinging bridge, the Foothills Trail leads over Toxaway Creek to the shaded camping area and then goes along Lake Jocassee. To your right, the Foothills Trail leads to the long swinging bridge over the Toxaway River. Take your time and explore the locale, gathering views from the bridges, fishing, swimming, and perhaps camping overnight.

Mileages	0.0	Frozen Creek access
	0.8	Canebrake Trail
	5.2	Foothills Trail
	5.3	Toxaway River swinging bridge
	10.6	Frozen Creek access

3   MOUNT MITCHELL CIRCUIT
Mount Mitchell State Park

Hike North Carolina's first state park while visiting the state's highest peak and its treasured spruce-fir high-country forests. Begin more than a mile high to hike along the fabled Black Mountain crest to Mount Mitchell. Enjoy 360-degree vistas, then return to the trailhead amid more evergreen forests broken with more panoramas to the lands beyond. Note: The park is often closed in winter due to snow on the roads. If in doubt, call the park about access.

Although you start at the highest trailhead in this guide, 6,200 feet, it is also one of the few trailheads where you can grab a meal before or after your hike—in season, of course. See, Stepps Gap is also home to Mount Mitchell State Park's restaurant, one of the highest-elevation restaurants in the East, if not the highest. Of course, at Mount Mitchell State Park you get used to such superlatives, since it is the highest point in North Carolina, the highest point east of the Mississippi River, with the highest campground in the East, and so on.

Distance 5.6-mile loop

Hiking time 3.3 hours

Difficulty Moderate to difficult, does have some
    irregular, challenging trail segments

Highlights Highest point in the East, views, spruce-fir forests

Cautions Wet, sloped stone trail segments

Best seasons May through early October

Other trail users None

Hours November–February, 7 a.m.–6 p.m.; March–April,
    7 a.m.–8 p.m.; May–August, 7 a.m.–10 p.m.; September–
    October, 7 a.m.–9 p.m.; closed Christmas Day

Trail contact Mount Mitchell State Park, 2388 NC 128, Burnsville, NC
    28714, 828-675-4611, www.ncparks.gov/mount-mitchell-state-park

Finding the trailhead From Asheville, take the Blue Ridge Parkway
    north 34 miles to milepost 355. Turn left on NC 128 into
    Mount Mitchell State Park. Follow NC 28 for 3.0 miles to
    the large state park restaurant parking on your right.

GPS trailhead coordinates 35.752566, –82.273417

And one more remarkable consummate aspect: Your hike begins on the historic Old Mitchell Trail, around since the 1830s. The restaurant is a much newer addition. Nevertheless, join the Old Mitchell Trail, heading north from a small building north of the park restaurant, trekking a narrow path bordered by Fraser fir, common up here but rare in the rest of the Southern Appalachians and nonexistent beyond these highlands. The path rolls over a peak as it runs parallel to the summit access road. At .4 mile, the trail and road separate. Here the Old Mitchell Trail becomes challenging—water seeps flowing over irregular, uneven rocks and mud. At this elevation the terrain rarely dries out. The worst spots have been spanned with land bridges, but expect slow progress nonetheless.

Pass under a transmission line at .6 mile. Begin an extended uptick, tromping golden evergreen needles bordered by moss-covered stone. Reach an intersection at .8 mile. Here the Camp Alice Trail shortcuts our loop, leaving right for Lower Creek. Come to another intersection at 1.0 miles. Here the Campground Spur Trail heads left to the small but recommended tent-only campground. Continue climbing the Old

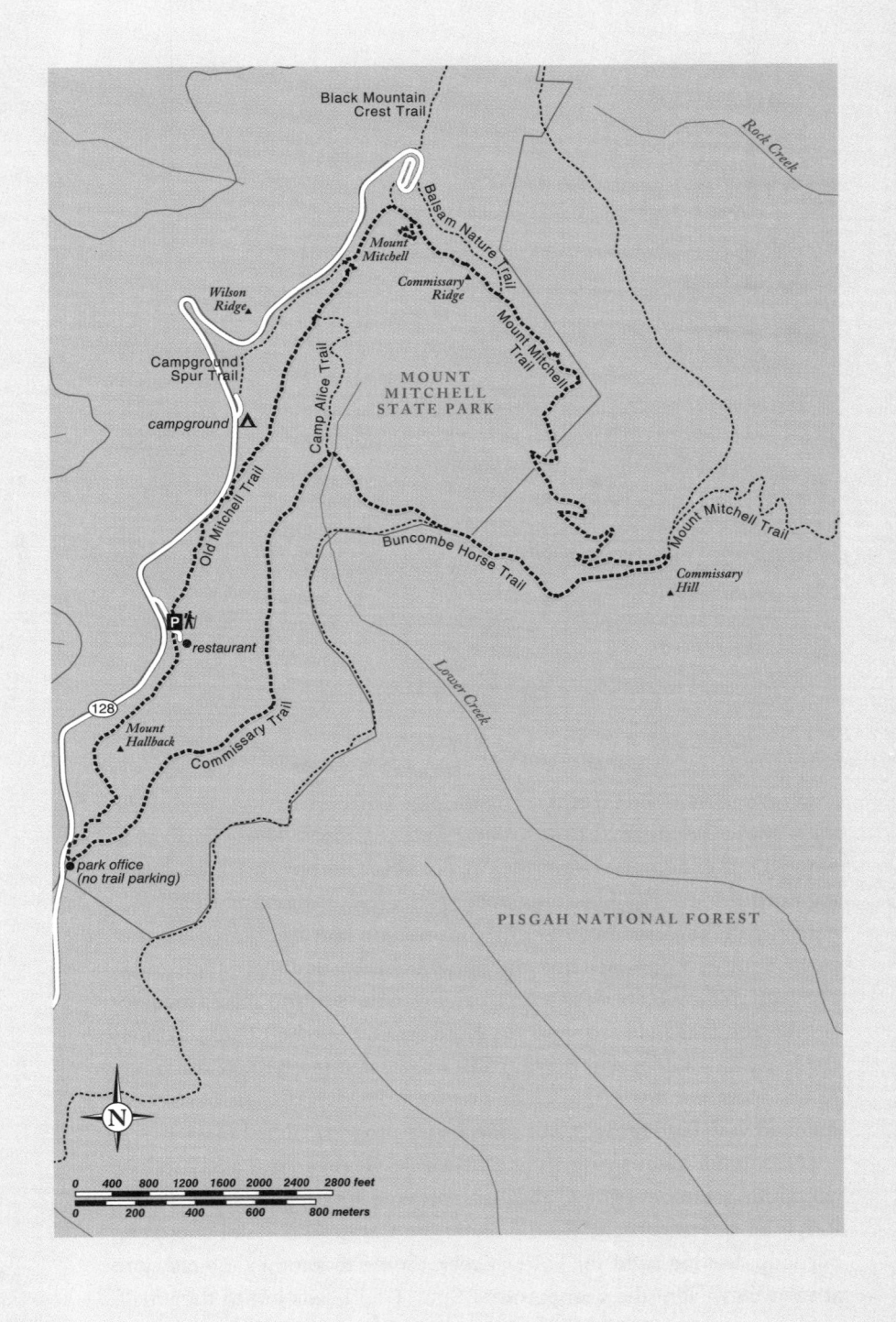

Autumn daisies grace the highlands of Mount Mitchell.

Mitchell Trail for .2 mile, then split right, joining the Summit Trail, the wide concrete path enjoyed by thousands who make the quarter-mile jaunt to Mount Mitchell via the nearby parking area. Ahead you will pass the park environmental education building and the Balsam Nature Trail.

At 1.4 miles, reach 6,684-foot Mount Mitchell. From the observation platform you can see in all directions, and helpful signage identifies distant peaks, valleys, and other lands. Hopefully the sky is clear on your visit. Visitors are often disappointed by cloudy, rainy, and foggy conditions atop the mount. To continue the loop, take the paved trail back down to turn right, picking up the other end of the Balsam Nature Trail, a natural surface trail. Pass old ranger quarters and rock outcrops, then at 1.7 miles pick up the Mount Mitchell Trail, usually a much quieter experience than you'll have atop Mount Mitchell. Temporarily leave state park boundaries at 2.1 miles to enter the Pisgah National Forest, though the highland scenery doesn't change. Switchback downward, gaining partial views while passing rock outcrops. At 2.6 miles, tread steps cut into the rock itself.

At 2.9 miles, reach another intersection, where you split right to join the Buncombe Horse Trail / Commissary Trail. Look left for the Commissary Hill backcountry campsite. The wide and nearly level path is a major contrast from the craggy Old Mitchell Trail. Berry bushes border the track, and at 3.2 miles it opens onto a fine vista where the trail curves above the Blue Ridge Parkway and below the state park office and restaurant.

At 3.5 miles, stay right with the Commissary Trail when the Buncombe Horse Trail splits left. On clear days, montane vistas continue as far as you can see. Trace an old railroad grade via which tourists of yesteryear visited Mount Mitchell. Ahead, reenter the state park. Cross Lower Creek and meet the other end of the Camp Alice Trail at 3.8 miles. Camp Alice was an early tourist destination for Mitchell visitors. You could eat in the dining hall and sleep in a genuine platform tent back more than a century ago. The hiking remains easy, and you reach state park office at 4.9 miles (no hiker parking). At this point, Stepps Gap, resume the Old Mitchell Trail from the front of the office. Wind north in low red spruce and Fraser fir rising over Mount Hallback before dropping to the hike's end near the park restaurant at 5.6 miles, completing the highest hike in North Carolina.

Mileages	
0.0	State park restaurant trailhead
1.4	Mount Mitchell
3.2	Stellar view
4.9	Park office
5.6	State park restaurant trailhead

4 **LAKE JAMES HIKE**
▇ Lake James State Park

Take a walk on the watery side at Lake James State Park and explore the attractive shores of Lake James. First cruise along the Paddys Creek embayment, viewing an old homesite before joining the Mill Creek Trail. Pass by the park swim beach along with other facilities before hiking among pines and hardwoods along intimate lake coves to close the loop. Be prepared to add other activities at this first-rate state park.

Lake James State Park is ideal for active visitors. Not only does it have over 10 miles of trails for hikers like us, but it also features 15 miles of mountain bike trails; paddling, swimming, and fishing opportunities; drive-in, walk-in, and paddle-in camping sites; and picnicking. So when you come here to hike, consider incorporating other activities into your visit.

Lake James is situated at the base of the Blue Ridge, where the Linville River and Catawba River have been dammed up, creating a 6,812-acre impoundment from which rise scenic mountains and one alluring body of water. The state park is situated on two segments of forested shoreline, creating an ideal setting for outdoor adventures. Our hike takes place in the Paddys Creek Area of the preserve. The other part of the state park is known as the Catawba River Area. Leave the trailhead parking lot, crossing the park road to head east on a grassy track that quickly morphs to singletrack path through woods of pine, holly, sweetgum, and other hardwoods. Ahead, a spur descends right toward a fishing area at the mouth of Paddys Creek, but we stay with the hiker-only Paddys Creek Trail as it parallels the shoreline of the lake before turning into a tributary at .3 mile. Note the preserved hemlocks in this hollow.

The path returns to the shore. At .5 mile, the Homestead Trail leaves left. Ahead you will wander through a former homesite. Note the rock fences and crumbled chimney. The former clearing is growing over. At .6 mile, the Paddys Creek Trail crosses another streamlet, returning to the shore yet again. At lower lake levels you can find a small beach here. At .9 mile, the Mill Creek Trail enters on your left—this will be your return route. For now, stay straight, still paralleling the shoreline and enjoying watery views. Curve into an embayment before emerging onto

Distance 5.1-mile balloon loop

Hiking time 2.4 hours

Difficulty Moderate

Highlights Lake views, pre-park history, additional park activities

Cautions None

Best seasons Early fall through late spring

Other trail users None

Hours December–February, 7 a.m.–7 p.m.; March–April,
October, 7 a.m.–9 p.m.; May–September, 7 a.m.–10 p.m.;
November, 7 a.m.–8 p.m.; closed Christmas Day

Trail contact Lake James State Park, 7321 NC 126, Nebo, NC 28761,
828-584-7728, www.ncparks.gov/lake-james-state-park

Finding the trailhead From Asheville, take I-40 East to Exit 90, Nebo / Lake
James. Turn right and join Harmony Grove Road, then pass over the
interstate. After .6 mile reach an intersection and stay right on Harmony
Grove Road, following it for 2.2 more miles to reach the intersection with
US 70 in Nebo. Turn left and follow US 70 West just a short distance,
then turn right on NC 126. Follow NC 126 for 5.0 miles, passing the
Catawba River section of Lake James State Park to turn right into
the Paddys Creek area. Follow the main park road for .9 mile to the
hiker trailhead on your left, just after the bridge over Paddys Creek.

GPS trailhead coordinates 35.754250, –81.891750

a paved path at 1.1 miles. You are now in the greater fishing, paddling, swim beach area of the park, including park ranger offices, restrooms, and changing rooms. Follow the paved path right, then come to the swim beach. Here, you trace the sandy shoreline through developed facilities, including a shoreline picnic area. This area is crowded during summer, the least popular time for hiking at Lake James State Park. In the cooler times—when you are more likely to be hiking—the beach will be deserted. Emerge near the East Shelter at 1.5 miles. Officially join the natural-surface Mill Creek Trail, crossing a park-personnel-only boat ramp, then reenter thick woods. The Mill Creek Trail turns up an embayment. Keep rolling through a hilly segment of the hike as lake glimpses open and close. Look for old roadbeds crossing the marked path. By 2.3 miles, you are directly along the shore open to the water. Enjoy the wide view to the east before turning away from the impoundment and cruising around

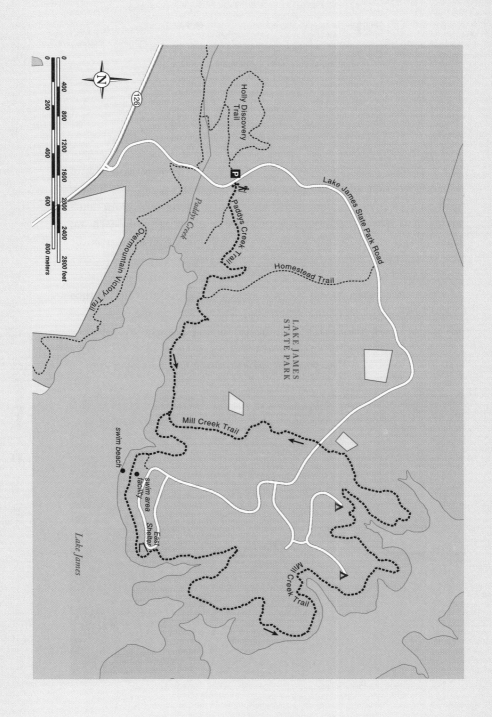

Lake James State Park

Holly Discovery Trail

126

Overmountain Victory Trail

Paddys Creek

Paddys Creek Trail

P

Lake James State Park Road

Homestead Trail

LAKE JAMES
STATE PARK

Mill Creek Trail

swim beach

swim area
facility

East
Shelter

Mill Creek Trail

Lake James

N

0   400   800   1200   1600   2000   2400   2800 feet

0   200   400   600   800 meters

Lake James State Park offers miles of wooded shoreline.

a small cove bisected with an intermittent streambed. By 2.7 miles, you are below the park's auto-accessible campground. Here user-created trails connect the camp to the trail. Stay with the blazed track.

Turn away from the campground for good at 3.2 miles. Here the Mill Creek Trail makes one last run for Lake James, coming near the reservoir a final time before heading west and climbing at 3.5 miles. Ahead, cross the paved park access road and roll southbound through rich woods, going more downhill than not. At 4.2 miles, meet the Paddys Creek Trail, having completed the loop portion of the hike. From here backtrack .9 mile to the trailhead.

Mileages	**0.0** Paddys Creek trailhead
	0.6 Homestead Trail heads left
	0.9 Mill Creek Trail heads left
	1.5 Leave swim beach area
	3.2 Leave campground area
	4.2 Complete Mill Creek Trail loop
	5.1 Paddys Creek trailhead

5   VIEWS FROM THE SOUTH MOUNTAINS
■■■ South Mountains State Park

This hike presents multiple panoramas while exploring a less-visited part of South Mountains State Park. Climb away from Jacob Fork on the River Trail, rising only to drop and cross the Little River, passing near a waterfall. From there, rise to ridgelines, where you gain views of adjacent mountains, including developed overlooks that deliver a punch, with looks at valleys and ridges, even High Shoals Falls. Don't fear the climbs and descents: the difference between points high and low is less than 1,000 feet.

Hiking is on the front burner here at South Mountains State Park, as is evidenced by 40 miles of trails coursing through this range of lower peaks south and east of the Blue Ridge. But make no mistake: these are indeed mountains, with the vertical variation, flora, and fauna to back it up. Along with getting to admire views aplenty, you will also observe fire ecology. In November 2016, one-third of the park was burned in a month-long wildfire. Its effects will be seen for a long time to come. You will notice skeletal standing trees, burned trunk bases, and renewed growth of fire-dependent species such as Table Mountain pine. Even though these are mountains, the recommended hiking season is early fall through late spring to avoid summer heat, as most elevations in the 20,000-plus-acre preserve range between 1,200 and 2,300 feet, with a few higher exceptions.

This hike starts along Jacob Fork. With your back to Jacob Fork, pick up the Little River Trail heading north away from the water, splitting between a ranger residence to your left and a park maintenance building to your right on a less-used route. The Little River Trail climbs away from Jacob Fork, curving around some heavily wooded hollows, rich with tulip trees and holly. At .7 mile, the Raven Rock Trail enters on your right. Stay straight, rising with the doubletrack Little River Trail to a piney ridgecrest complemented with sourwood, sweetgum, and chestnut oak.

At 1.2 miles, keep straight where the Turkey Ridge Trail leaves right. Partial views open to the east. At 1.4 miles, a trail leaves left to Little River campsites, one of seven reservable backcountry camps in the park. Soon top out, then descend to bridge the Little River at 1.7 miles. Leave the

Distance 8.6-mile balloon loop

Hiking time 4.2 hours

Difficulty Moderate to difficult due to distance

Highlights Remote ridges, multiple views, backpacking possibilities

Cautions None

Best seasons Early fall through late spring

Other trail users Equestrians on some trails

Hours December–February, 7 a.m.–7 p.m.; March–April,
October, 7 a.m.–9 p.m.; May–September, 7 a.m.–10 p.m.;
November, 7 a.m.–8 p.m.; closed Christmas Day

Trail contact South Mountains State Park, 3001 South Mountain
Park Avenue, Connelly Springs, NC 28612, 828-433-4772,
www.ncparks.gov/south-mountains-state-park

Finding the trailhead From Exit 118 on I-40 west of Hickory, take
Old NC Highway 10 South for 1.1 miles and keep straight to join
Shoupes Grove Church Road. Follow it for .8 mile, turn left onto
Miller Bridge Road, and follow it for 5.3 miles to turn left onto NC
18 South. Follow NC 18 South 2.0 miles, then turn acutely right
onto Sugar Loaf Road. Follow it 4.2 miles to turn left onto Old NC
18, and follow it 2.7 miles to turn right onto Ward Gap Road. Follow
Ward Gap Road for 1.4 miles to enter South Mountains State Park.
After 3.3 miles, dead-end at the High Shoals Falls parking area.

GPS trailhead coordinates 35.602805, –81.627909

perched stream vale to reach a sharp left turn at 1.9 miles. Here user-cre-ated trails lead right toward Little River Falls, a long caroming spiller. It's positively dangerous to reach the base of this waterfall, so be content with a glance down from the upper edge, and don't descend to the bottom.

At 2.1 miles, stay left to join the Upper CCC Trail as a road leaves right, toward the park boundary. The trail name comes from the Civilian Conservation Corps. Back in the 1930s, the public works group built roads and managed the forest here in the South Mountains, well before it became an official North Carolina state park in 1974. Continue up more than not, passing the Sawtooth Trail and a potential shortcut of the loop at 2.5 miles. Roll through xeric pine woods with sporadic views in this remote area. At 3.7 miles, come to a gate and intersection. Head left here on the Horseridge Trail, initially climbing sharply in oaks and hickories,

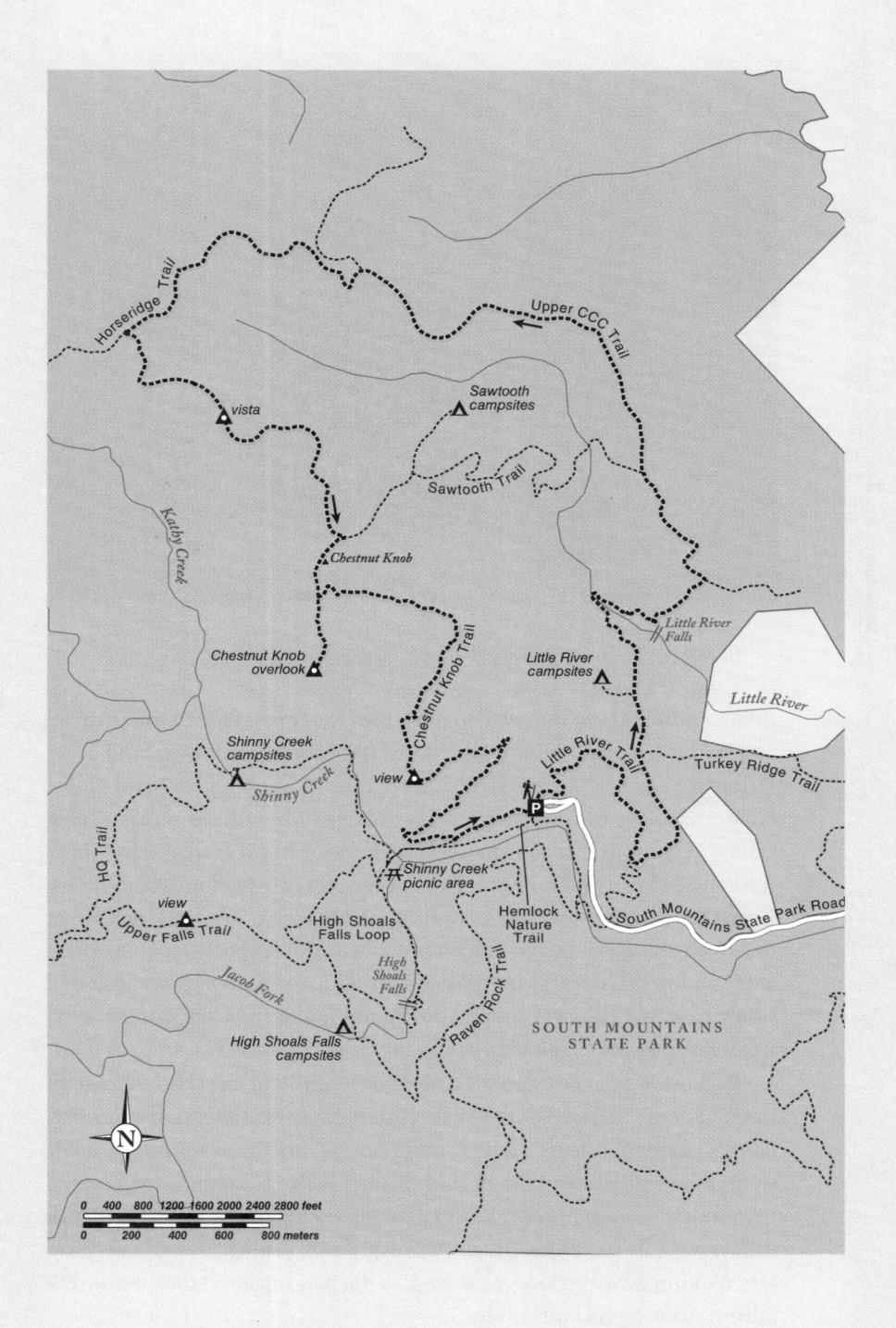

Horseridge Trail

Upper CCC Trail

vista

Sawtooth campsites

Kathy Creek

Sawtooth Trail

Chestnut Knob

Chestnut Knob overlook

Little River Falls

Little River campsites

Little River

Chestnut Knob Trail

Shinny Creek campsites

Shinny Creek

view

Little River Trail

Turkey Ridge Trail

P

HQ Trail

Shinny Creek picnic area

view

Upper Falls Trail

High Shoals Falls Loop

Hemlock Nature Trail

South Mountains State Park Road

Jacob Fork

High Shoals Falls

Raven Rock Trail

SOUTH MOUNTAINS STATE PARK

High Shoals Falls campsites

N

0   400   800 1200 1600 2000 2400 2800 feet

0   200   400   600   800 meters

Gazing across the Jacob Fork valley from Chestnut Knob Overlook.

then undulate along the ridge to meet the other end of the Sawtooth Trail at 4.7 miles. Turn left here to head south. More views open, and at 5.1 miles you come to a cleared view with a horse-hitching post and picnic table. Distant views open across the Shinny (pronounced *shiney*) Creek valley. At 5.8 miles, head right on the Chestnut Knob Trail and pass over the actual Chestnut Knob; you'll reach another intersection at 6.0 miles. Keep straight here toward Chestnut Knob Overlook. The wide path soon narrows to singletrack and descends out to a boulder-pocked point where, at 6.2 miles, extensive panoramas open south and east of mountains and valley near and far, clear toward the Piedmont. Scenes like this are what we come to expect at North Carolina state parks.

Backtrack and continue the Chestnut Knob Trail, descending east on the hiker-only pathway. It is downhill all the way from here. At 7.4 miles, come to a cleared view on a bluff above Jacob Fork. Scan across the valley to find the uppermost part of High Shoals Falls in the distance, framed by wooded mountains. Wow! After that, switchback into the Jacob Fork valley, meeting the High Shoals Falls Loop at 8.4 miles. From here, head left, making the easy, level walk back to the parking area, completing the adventurous loop at 8.6 miles.

6   HIGH SHOALS FALLS HIKE
South Mountains State Park

This trek at South Mountains State Park takes you on a circuit leading to the preserve's signature feature—High Shoals Falls. This 80-foot spiller is the denouement of a series of cascades you will see along Jacob Fork. First, however, enjoy interpretive information on the Hemlock Nature Trail, then visit the falls before climbing into the park's higher terrain to revel in mountain views, and finally descend to Shinny Creek, with its own waterfalls. Be apprised that much of the hike can be busy. Solitude seekers will want to undertake this venture during off times.

The waterfalls of Jacob Fork are truly scenic and deserve your attention. This loop will take you to them but also to a less-visited part of the park on quiet ridges and along upper Shinny Creek and its rugged, difficult-to-reach falls. Plan your hike for morning or evening or during the week should you want solitude. The rewarding hike first joins Hemlock Nature Trail, one of the best interpretive trails in the Southeast. Take your time and you can learn a lot. Pick up the trail directly along Jacob Fork, which makes a scenic white rush. Head upstream under preserved hemlocks, sycamore, Fraser magnolia, and rhododendron. A shaded picnic area lies to your right. Come to the first of many interpretive panels detailing the flora and fauna of the South Mountains, from minnows to fish, from raccoons to bears, and from wildflowers to trees. At .3 mile, continue upstream, joining the High Shoals Falls Loop Trail. Cross Shinny Creek near its confluence with Jacob Fork, reaching Shinny Creek picnic area at .5 miles. Stay left with the High Shoals Falls Loop,

Distance 4.9-mile loop

Hiking time 2.3 hours

Difficulty Moderate

Highlights High Shoals Falls, other cascades,
   extensive interpretive information

Cautions Be careful around falls

Best seasons Year-round

Other trail users Equestrians on a few trails

Hours December–February, 7 a.m.–7 p.m.; March–April,
   October, 7 a.m.–9 p.m.; May–September, 7 a.m.–10 p.m.;
   November, 7 a.m.–8 p.m.; closed Christmas Day

Trail contact South Mountains State Park, 3001 South Mountain
   Park Avenue, Connelly Springs, NC 28612, 828-433-4772,
   www.ncparks.gov/south-mountains-state-park

Finding the trailhead From Exit 118 on I-40 west of Hickory, take
   Old NC Highway 10 South for 1.1 miles and keep straight to join
   Shoupes Grove Church Road. Follow it for .8 mile, turn left onto
   Miller Bridge Road, and follow it for 5.3 miles to turn left onto NC
   18 South. Follow NC 18 South 2.0 miles, then turn acutely right
   onto Sugar Loaf Road. Follow it 4.2 miles to turn left onto Old NC
   18, and follow it 2.7 miles to turn right onto Ward Gap Road. Follow
   Ward Gap Road for 1.4 miles to enter South Mountains State Park.
   After 3.3 miles, dead-end at the High Shoals Falls parking area.

GPS trailhead coordinates 35.602805, –81.627909

keeping up along crashing and dashing Jacob Fork. Enjoy looks at the
water, ascending on stone steps amid trailside rock slabs and boulder
gardens. The valley is rocky to the extreme, yet black birches rise and
moss grows on anything that doesn't move. At .8 mile, cross Jacob Fork
on a bridge in front of a multitiered cascade. You might as well keep your
phone or camera out, because the waterfalls come fast and furious now.
White noise echoes into your ears as you climb stone steps set in boulders
where the waters of Jacob Fork follow gravity's orders amid rocky chaos.

   You are working up the left bank of Jacob Fork on very steep steps
while the whitewater caroms down to your right. At .9 mile, take the spur
right to 80-foot High Shoals Falls. Here Jacob Fork freefalls from a stone
lip, straight down, faucet-style, before splattering and making a second
shorter drop, emitting mist into air and onto the viewing deck. Whoa.

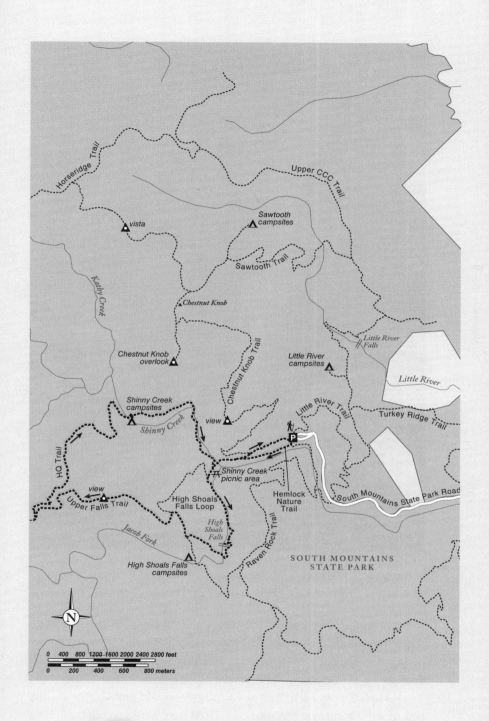

High Shoals Falls makes its two-tiered dive.

Continue steeply beyond the falls, saddling alongside a sheer bluff. Ahead you come to a smaller fall, making a pretty little two-tiered 15-foot drop before pushing over the edge as High Shoals Falls. Bridge Jacob Fork at 1.2 miles, rising on a milder uptick to meet the Upper Falls Trail / High Shoals Falls Trail at 1.3 miles. You will probably notice the lack of water song entering your ears. Head right here, leaving Jacob Fork in pines and mountain laurel. At 1.5 miles, the High Shoals Falls Trail leaves right—along with the crowds—but we stay straight, climbing into pines and mountain laurel on the Upper Falls Trail, which is nowhere near water at this point. You are on the ridge dividing Shinny Creek from Jacob Fork, and at 1.9 miles you will reach a cleared view to the south, where mountains stretch out beyond the Jacob Fork valley.

Beyond the view, continue rolling on the ridge to turn right onto the HQ Trail at 2.5 miles. More partial views are open at this point. It is mostly downhill from here, trekking through mountain laurel, pines, rhododendron, and holly—a lot of evergreen. By 3.5 miles, you are heading downstream along Shinny Creek, bridging it at 3.6 miles and reaching the Shinny Creek campsites, complete with fire ring and picnic table. Climb a bit before dropping again to bridge Shinny Creek at 4.2 miles. Here the waterway cuts a gorge and begins tumbling in multiple cataracts. Unfortunately, no developed trails descend to these falls, so viewing them is a dangerous proposition. At 4.4 miles, you are back at the Shinny Creek picnic area. Backtrack here and stay with the wide High Shoals Falls Loop, returning to the trailhead at 4.9 miles.

Mileages		
	0.0	High Shoals Falls trailhead
	0.9	High Shoals Falls
	1.5	Stay with Upper Falls Trail
	1.9	Cleared view
	2.5	Right on HQ Trail
	3.6	Shinny Creek campsites
	4.9	High Shoals Falls trailhead

7   PROFILE TRAIL

█ Grandfather Mountain State Park

This stellar hike uses the iconic Profile Trail at Grandfather Mountain State Park to climb to multiple views from Calloway Peak and nearby crags. The challenging trek follows a well-maintained trail before traversing a boulder-strewn slope, slowing progress. Rise into spruce-fir highlands to find a panorama of Grandfather Mountain from a cliff before topping out on Calloway Peak with vistas into a mosaic of western North Carolina mountains, valleys, and adjacent high-country communities.

Distance 8.2-mile out-and-back

Hiking time 5.1 hours

Difficulty Difficult due to elevation gain and rocky trail

Highlights Multiple vista points, spruce-fir forest

Cautions Rocky trail segments

Best seasons Whenever the skies are clear and trail dry

Other trail users None

Hours November–February, 8 a.m.–6 p.m.; March–May, September–October, 8 a.m.–8 p.m.; June–August, 8 a.m.–9 p.m.

Trail contact Grandfather Mountain State Park, 9872 NC 105 South, Suite 6, Banner Elk, NC 28604, 828-963-9522, www.ncparks.gov/grandfather-mountain-state-park

Finding the trailhead From the intersection of US 221 and NC 105 in Linville, take NC 105 North for 4.6 miles to the signed right turn toward the Grandfather Mountain State Park Profile trailhead. Follow the entrance road a short distance to end at a large parking area with water and restrooms.

GPS trailhead coordinates 36.119158, –81.833067

Grandfather Mountain has long been a storied summit in the fabled mountains of North Carolina. Visitors most often became familiar with the peak while visiting the private attraction atop much of the mountain,

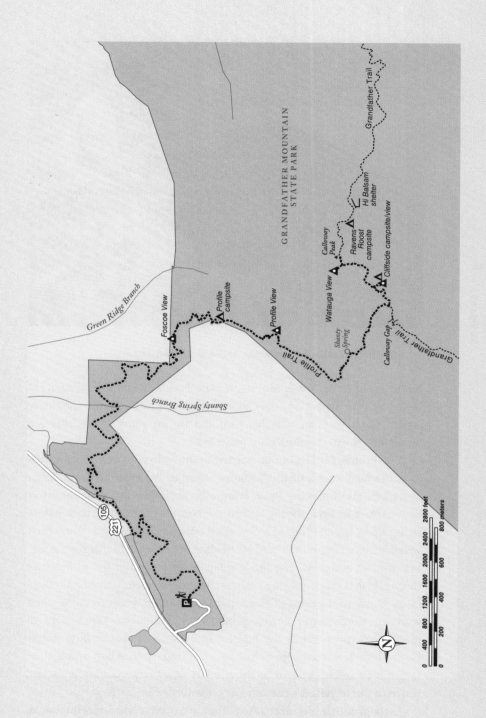

GRANDFATHER MOUNTAIN
STATE PARK

Green Ridge Branch

Shanty Spring Branch

Foscoe View

Profile campsite

Profile View

Profile Trail

Shanty Spring

Watauga View

Callaway Peak

Ravens Roost campsite

Hi Balsam shelter

Callaway Gap

Cliffside campsite/view

Grandfather Trail

Grandfather Trail

105

221

P

N

0   400   800   1200   1600   2000   2400   2800 feet

0   200   400   600   800 meters

Hiker looks south on the jagged ridge of Grandfather Mountain.

but in 2009 Grandfather Mountain State Park was established adjacent to the private attraction, only increasing the Profile Trail's legendary status. Today you can take this path and see for yourself why this is a "must-do" North Carolina state parks hike.

The Profile Trail links our starting point—already over 4,000 feet—near the headwaters of the Watauga River to the crest of Grandfather Mountain and Calloway Peak. Ironically, we follow the Watauga River downstream at first, staying within the bounds of the state park before rising along Green Ridge to a view amid northern hardwoods. Your climb winds through incredible boulder fields that, while scenic, make the hiking difficult and slow. The grade steepens as you enter the rare-spruce fir forests that cloak only the highest mantles of North Carolina's mountains. Once on the crest of Grandfather Mountain, you can enjoy some warm-up views from rocky crags before topping out on 5,964-foot Calloway Peak, purportedly the highest spot along the entire Blue Ridge. Grab a last view from here before backtracking. Note: Allow ample time to climb up and back down, as the going is slow in the boulder fields, and much of the terrain is generally rugged and steep.

Incongruously, the first part of the trek is on a wide, nicely graded, easy trail. Leave the large parking area after registering (rangers are sticklers about making sure everyone not backpacking overnight is safe and out of the parking area). Head east winding through coves enhanced with preserved trailside hemlocks. At .1 mile, a steel bridge leads you over a small stream, keeping east within the narrow state park corridor. Cross other feeder branches of the Watauga River before descending to reach the Watauga River at .8 mile. Here on the slopes of Grandfather Mountain, the Watauga River is a mere pup of a creek rather than the brawling whitewater torrent it becomes later, only to settle down on entering Tennessee, dammed in the Volunteer State before giving its waters to the Holston River. Here in the state park the pretty watercourse shimmers among boulders shaded by rhododendron, hemlock, and yellow birch.

You are at the low point of the hike as the Profile Trail turns south away from the Watauga River and begins its 2,096-foot ascent. Cherry, beech, and buckeye trees line the track as it comes to entertainingly named Shanty Spring Branch at 1.6 miles. No bridge here, just stepping-stones. Beyond the creek, enter a nest of big boulders through which you traverse. This is the end of the wide and easy trail. The more primitive track winds upward using switchbacks, opening onto Green Ridge and signed Foscoe View at 2.4 miles. Here the cleared panorama opens north to the town of Boone and Elk Knob State Park and onward into the Old Dominion.

You are near 4,400 feet now, and the yellow birches on Green Ridge display the effects of north winds blowing them into gnarled vestiges of their kindred down on the Watauga River. The higher you go, the more troublesome may prove trailside stinging nettle, a summertime nuisance that leaves barelegged hikers scratching their shins, despite park personnel's efforts to keep it cut back. At 2.7 miles, a short spur leads to Profile campsite, one of several advance-reservation-only backpacker camps in the state park.

Ahead, as you hike along trail enhanced with elaborate rock work, find the first red spruce trees adding their fragrance to the forest, soon to be joined by Fraser fir. At 2.9 miles, the Profile Trail comes alongside a colossal rock face, then to signed Profile View. This less-than-stellar vista opens east. Keep climbing into steeper and rockier terrain. Reach signed Shanty Spring at 3.4 miles. This is the last place on the hike where water is available.

Pass a stone cliff and come to the rock obstacle course through which the trail traverses. Make every step count among the irregular boulders. Top out before making a brief descent to find a trail intersection at 3.7

miles amid the spruce-fir forest so rare in the Southern Appalachians. Here turn left on the Daniel Boone Scout Trail, aiming for Calloway Peak. Climb to meet the spur trail to Cliffside campsite at 3.8 miles. Follow the spur through the campsite, then come to an open jagged cliff with a worthy view south along the ridge of Grandfather Mountain, where you might spot hikers on the Grandfather Trail. The Blue Ridge Parkway below is easy to see, while Table Rock stands farther in the distance. Still farther east, mountains give way to the Piedmont.

More views are ahead. Keep climbing to turn left at the spur to Watauga View at 4.1 miles, my personal favorite. Here, gaze from outcrops west down to Linville and beyond to the state-line crest dividing North Carolina and Tennessee. Elk Knob rises to the northwest. From there, resume the main trail, climbing a ladder at 4.2 miles to open onto the gray outcrop that is Calloway Peak. The smallish stone crown rises above wind-sculpted spruce and fir, offering panoramas to the west and north, a host of North Carolina highland peaks and valleys. Absorb the view for a while, and then use care as you head back down.

Mountains

Mileages	0.0	Profile Trail parking
	0.8	Watauga River
	1.6	Shanty Spring Branch
	2.7	Profile campsite
	3.7	Daniel Boone Scout Trail
	3.8	Cliffside campsite
	4.2	Calloway Peak
	8.4	Profile Trail parking

8 CRAGWAY HIKE
Grandfather Mountain State Park

*Make a loop on the east side of Grandfather Mountain, gaining
first-rate vistas while walking in the high country. Start from the
Blue Ridge Parkway, then cross Boone Fork on a swinging bridge.
After that angle up the slope of Grandfather, opening onto multiple
rock outcrops revealing a host of mountains in the distance. Rise
into spruce forest, flirting with the 5,000 feet elevation mark before
dropping back to the Parkway.*

Distance 3.7-mile balloon loop

Hiking time 2.0 hours

Difficulty Moderate due to distance

Highlights Numerous views from outcrops, spruce woods, swinging bridge

Cautions Hike has 1,000-foot climb

Best seasons Whenever the skies are clear and trail dry

Other trail users None

Hours November–February, 8 a.m.–6 p.m.; March–May,
September–October: 8 a.m.–8 p.m.; June–August, 8 a.m.–9 p.m.

Trail contact Grandfather Mountain State Park, 9872 NC
105 South, Suite 6, Banner Elk, NC 28604, 828-963-9522,
www.ncparks.gov/grandfather-mountain-state-park

Finding the trailhead From the intersection of US 221 and NC 105 in
Linville, take US 221 North for 3.1 miles to split left onto the Blue
Ridge Parkway. Follow the Parkway for 5.9 miles to the Boone Fork
parking area on your left, Blue Ridge Parkway milepost 299.8.

GPS trailhead coordinates 36.119984, –81.781194

A name like Cragway accurately depicts this rugged yet very scenic parcel
of Grandfather Mountain State Park. The name comes from one of the
pathways used on this loop hike—the Cragway Trail. Along that path are
rock outcrops—crags, you might say—that provide stellar views to the
crest of Grandfather Mountain and toward distant horizons, seemingly

all the way to Raleigh. More views can be had elsewhere on the hike. You will also enjoy looking from the swinging bridge down into Boone Fork as well as lapping up the trailside scenery along the loop hike, where a highland forest of northern hardwoods mix with fragrant spruce trees and rock outcrops, melding into the Blue Ridge splendor you expect.

The hike is relatively short, at 3.6 miles, and is doable by most hikers. You should factor in the climb, however. Grandfather Mountain is one of North Carolina's iconic peaks. Luckily, a portion of the mountain is preserved as a North Carolina state park. Part of the mountain is privately owned, with houses and condos as well as a private attraction. Another part is a parcel of the Blue Ridge Parkway, and that is where we begin this hike. Leave the southwest corner of the Boone Fork parking area on a connector trail, starting out almost 4,000 feet high. Shortly you'll pass the Upper Boone Fork Trail leaving left, then meet the Tanawha Trail. Stay left with the Tanawha Trail, entering the state park. Come to the swinging bridge over crystalline Boone Fork, flowing swift and cold down Grandfather Mountain. Overhead, yellow birch, beech, and cherry shade the waterway and trail, along with rhododendron.

Beyond the swinging bridge, the Asutsi Trail leaves left for US 221. Stay right with the Tanawha Trail, passing a signboard detailing the state park backcountry camping here. Come to yet another trail intersection at .4 mile. Here split right on the Nuwati Trail. You may see a Permit Required sign: don't worry, that means a camping permit is required to overnight at one of the campsites on the Nuwati Trail, not to day-hike along the path. Angle up a mountain slope among tightly grown rhododendron and wind-shortened hardwoods broken by occasional spring branches flowing over the path.

At 1.1 miles, turn left on the Cragway Trail, continuing the climb. Spruce trees begin to appear. The path narrows, squeezing through rocks and tight-knit evergreens, but soon opens onto one of the crags, an angled rock jutting into the sky above the woods. Once you climb the crag, the mountains open before you. The mile-high crest of Grandfather rises above, with more outcrops jutting from the forest ahead. To the east, a host of mountains and valleys and lakes falls away, a mosaic of Carolina highlands. More views open uptrail, then you reach the aptly named Top Crag View at 1.4 miles. It is an open and large rock slab that presents first-rate panoramas up and down the mountain, across Boone Fork and beyond. This is a place to linger.

Carry on the Cragway Trail in increasing spruce woods, running

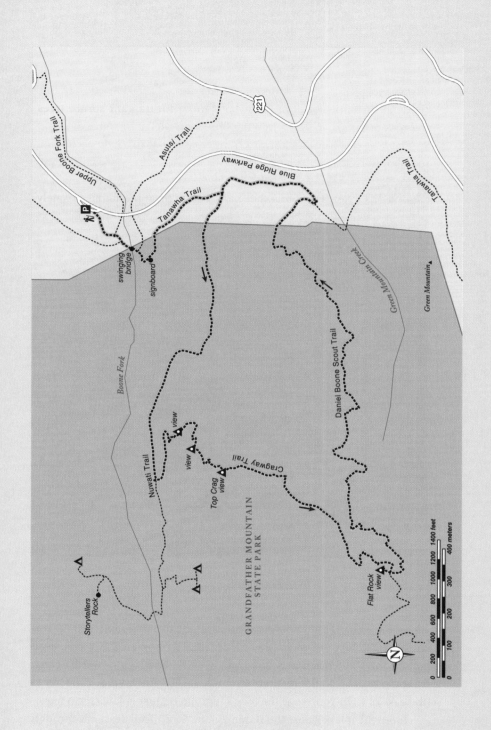

Hiker stands on crags above Boone Fork.

along the brow of outcrop. At 2.0 miles, come to a trail intersection. You are on a shoulder of Grandfather Mountain. To complete the circuit, head left on the Daniel Boone Scout Trail, but first aim right toward a crack in some nearby boulders, then scramble to Flat Rock View. It opens to the east as well. You are at the hike's high point, just below 5,000 feet.

From the intersection, the Daniel Boone Scout Trail descends through spruce and stunted yellow birch. The path is rocky, rooty, and slow going. Take your time as the track switchbacks downhill. Leave state park property just before meeting the Tanawha Trail at 3.2 miles. Head left, northbound, on the Tanawha Trail. Complete the loop portion of the hike at 3.3 miles. From here, backtrack over the Boone Fork swinging bridge, then return to the parking area, completing the hike at 3.7 miles.

Mileages		
	0.0	Boone Fork parking area
	0.4	Nuwati Trail
	1.1	Cragway Trail
	1.4	Top Crag view
	2.0	Daniel Boone Scout Trail
	3.7	Boone Fork parking area

9 ELK KNOB HIKE
Elk Knob State Park

This is a mountain hike in its truest sense and takes place at one of the Tar Heel State's newer preserves, developed with an eye on conserving the resource. Take a finely graded track from a high gap where you switchback ever upward to the top of angled Elk Knob. Here, feast on the panoramas from two major vista points: mountains galore extend from this Southern Appalachian grandstand.

The 1,000-foot climb to the top of Elk Knob is well worth it, and we should be grateful the park is here in the first place. See, this mountain outside Boone has stood proud on the horizon for time untold, making its mark on the scenic landscape of western North Carolina. Locals took its natural majesty for granted. Then one day news came out that Elk Knob was slated for a housing development. A movement began: Elk Knob was purchased by the Nature Conservancy, then turned over to North Carolina for inclusion in its state park system.

Thus, in 2003, Elk Knob State Park came to be. It has taken awhile to get the park going. More trails are in the works. For now, enjoy the Elk Knob Summit Trail and its views, knowing this summit will remain in its natural glory, a diamond on the horizon, protecting the headwaters of

Distance 3.8-mile out-and-back

Hiking time 2.2 hours

Difficulty Moderate

Highlights Mountaintop vistas, high-country forest

Cautions Winter can be very cold and trail inaccessible

Best seasons March through November

Other trail users None

Hours November–February, 7 a.m.–6 p.m.; March–May,
7 a.m.–8 p.m.; June–August, 7 a.m.–9 p.m.; September–
October, 7 a.m.–8 p.m.; closed Christmas Day

Trail contact Elk Knob State Park, 5564 Meat Camp Road, Todd, NC
28684, 828-297-7261, www.ncparks.gov/elk-knob-state-park

Finding the trailhead From the intersection of US 421 and NC 194 in Boone,
take NC 194 North for 4.3 miles to turn left on Meat Camp Road, then
follow it for 5.4 miles to turn left into Elk Knob State Park. Enter the
park and drive a short distance to the Elk Knob Trail parking area.

GPS trailhead coordinates 36.331583, –81.689111

the North Fork New River, which flows from northern hardwood forests where the rare Gray's lily and large purple fringed orchid thrive.

Elk Knob stands at 5,520 feet. Your route to the top starts in an un-named gap, elevation 4,560 feet, to the west of Elk Knob. Pick up the Elk Knob Summit Trail beyond a pole gate. You are in a grand northern hardwood forest of buckeye, along with northern red oak, red maple, yellow birch, and beech, with a grassy understory in many places.

Yellow buckeyes, also referred to simply as buckeyes, are primarily found in mountainous areas in the western part of the Tar Heel State; Great Smoky Mountains National Park is a stronghold. Buckeyes are found from around 1,500 to 5,250 feet in elevation. The buckeyes on Elk Knob are near the upper end of their elevation tolerance. The buckeye's fruit—a smooth brown orb with a singular lighter spot, the "eye"—is its most easily identifiable feature. Leaves are usually found in clusters of five. The fruit does recall the eye of a deer. The bark is grayish brown and often mottled. In spring, clusters of large, showy yellow flowers rise 2 to 3 inches from the leaves. Buckeyes are among the first trees to leaf out in spring and also one of the first trees to turn color in the fall.

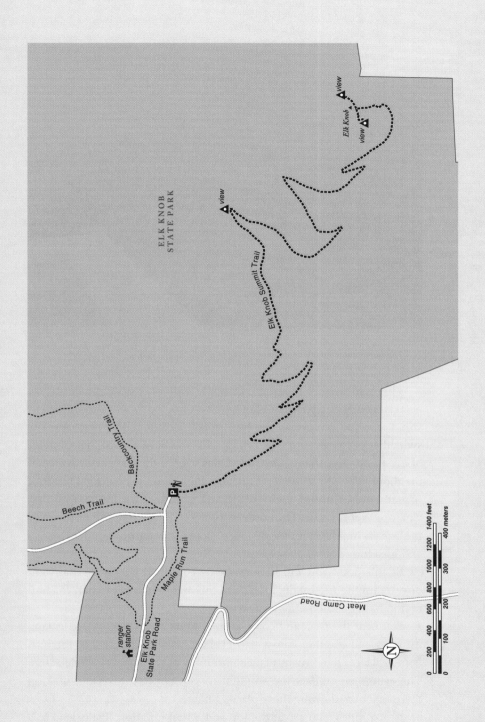

ELK KNOB
STATE PARK

view

Elk Knob Summit Trail

view

Elk Knob

view

Backcountry Trail

Beech Trail

P

Maple Run Trail

ranger
station

Elk Knob
State Park Road

Meat Camp Road

N

0   200   400   600   800   1000   1200   1400 feet
0   100   200   300   400 meters

The overlook at Elk Knob delivers hikers to a rewarding vista.

This trail doesn't follow some settler path or logging grade. It has been laid out with precision—not too steep, not too rough. Unfortunately, stinging nettle can crowd the trail in late summer. The first of many switchbacks comes at .2 mile. By .7 mile you have gained the shoulder of Elk Knob. From here, the trail angles over to the cooler north side of the mountain, where the trees are also subject to the continual blasts of winter winds, stunting their growth and molding their limbs. Your first view opens at 1.0 mile. The northwestern mountains of Carolina give way to Virginia highlands in the distance. Note the patchwork quilt of woods and meadows among the peaks and valleys.

By this point you will have crisscrossed an old jeep track that went directly up the mountain. Don't use this track. It is kept open for trail maintenance and emergency use only.

You near the peak and curve around to its south side before leaving the trees and opening onto a "laurel slick," as old timers called them. A laurel slick is a low, brushy plant community of scrub and rhododendron. The evergreens reflect the sunlight more than tree covering, making them "slick" and giving these places a name.

At 1.9 miles, you are at the top and a trail junction. Trails lead to a north view and a south view. From the south view, Grandfather Mountain and Mount Mitchell stand on the distant horizon. Snake Mountain, Beech Mountain, and Humpback Mountain stand in the near. Enjoy the north view from the peak itself. A clearing presents a panorama opening north toward Virginia, where its high point of Mount Rogers prevails above a melding of rivers, peaks, woods, farms, and communities. After reveling in the views from the top, you will agree that the climb is easily worth it.

Mileages	0.0	Trailhead
	1.0	First view
	1.9	Top of Elk Knob
	3.8	Trailhead

10 VIEWS FROM MOUNT JEFFERSON
Mount Jefferson State Natural Area

This mountain trek leads you to several overlooks at iconic Mount Jefferson State Natural Area. Start at Sunset Overlook, then ascend through rich but rocky woods to gain looks from Sunrise Overlook, Jefferson Overlook, the peak of Mount Jefferson, and my personal favorite, Luther Rock. Loop the mountain crest before backtracking to your starting point.

Originally established in 1956 as Mount Jefferson State Park, this preserve now bears the name Mount Jefferson State Natural Area, which reflects its status as an important flora and fauna harborage. Widely varied vegetation cloaks its slopes, from dogwoods to big-toothed aspens. Administrated by North Carolina State Parks, the registered National Natural Landmark rises 1,600 feet above the surrounding landscape, to 4,683 feet in elevation. Named for our third president, Thomas Jefferson, who with his father owned land in the area, the peak now offers hikers a chance to hike to view after view, to vista after vista. Parts of the adventure parallel a scenic road built by the Civilian Conservation Corps in the 1930s.

We use part of that road to reach the Sunset Overlook trailhead. The

Distance 4.7-mile balloon loop with spur

Hiking time 2.3 hours

Difficulty Moderate, does have 1,000-foot climb

Highlights Views galore

Cautions None

Best seasons Whenever the skies are clear

Other trail users None

Hours November–February, 7 a.m.–6 p.m.; March–April, September–October, 7 a.m.–8 p.m.; May–August, 7 a.m.–9 p.m.; closed Christmas Day

Trail contact Mount Jefferson State Natural Area, 1481 Mount Jefferson State Park Road, West Jefferson, NC 28694, 336-246-9653, www.ncparks.gov/mount-jefferson-state-natural-area

Finding the trailhead From the intersection of NC 194 and US 421 in Boone, take US 421 East for 8.9 miles to US 221 North. Drive north on US 221 for 14 miles, then turn right onto Mount Jefferson State Park Road and follow it for 2.0 miles to Sunset Overlook and a parking area.

GPS trailhead coordinates 36.401707, –81.469773

rest of the climb is by foot, though others will be making the drive to the top. At the trailhead, you will be wowed by the views from Sunset Overlook. Here Grandfather Mountain and a swarm of other peaks stand to the west, while the town of West Jefferson occupies the valley below. Of course, the best views are earned on foot. Therefore we take the single-track, natural-surface Spur Trail from the north side of Sunset Overlook, climbing into sloped woods of chestnut oaks and sugar maple on the west side of the mountain. Exposure—north, east, south, or west—goes a long way in determining forest type on the slopes of Mount Jefferson. It isn't long before the Spur Trail makes a switchback using stone steps, then rises to meet the Mountain Ridge Trail at .3 mile. At this intersection head right, south, toward Sunrise Overlook. Traverse rocky woods, emerging at the Civilian Conservation Corps–built mountain road and Sunrise Overlook at .5 mile. Here your best view is to the south—and east—over the Beaver Creek valley, as well as Frenches Knob, Nettle Knob, and Mulatto Mountain.

Backtrack for .2 mile, then continue on a new pathway, rising on the Mountain Ridge Trail. Below, through the trees, are the towns of Jefferson

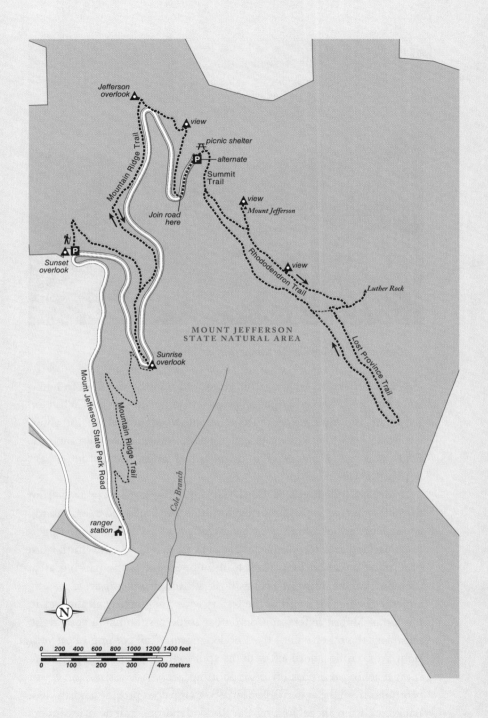

Jefferson overlook

view

picnic shelter

P

alternate

Summit
Trail

Mountain Ridge Trail

Join road
here

view
Mount Jefferson

view

Rhododendron Trail

Luther Rock

Sunset
overlook

P

Lost Province Trail

MOUNT JEFFERSON
STATE NATURAL AREA

*Sunrise
overlook*

Mountain Ridge Trail

Mount Jefferson State Park Road

Cole Branch

ranger
station

N

| 0 | 200 | 400 | 600 | 800 | 1000 | 1200 | 1400 feet |

| 0 | 100 | 200 | 300 | 400 meters |

Distant mountains rise above Mount Jefferson from Luther Rock.

and West Jefferson. After a gentle climb, at 1.2 miles, you'll reach Jefferson Overlook. This open outcrop reveals distant panoramas of Whitetop Mountain and Mount Rogers—two notable Virginia peaks rising above the North Fork New River valley, along with innumerable hills, mounts, fields, and flats, a mosaic of wild and tamed lands. Wind-stunted oaks border the wide outcrop.

Continue the Mountain Ridge Trail, climbing stone steps away from the Jefferson Overlook. Join a ridgeline with wind-affected trees, passing a smaller overlook offering a view directly north. Emerge at the uppermost parking area for Mount Jefferson at 1.5 miles. All who climb from here must do so on foot. Walk to the upper end of the parking area, then pick up the Summit Trail as it rises through a picnic area, passing a picnic shelter. This part of the trail is wide and gravelly all the way to the top of Mount Jefferson. Come near some restrooms on your right, then pass the other end of the Rhododendron Trail coming in on your right. At 1.9 miles, head left with the spur to the top of Mount Jefferson, soon reaching the possibly disappointing peak. A transmission tower protrudes from the apex, while a small outcrop does provide a north view. Backtrack from there, joining the Rhododendron Trail as it meanders almost level, heading southeast along the edge of the mountain. This drop-off allows almost continual views to the east. Outcrops beckon you to additional vistas. You get a real sense of being atop a mountain here, and this is arguably the best part of the hike. Trailside interpretive information enhances the experience. At 2.3 miles, head left to Luther Rock. Pop out on open stone and a fantastic view along a narrow spine of rock. The peak of Mount Jefferson rises to your left, while the South Fork New River valley meanders to the east. Walk all the way down the rock spine to grasp more panoramas north and south.

After luxuriating in the scenery, resume the Rhododendron Trail and quickly head left on the Lost Province Trail. Lost Province was the nickname for this once-isolated part of the Tar Heel State, due to the lack of roads through the mountain ramparts. The Lost Province Trail is mostly level and circles to the south end of the peak and back to meet the Rhododendron Trail at 3.0 miles. Stay left here, continuing in highland woods to loop atop Mount Jefferson before meeting the Summit Trail again at 3.4 miles. From here, backtrack 1.3 miles to the trailhead at Sunset Overlook, almost all downhill this time. Enjoy the walk.

Mileages	0.0	Sunset Overlook / trailhead
	0.5	Sunrise Overlook
	1.2	Jefferson Overlook
	1.9	Top of Mount Jefferson
	2.3	Luther Rock
	3.4	Backtrack toward trailhead
	4.7	Sunset Overlook / trailhead

11 RIVERBEND TRAIL
New River State Park

This fine day hike or overnight backpacking trip takes place at the Wagoner access of New River State Park. Leave the South Fork New River bottoms, then join the Fern Nature Trail. Rise on slopes above the water, then pick up the Riverbend Trail. It takes you along the slopes of The Peak. Finally, hike a ridge forming a sharp bend in the South Fork New River. Drop to the waterway and reach a remote shoreline of the park, where campsites await backcountry travelers.

Distance 7.7-mile out-and-back, including subloop

Hiking time 3.8 hours

Difficulty Moderate, much level hiking

Highlights River views, backcountry camping

Cautions None

Best seasons Spring through fall

Other trail users None

Hours December–February, 7 a.m.–6 p.m.; March–April, 7 a.m.–9 p.m.;
May–September, 7 a.m.–10 p.m.; October, 7 a.m.–9 p.m.;
November, 7 a.m.–8 p.m.; closed Christmas Day

Trail contact New River State Park, 1447 Wagoner Access Road, Jefferson,
NC 28640, 336-982-2587, www.ncparks.gov/new-river-state-park

Finding the trailhead From the intersection with US 421 on the west side
of Wilkesboro, take NC 16 North 23 miles to NC 88. Turn right, heading
east on NC 88, and follow it 1.4 miles to Wagoner Access Road. Turn
left on Wagoner Access Road and follow it 1 mile to enter the park.
Follow the park access road to its end on the South Fork New River.

GPS trailhead coordinates 36.415867, –81.386658

With a name like New River State Park, it stands to reason the preserve would be water-centric, and the South Fork New River does play a large role in park recreation. However, the Wagoner access offers a swath of riverside lands large enough to create a 7-plus-mile there-and-back hike to backcountry campsites on a sharp bend along the South Fork. Don't sweat it if you are not a backpacker and prefer day hiking. Most users of the Riverbend Trail—your main pathway conduit for this trek—do it as a day hike. However, for those inclined, the hike visits six backcountry campsites: two on the slopes of The Peak, and four alongside the South Fork New River. Reservations are required for these primitive camps.

The hike also travels beside the Wagoner access walk-in campground, riverside camps just a short distance from the trailhead. These sites may draw you in to overnight as well. The hike itself starts at the walk-in campground parking area. Leave from the parking area's south end on a wide gravel path, then cross an open grassy area with picnic tables. Next, walk by the group campground—an old homesite—to enter the

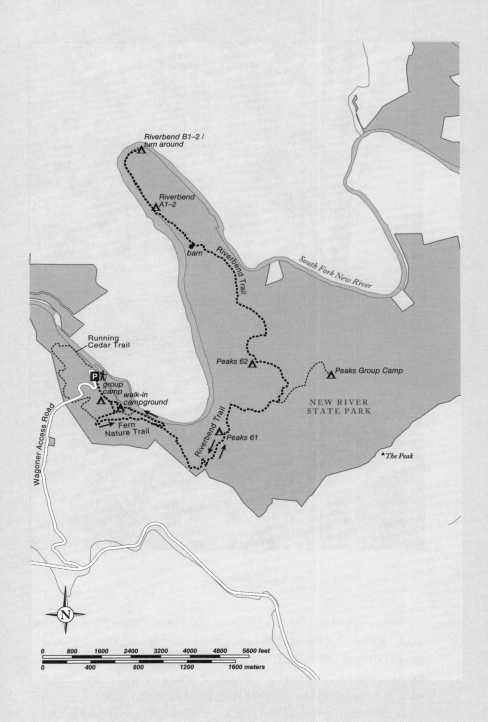

Riverbend B1–2 /
turn around

Riverbend
A1–2

barn

Riverbend Trail

South Fork New River

Running
Cedar Trail

Peaks 62

Peaks Group Camp

group
camp
walk-in
campground

NEW RIVER
STATE PARK

Fern
Nature Trail

Riverbend Trail

Peaks 61

The Peak

Wagoner Access Road

N

| 0 | 800 | 1600 | 2400 | 3200 | 4000 | 4800 | 5600 feet |

| 0 | 400 | 800 | 1200 | 1600 meters |

The New River rushes past a trailside sandbar.

walk-in campground. At .2 mile, head right on the signed Fern Nature Trail, located near the walk-in campground bathhouse. The singletrack, natural-surface foot trail turns up a hollow, passing an intersection with the Running Cedar Trail at .3 mile. Climb onto a wooded slope above the walk-in campground to meet the Riverbend Trail at .7 mile.

Begin heading toward the "back 40" of the Wagoner access under buckeye, black birch, and maples with a ferny understory on the singletrack Riverbend Trail. Circle in and out of attractive wooded coves, each with its own streambed, aiming for the South Fork New River 300 feet below. At points you will get off the singletrack trail and hike on old mountain roads. But the way is blazed, clear, and well maintained. At 1.4 miles, come to signed Peaks 61 backcountry campsite, located on a side ridge, a simple affair with just a fire ring. Bring your own water.

Curve around a rib ridge of The Peak at 1.6 miles, entering more coves. At 1.9 miles, come to an intersection. Here a signed spur trail leads right to the Peaks Group Camp. The Riverbend Trail heads abruptly left, bisecting a rhododendron thicket before crossing a linear boulder garden running toward the river at 2.1 miles. Reach the Peaks 62 backcountry campsite at 2.2 miles. It is also set on a flat adjacent to the trail, equipped with a fire ring.

Ahead, at 2.4 miles, step over a small stream with a short boardwalk over a wetland. Just ahead, cross a doubletrack jeep road with which the Riverbend Trail plays tag, going on and off it. For now, the Riverbend Trail winds along a side slope above Macks Creek before returning to the jeep track at 2.7 miles, amid a grove of planted white pines. Continue out the ridge around which the entire South Fork New River bends. The waterway is visible through the trees as the ridge steepens and narrows. Cut under a powerline at 3.1 miles. Walk through more even-aged planted pines, which create a strange fairyland-like atmosphere with the endless brown trunks and needle floor. Stranger still, the Riverbend Trail leads directly through an old barn, now surrounded by thick woods, at 3.2 miles. Of course, this arrangement could come in handy during a thunderstorm.

Continue descending toward the South Fork New River, and by 3.5 miles you will reach Riverbend backcountry campsites A1 and A2, also under white pines, next to the moving water. These sites also only have a fire ring. The path presents good looks at the South Fork, and you continue in riparian woods, bending to finally reach Riverbend backcountry campsites B1 and B2. Here the path ends at a sandbar and paddler campsite access at 3.9 miles. Relax a bit and have a snack, or pitch your tent if overnighting it. Either way, you'll find the experience rewarding. On the return trip, continue the loop of the Fern Nature Trail, taking in more river scenes and passing through the walk-in campground.

Mileages	0.0	Parking area
	0.7	Join Riverbend Trail
	1.4	Peaks 61 campsite
	2.2	Peaks 62 campsite
	3.2	Old barn
	3.5	Riverbend campsites A1 and A2
	3.9	Riverbend campsites B1 and B2; turn around here
	7.1	Rejoin Fern Nature Trail, walk-in campground
	7.7	Parking area

12 RIVER RUN HIKE

New River State Park

Ramble through a parcel of New River State Park, making a circuit that explores the lands and waters along the South Fork New River. Leave the ridgetop visitor center on the Hickory Trail as it wanders through rich forest down to the South Fork New River. Join the River Run Trail, then curve along the bend of the alluring waterway, visiting the former Stump homesite on the way. The final part of the hike climbs back to the visitor center.

New River State Park comprises several tracts along the South Fork New River and the main stem of the New River. Located in mountainous northwestern North Carolina, the New River cuts a scenic valley through the Southern Appalachians before flowing into Virginia. Luckily for us, the North Carolina state park system has been acquiring and continues to acquire riverside tracts that present paddling, camping, and of course hiking possibilities, along with preserving the resource for future North Carolinians to enjoy.

This beautiful hike takes place in the US 221 access tract of New River State Park, situated on the inside of a big bend in the South Fork New River, where the waterway curves around sloping Huckleberry Ridge. This land, like many other park tracts, was once farmed, and parts of it are returning back to nature. The park system's integrated recreation-based infrastructure allows us to engage with the park whether we are floating down the river in a canoe or kayak, fishing for smallmouth bass, hiking through mixed woods and fields, having a picnic, or

Distance 2.5-mile balloon loop

Hiking time 1.2 hours

Difficulty Easy to moderate

Highlights River views, Stump homesite

Cautions None

Best seasons Year-round

Other trail users None

Hours December–February, 7 a.m.–7 p.m.; March–April,
    7 a.m.–9 p.m.; May–September, 7 a.m.–10 p.m.; October,
    7 a.m.–9 p.m.; November, 7 a.m.–8 p.m.; closed Christmas Day

Trail contact New River State Park, 1447 Wagoner Access Road, Jefferson,
    NC 28640, 336-982-2587, www.ncparks.gov/new-river-state-park

Finding the trailhead From Sparta, take US 21 North for 2.9 miles, then
    turn left onto US 221 South and follow it for 13.2 miles to turn left
    into the US 221 access of New River State Park. Follow the main
    park road for .2 mile, then turn right toward the park campground
    and make an immediate left into the visitor center parking area.

GPS trailhead coordinates 36.465516, –81.341498

camping in the developed drive-up campground or the riverside walk-in campground. And you can undertake all the above activities just here at the US 211 access!

Start the hike on the Track Trail. As you face the park visitor center, walk around the left side of the building and join the Track Trail as it leaves the grassy building yard and then descends into hardwoods of maple, oak, and white pine. You'll quickly meet the Campground Spur Trail. Head left on the singletrack Campground Spur Trail, contouring along the slope of Huckleberry Ridge. Meet the Hickory Trail at .2 mile. Stay right here and continue down the grade, which ultimately leads to the South Fork New River, 200 or so feet lower in elevation. The path weaves through regenerated fields: now pioneer species walnut, locust, and tulip trees rise where cattle once grazed.

At .6 mile, come to a trail junction. Stay right here as the loop portion of the Hickory Trail goes left. Then, just ahead, a short trail heads left to the park Community Building. We stay right with an arm of the still-descending Hickory Trail to emerge at a parking area at .8 mile. On your

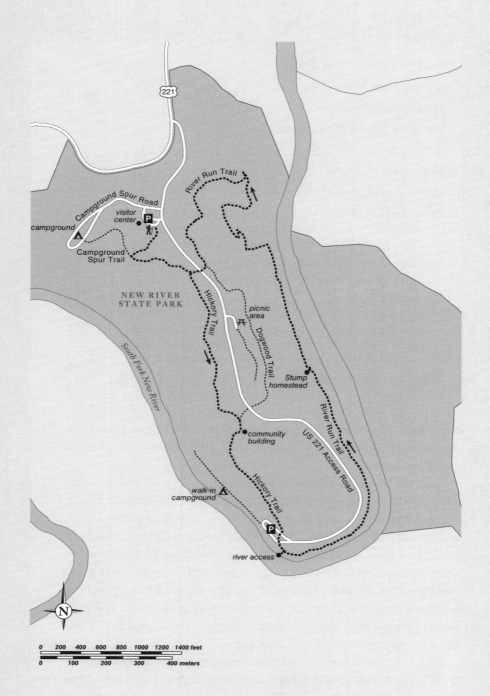

221

Campground Spur Road

visitor
center

P

campground

Campground
Spur Trail

River Run Trail

NEW RIVER
STATE PARK

Hickory Trail

picnic
area

Dogwood Trail

South Fork New River

Stump
homestead

River Run Trail

community
building

US 221 Access Road

walk-in
campground

Hickory Trail

P

river access

N

0   200   400   600   800   1000 1200 1400 feet

0   100   200   300   400 meters

The River Run Trail traverses a host of vegetation along the New River.

right lies the recommended walk-in campground, with shaded camp-sites along the banks of the South Fork New River. Our hike angles left across the parking lot, aiming for the park's canoe/kayak launch. Here, at a sandy bend in the wide waterway, paddlers launch, often making a day-trip float 8 miles downstream to the Kings Creek access off Kings Creek Road. The state park has designated primitive camping sites at various points along the river, allowing for multinight canoe and kayak camping trips.

Join the River Run Trail after checking out the river. This path stays at water level, curving with the South Fork as it makes a hairpin turn around Huckleberry Ridge. User-created spur trails lead to the water's edge, where you can observe the waterway and the hills that rise from its banks. Sycamore, white pine, and willow as well as mixed brush border the grassy, sometimes sandy path. The South Fork New River bustles along in Class I shoals. At 1.2 miles, the trail bisects a pine grove. By 1.4 miles, the valley opens, and you soon come to the signed Stump homesite. Here a springhouse, chimney, and root cellar remain from this farm that was in existence from 1937 to 1956. Quay and Lester Stump primarily grew corn in the riverside flats, but in 1956 a fire burned down the house. After that, the Stumps moved on to greener pastures, and eventually the state of North Carolina bought the land for this park.

Beyond the Stump homesite, the River Run Trail enters a white pine grove overlooking the clear, 120-foot-wide South Fork New River. The banks alternate between overhanging brush and sandy spots, overwash from periodic high-water events. At 1.7 miles the trail leaves the South Fork and turns up a hollow. From there, switchbacks ease the ascent, and by 2.2 miles you are alongside the main park road. At 2.3 miles, intersect the Hickory Trail. From here, head right, crossing the main park road to soon complete the loop portion of the hike. From there, backtrack .2 mile to the visitor center, concluding the adventure. Consider incorporating other activities into your visit to the US 221 access of New River State Park.

Mileages	0.0	Visitor center
	0.8	Lower parking area / walk-in campground
	1.4	Stump homesite
	2.3	Complete loop
	2.5	Visitor center

13 STONE MOUNTAIN LOOP

■■ Stone Mountain State Park

This highlight reel of a hike takes you on a first-rate exploration of Stone Mountain State Park. First, climb to Wolf Rock and the first of several huge granite domes that present fascinating geology and even better views. Descend to explore the preserved Hutchinson Farm, with its restored buildings and interpretive information. From there, head to Big Sandy Creek to view three waterfalls, including 200-foot Stone Mountain Falls. Close the loop with a climb over Stone Mountain itself, which offers vistas galore. Allow plenty of time to enjoy the many sights here.

First-time visitors will be happily surprised with Stone Mountain State Park. Not only does it feature highlights galore on its 18-mile trail system, but additional park amenities range from picnicking grounds to a ninety-site drive-up campground—plus backpacking—to fishing 20 miles of trout streams to rock climbing and horseback riding. Come and let it all soak in.

Covering 14,000 acres, the granite domes—and the waterfalls that flow over them—are the preserve's signature features. Established in 1969, Stone Mountain State Park received the prestigious National Natural Landmark designation in 1975. Start the adventure at the lower trailhead, replete with restrooms, on a connector trail linking to the balance of pathways. Hike along a small creek ensconced in rhododendron and reach an intersection. Here, head right for Wolf Rock and the Hutchinson Homestead, descending to cross the creek below. At .2 mile, split right on the Wolf Rock Trail and begin a prolonged ascent in fire-managed woods of tulip trees and pines. Stone Mountain is visible through the trees to your left. By .9 mile, reach a flat and the crown of Wolf Rock, joining an old roadbed under black gum and oaks, walking parallel to an old stone wall.

At 1.2 miles, reach the signed spur leading you right to Wolf Rock. Soon the trail opens onto a football-field-sized (or bigger) sloping stone expanse, pocked with a few stunted pines and water-cut rivulets. Instant and expansive panoramas open of the Roaring River valley below and the Blue Ridge rising to your right. Explore the outcrop, then return to the

65

Mountains

Distance 8.2-mile loop including spurs

Hiking time 4.4 hours

Difficulty Moderate to difficult

Highlights Granite domes, vistas, historic farm, waterfalls, attractive forest

Cautions Granite domes can be slick when wet

Best seasons Year-round

Other trail users None

Hours November–February, 7 a.m.–6 p.m.; March–April,
September–October, 7 a.m.–8 p.m.; May–August, 7 a.m.–9 p.m.;
closed Christmas Day

Trail contact Stone Mountain State Park, 3042 Frank Parkway, Roaring Gap,
NC 28668, 336-957-8185, www.ncparks.gov/stone-mountain-state-park

Finding the trailhead From Exit 83 on I-77 near Elkin, take US 21
Bypass toward Roaring Gap / Sparta and follow it 11 miles, then
turn left onto Traphill Road. Follow it 4.4 miles to turn right onto
John P. Frank Parkway. Stay on the parkway for 4.0 miles, then veer
right onto Stone Mountain Road and follow it 1.4 miles to what
is known as the Stone Mountain State Park lower trailhead.

GPS trailhead coordinates 36.397986, –81.051071

Wolf Rock Trail, descending through hickory, cedar, and oak (a typical forest found on these thin-soiled granite slopes) to pass a crumbling hunt shack on your right. At 1.6 miles you'll meet the Cedar Rock Trail and Black Jack Ridge Trail. Turn left here onto the Cedar Rock Trail, ascending naked slickrock to open onto sloped and wide Cedar Rock and another staggering view, this time to the east. Ahead, Stone Mountain stretches wide in all its glory, with the Big Sandy Creek valley below and wooded hills beyond. From here, angle up and to the left to rejoin the trail after crossing Cedar Rock.

The path descends to intersect the other end of the Black Jack Ridge Trail at 2.1 miles. Stay left here and descend a doubletrack to meet the Stone Mountain Loop Trail at 2.4 miles. Head left here, passing through meadows, and you'll soon meet the Hutchinson Homestead, situated in a valley at the base of Stone Mountain. Explore the outbuildings and home, learning about the family and their way of life through the decades through interpretive signage. Seems like it sure was simpler then. After

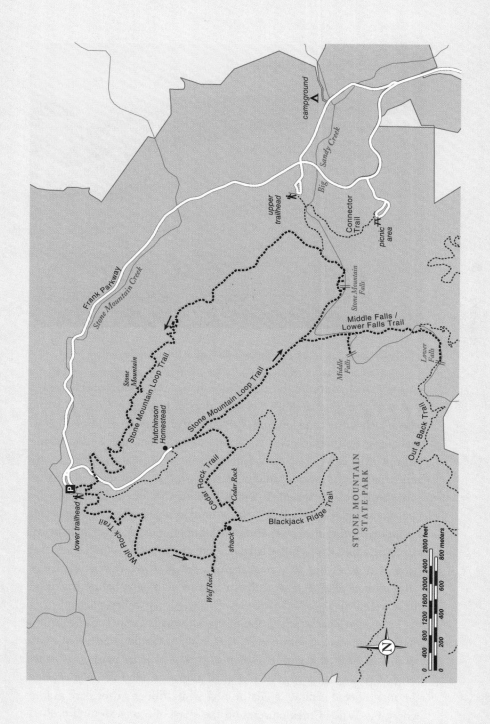

camground

Big Sandy Creek

Connector Trail

picnic area

upper trailhead

Frank Parkway

Stone Mountain Creek

Stone Mountain Falls

Middle Falls / Lower Falls Trail

Stone Mountain Loop Trail

Stone Mountain Loop Trail

Middle Falls

Lower Falls

Out & Back Trail

Stone Mountain

Hutchinson Homestead

Cedar Rock Trail

Cedar Rock

Blackjack Ridge Trail

shack

Wolf Rock Trail

Wolf Rock

lower trailhead

P

STONE MOUNTAIN STATE PARK

N

0   400   800   1200   1600   2000   2400   2800 feet
0   200   400   600   800 meters

Pockmarked Cedar Rock provides an open vista of Stone Mountain.

backtracking, continue the Stone Mountain Loop Trail, southbound in woods, dipping to parallel a clear tributary of Big Sandy Creek in scenic woods rich with rhododendron. Bridge the tributary several times before reaching a trail intersection at 3.3 miles. Head right here on the Middle Falls / Lower Falls Trail, now following along Big Sandy Creek. At 3.5 miles, split right toward Middle Falls, passing an oddly eroded rock before coming to the waterfall, which forms an 18-foot slide cascade in a deep rock cleft, then slows in a stone-bordered pool. Return to the main trail, now aiming for Lower Falls, rock-hopping Big Sandy Creek before climbing a hill. Pass a horse barrier. Here an arm of the Out & Back Trail leaves left. Rock-hop the creek again to reach Lower Falls at 4.2 miles. This layered cataract first spills in narrow stairsteps before making a long, widening 25-foot slide to slow in a large, crystalline pool.

From here, backtrack to the Stone Mountain Loop Trail, resuming the loop, to reach a set of stairs that leads to fabulous 200-foot Stone Mountain Falls at 5.4 miles. Interestingly, its official name on United States Geological Survey (USGS) quad maps is Little Falls. Name aside, the magnificent cataract spills in long white ribbons over bare granite where Big Sandy Creek plunges off the slope of Stone Mountain. Boulders at the base offer natural seating. Continue up a long staircase to reach a second, then third top-down view at Stone Mountain Falls, with the Blue Ridge forming a backdrop—first-rate North Carolina state park scenery. The slope has eased as you pass a spur trail leading right to the upper trailhead at 5.7 miles. A chimney stands nearby. Stay left here, still on the Stone Mountain Loop Trail, climbing through pines and hickories. The trail leads across granite slabs, revealing photo-worthy scenes of the hills and valleys—and other granite slabs—in the distance. Cut through a gap before ascending by switchbacks to make the top of Stone Mountain at 7.2 miles. Nearby outcrops provide still more views.

From the top, the downgrade is steep in places, bisecting small slabs ahead, yet eased by steps and staircases. Make a couple of wide switchbacks before crossing the access road to Hutchinson Homestead at 8.1 miles. Keep downhill to reach an intersection just before completing the loop. Head right here and walk a short distance back to the trailhead, completing the hike at 8.2 miles.

Mileages		
	0.0	Lower trailhead
	1.2	Wolf Rock
	1.6	Cedar Rock
	2.4	Hutchinson Homestead
	3.3	Right to Middle/Lower Falls
	5.4	Stone Mountain Falls
	7.2	Top of Stone Mountain
	8.2	Lower trailhead

Soak up this view of the Yadkin River while hiking at Pilot Mountain State Park.

■ *Piedmont*

Hikers and climbers enjoy the outcrops atop Crowders Mountain.

14 CROWDERS MOUNTAIN CIRCUIT

■ Crowders Mountain State Park

This busy and rewarding hike at Crowders Mountain State Park will surprise. Leave the trailhead to ramble through woods and come along the west slope of Crowders Mountain. Then climb the peak to a rocky overlook where exclamatory views extend as far as the eye can see. Maneuver along the stony to the extreme Rocktop Trail, enjoying more distant vistas before completing the loop. The going is slow on the Rocktop Trail, and the trailhead parking area—and trails—can fill on weekends.

Distance 5.4-mile balloon loop

Hiking time 3.0 hours

Difficulty Moderate, does have rocky, slow sections and 500-foot climb

Highlights Views, geology

Cautions Rocktop Trail involves a bit of clambering among boulders

Best seasons Year-round, though summer can be torrid

Other trail users None

Hours December–February, 8 a.m.–6 p.m.; March–April, October, 8 a.m.–8 p.m.; May–September, 8 a.m.–9 p.m.; November, 8 a.m.–7 p.m.; closed Christmas Day

Trail contact Crowders Mountain State Park, 522 Park Office Lane, Kings Mountain, NC 28086, 704-853-5375, www.ncparks.gov/crowders-mountain-state-park

Finding the trailhead From Exit 13 on I-85 east of Gastonia and west of Charlotte, take Edgewood Road South for .7 miles, then turn right onto US 74W / US 29S. Follow it for 1.8 miles to turn left onto Sparrow Springs Road. Follow Sparrow Springs Road for 2.5 miles, then veer right to stay on Sparrow Springs Road. Follow it for .6 mile farther to turn right into the state park, and follow the main road to turn right to the park visitor center.

GPS trailhead coordinates 35.213306, –81.293556

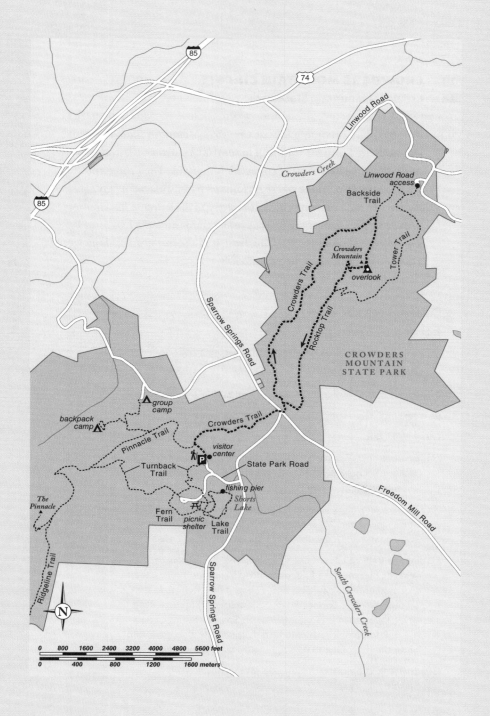

85

74

Linwood Road

Crowders Creek

Linwood Road
access

Backside
Trail

85

Crowders
Mountain

Tower Trail

overlook

Crowders Trail

Rooftop Trail

CROWDERS
MOUNTAIN
STATE PARK

Sparrow Springs Road

group
camp

backpack
camp

Crowders Trail

Pinnacle Trail

visitor
center

P

State Park Road

Turnback
Trail

Freedom Mill Road

The
Pinnacle

fishing pier

Shorts
Lake

Fern
Trail

picnic
shelter

Lake
Trail

Ridgeline Trail

Sparrow Springs Road

South Crowders Creek

N

| 0 | 800 | 1600 | 2400 | 3200 | 4000 | 4800 | 5600 feet |

| 0 | 400 | 800 | 1200 | 1600 meters |

The two peaks of Crowders Mountain State Park—Crowders Mountain and The Pinnacle—rise from the Piedmont in stony splendor, providing this growing area a place to enjoy nature while hiking. And did I mention the views? You will be well rewarded for your efforts with first-rate vistas from montane cliffs rising above the lowlands below. However, the park's popularity may be its primary detraction. If possible, avoid the crowds by visiting in the morning or evening and avoiding obvious times when the park will be crowded. Your experience will be better that way, and you'll reduce the strain on the park's resources from overly concentrated visitation.

By all means do visit. You can't miss the views. Start out by finding the correct trailhead. As you face the park visitor center, look left for a map and kiosk. Join the wide natural-surface track, heading northbound. Cruise through flatwoods. At .1 mile, turn right with the Crowders Trail, as the Pinnacle Trail leads left. Hickories and oaks shade the heavily used trail, with many an exposed root. At .4 mile, cross a small stream under boughs of mountain laurel.

At .8 mile emerge onto and cross Sparrow Springs Road. By now you will have noticed trailside markers adorned with a number, helping rangers locate hikers when trouble arises. At .9 mile, come to a trail intersection. Head left here, staying with the Crowders Trail under pine oak, hickory, sourwood, and sweetgum, along with wild azalea and sparkleberry. Begin working north along the west slope of Crowders Mountain. Standing boulders and outcrops are common. Cross occasional wet-weather drainages flowing off Crowders Mountain.

At 2.1 miles, the trail becomes rockier, traversing little boulder fields. Circle to the north side of the mountain, reaching a trail intersection at 2.6 miles. Here, turn right on the Backside Trail, climbing a doubletrack. Stone cliffs rise to your left. At 3.0 miles, the trail angles left, where you'll make the final climb using seemingly endless steps. Come to a crag on the ridgecrest at 3.1 miles. Carefully explore these cliffs, which open onto implausible panoramas, mostly to the east. Charlotte's skyline rises in the distance, along with hump-like hills escalating above the Piedmont. Be careful—the rock is jagged and irregular—but do look around, to the south and also north.

From the overlook, pick up the Rocktop Trail, heading south to climb to radio towers at the peak. Scoot directly beside the towers to reach a doubletrack tower access road. Here the Rocktop and Tower Trails run in conjunction. Descend by switchbacks to reach an intersection at 3.6

miles. At this juncture, the doubletrack Tower Trail splits left and continues a downgrade, while we stay right on the now-narrow Rocktop Trail, keeping south along the ridge. Here the path becomes unbelievably rocky in places, scattered with pines and offering many a vantage point to both east and west from adjacent outcrops. Look for The Pinnacle to the south. In places you will scramble amid boulders, following the red blazes, sometimes painted onto the rock, to help you through the maze. The hiking is fun, but slow. Allow for the extra time so you can enjoy the ride.

At 4.4 miles, continue descending past eye-catching rock crags rising to your left. Just ahead, leave the stony razorback behind, traveling a dirt path through bucolic woods, quite a change from the adventure along the ridge of Crowders Mountain. At 4.5 miles, meet the Crowders Trail to complete the loop portion of the hike. From here, backtrack to the trailhead, finishing this rocky, exciting North Carolina state park adventure.

Mileages		
	0.0	Visitor center trailhead
	0.8	Cross Sparrow Springs Road
	1.5	Stay with Crowders Trail
	2.6	Join Backside Trail
	3.1	Vista
	4.5	Complete loop portion of hike
	5.4	Visitor center trailhead

15 THE PINNACLE HIKE
Crowders Mountain State Park

This first-rate hike at Crowders Mountain State Park makes a loop that first leads you to The Pinnacle, a rocky peak with extensive views from its stony summit. From there, the Turnback Trail takes you down to Shorts Lake. Circle the still waters in attractive woods, enjoying sights both high and low before returning to the trailhead.

The Pinnacle at Crowders Mountain State Park is aptly named. Rising like the crown of a king, with sheer cliffs at its apex, The Pinnacle rises nearly 700 feet from the surrounding Piedmont, making it not only a beacon but also an excellent vantage point, where you can see to the horizon in all directions. The park came to be in the 1970s, when mining interests

Distance 5.5-mile double loop

Hiking time 3.0 hours

Difficulty Moderate, does have 750-foot climb

Highlights Views, geology, lake

Cautions None

Best seasons Late summer through late spring

Other trail users None

Hours December–February, 8 a.m.–6 p.m.; March–April,
    October, 8 a.m.–8 p.m.; May–September, 8 a.m.–9 p.m.;
    November, 8 a.m.–7 p.m.; closed Christmas Day

Trail contact Crowders Mountain State Park, 522 Park
    Office Lane, Kings Mountain, NC 28086, 704-853-5375,
    www.ncparks.gov/crowders-mountain-state-park

Finding the trailhead From Exit 13 on I-85 east of Gastonia and west
    of Charlotte, take Edgewood Road South for .7 miles, then turn
    right onto US 74W / US 29S and follow it for 1.8 miles to turn
    left onto Sparrow Springs Road. Follow Sparrow Springs Road
    for 2.5 miles, then veer right to stay on Sparrow Springs Road.
    Follow it for .6 mile farther to turn right into the state park, and
    follow the main road to turn right to the park visitor center.

GPS trailhead coordinates 35.213306, –81.293556

wanted to extract minerals from the locale. Nearby Gastonia residents banded together and encouraged the state to instead purchase the land for a state park. It did, and Crowders Mountain State Park has since been expanded twice; it now links to Kings Mountain National Military Park in nearby South Carolina.

Today this is a very popular state park. This hike takes you to the views from The Pinnacle as well as to Shorts Lake, a relic impoundment of latter-year farm families who owned the land that became this preserve. Begin your adventure at the park visitor center. As you face the visitor center entrance, look left for a map board and kiosk. Join the wide natural surface track, northbound. Cruise through flatwoods. At .1 mile, head left with the Pinnacle Trail as the Crowders Trail leads right. Gently ascend among sourwood, hickory, oak, black gum, and pines. At .6 mile, a spur trail leads right to the park backcountry campground. It offers hike-to campsites with picnic table and fire ring. I've overnighted there myself

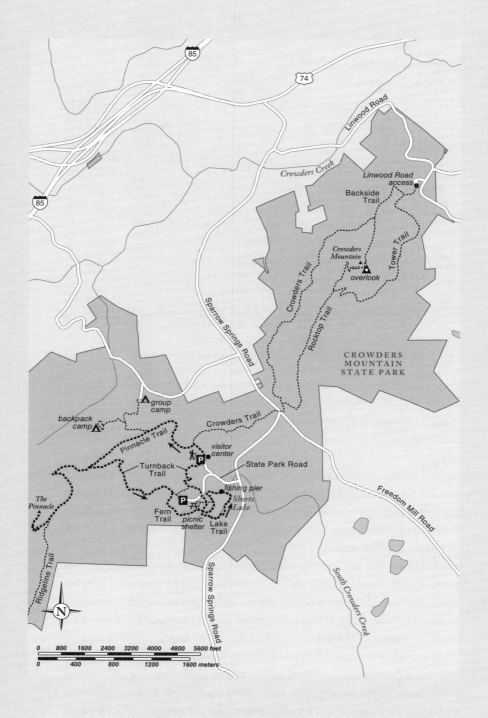

85

74

Linwood Road

Crowders Creek

Linwood Road
access

Backside
Trail

Crowders
Mountain
overlook

Tower Trail

85

Crowders Trail

Rocktop Trail

CROWDERS
MOUNTAIN
STATE PARK

Sparrow Springs Road

group
camp

backpack
camp

Crowders Trail

Pinnacle Trail

visitor
center

P

State Park Road

Turnback
Trail

fishing pier

Shorts
Lake

Freedom Mill Road

The
Pinnacle

P

Fern
Trail

picnic
shelter

Lake
Trail

Ridgeline Trail

N

Sparrow Springs Road

South Crowders Creek

| 0 | 800 | 1600 | 2400 | 3200 | 4000 | 4800 | 5600 feet |

| 0 | 400 | 800 | 1200 | 1600 meters |

The Piedmont stretches across the morning horizon from the Pinnacle Trail.

and recommend the experience. We stay with the Pinnacle Trail, running a piney ridgeline thick with rock outcrops and chestnut oaks.

At 1.1 miles, meet the Turnback Trail in a gap. You will return here later, but for now stay with the Pinnacle Trail, climbing steadily to swing around to the east side of the mountain. Avoid shortcuts. At 1.8 miles, at the base of The Pinnacle, the Ridgeline Trail goes south, eventually leaving North Carolina. We stay with the Pinnacle Trail. Keep rising and you reach the stone crown that is The Pinnacle. Here the path angles up a break in the cliffs using stone steps, and once you're at the top, jaw-dropping views open from outcrops and cliff edges. Walk along The Pinnacle's pine and boulder-pocked ridgecrest. To the south and east the panorama stretches out on the Piedmont. To the northwest runs I-85 and beyond that the town of Kings Mountain. Crowders Mountain and its towers are easily spotted to the northeast, as are the skyscrapers of Charlotte.

Find a perch and relax before continuing the trek by backtracking to the Turnback Trail and descending the southeast slope in rich woods. The terrain flattens out quickly, and you come along a stream before meeting the Fern Trail at 3.9 miles. Here's your chance to explore the lowlands, which first were grazing acreages for elk and buffalo, then family farms held for generations, before becoming a state park. The forest continues to reclaim former fields that once grew tobacco, corn, and cotton. The Fern Trail is much less used than the pathways you've walked thus far. Ahead, a spur goes left up to a picnic shelter just before reaching an intersection near a creek at 4.3 miles. The Fern Trail goes left, while the Lake Trail goes right and straight. Here you head right with the Lake Trail, crossing a small creek on a wooden bridge.

Once across the bridge, stay with the singletrack footpath of the Lake Trail, as a ranger road also circles 9-acre Shorts Lake. Cruise the bottoms as watery vistas open where you can observe the dam and a fishing pier. You may even see a kayaker paddling around in the warm season. Continue circling the impoundment, passing the pier at 4.7 miles. An alternate parking area is to your right. Keep along the shore of Shorts Lake to completely circle the impoundment, and at 5.0 miles you are back where you were before at 4.3 miles. Now head right on the Fern Trail, northbound, once again passing near the picnic shelter and crossing a park road to meet the Turnback Trail at 5.2 miles. Here you head right to hike along a meadow. The visitor center comes into view as you complete your high-and-low adventure at 5.5 miles.

Mileages		
	0.0	Visitor center trailhead
	0.6	Spur to the backcountry campground
	1.1	Meet the Turnback Trail
	2.1	Top of The Pinnacle
	3.1	Right on Turnback Trail
	4.3	Circle Shorts Lake
	5.5	Visitor center trailhead

16 LAKE SHORE TRAIL
Lake Norman State Park

*A local favorite, this hike lives up to its name, as the venture
makes a curvaceous loop along the shore of Lake Norman, at Lake
Norman State Park. The hiker-only circuit cruises amid pines and
hardwoods while rolling in and out of hollows on a peninsula that
juts into the impoundment. Lake views are abundant, and the path
often skirts intimate sand beaches.*

Distance 5.4-mile loop

Hiking time 2.5 hours

Difficulty Moderate

Highlights Lake views

Cautions None

Best seasons Year-round; mornings in summer

Other trail users None

Hours November–February, 7 a.m.–6 p.m.; March–April,
7 a.m.–8 p.m.; May–August, 7 a.m.–9 p.m.; September–
October, 7 a.m.–8 p.m.; closed Christmas Day

Trail contact Lake Norman State Park, 759 State Park Road, Troutman,
NC 28166, 704-528-6350, www.ncparks.gov/lake-norman-state-park

Finding the trailhead From Exit 42 on I-77 north of Charlotte, take US
21 North for 2 miles to turn left on Autumn Leaf Road. Follow it
for 1.9 miles, then turn left on Perth Road and follow it for .3 mile.
Turn right onto State Park Road and follow it for 5.1 miles, then
turn left onto Shortleaf Drive just before reaching the large swim
beach parking area. Follow Shortleaf Drive just a short distance
to immediately turn right and reach the Lake Shore Trailhead.

GPS trailhead coordinates 35.649725, –80.943879

A product of Duke Power's damming of the Catawba River for power
generation, Lake Norman State Park came to be in the 1960s. The preserve, originally named Duke Power State Park, was established on a little

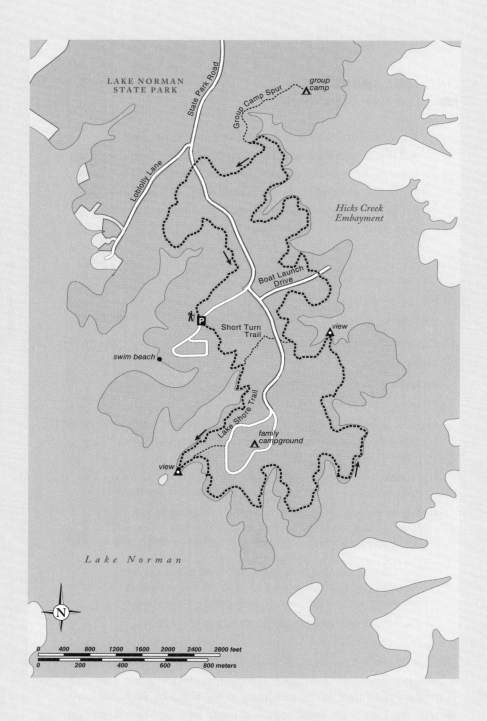

LAKE NORMAN
STATE PARK

State Park Road

Loblolly Lane

Group Camp Spur

group camp

Hicks Creek
Embayment

Boat Launch
Drive

view

Short Turn
Trail

swim beach

Lake Shore Trail

family
campground

view

Lake Norman

N

0   400   800   1200 1600 2000 2400 2800 feet
0   200   400   600   800 meters

The Lake Shore Trail leads you to Lake Norman views like this one.

over 1,300 acres of land on a peninsula set between the Hicks Creek arm and the main channel of the impoundment. Most of Lake Norman's 520 miles of shores are privately owned, making the state park all the more valuable for hikers and outdoor enthusiasts like us.

The Lake Shore Trail is Lake Norman State Park's premier hiker-only trail destination, following the narrowest part of the park peninsula and offering the best views as well. The park also features the 30-plus-mile network of pathways for mountain bikers known as the Itusi Trails. The Itusi Trails are open to hikers, but as a practical matter they are dominated by the two-wheeled set. Hikers who do tackle the Itusi Trails should keep their eyes and ears open for fast-moving mountain bikers.

Lake Norman State Park also offers a large and very popular swim beach, packed during the warm season. The natural shores are also enjoyed by paddlers. You can rent canoes, kayaks, pedal boats, and even paddleboards at the swim beach visitor center or bring your own watercraft and launch at Boat Launch Drive, a road you cross on this hike.

The hike is a good one, presenting beauty near and far. While making its circuit, the Lake Shore Trail repeatedly goes on and off old roads. Fear not, for the trail is well signed and heavily used. But as you hike, imagine this area a century back—dusty, rural farm country with rolling pastures and fields. Harken back still further to the American Revolution, when Patriot fighters took on England's Lord Cornwallis at the Battle of Cowan's Ford, now under the waters of Lake Norman, as the Americans were harassing and slowing Cornwallis's southern advance.

Begin your counterclockwise circuit, descending from Shortleaf Drive into woods of pine, hickory and oak, along with sweetgum and dogwood. Dip to your first hollow and meet the Short Turn Trail. Take this official shortcut if you want to cut your loop down to a 3-mile circuit. Notice how these hollows are populated by moisture-loving ironwood and river birch. All the hollows have wet-weather drainages, but you will see no perennial streams along the trail, though some drainages are bridged for when the streams flow, primarily winter through spring.

Winter is a good time to hike here, when the motorboats are stilled and migratory waterfowl can be spotted on the lake. I like fall, too, when the lake is quieter and the hardwoods are showing their autumn finery, contrasting with the emerald pines. If you come here during summer, especially the weekends, boat noise can be a problem. Come early in the morning during those times, to beat both the heat and the noise.

Continuing the Lake Shore Trail, views are immediate as you gaze down a cove into the body of Lake Norman to reach a wider vista at .6 mile. Here a small lone island stands in the foreground, while an expanse of water and shoreline stretches beyond. At .7 mile, a spur heads to the recommended family campground. With only thirty-three sites, the smallish camp delivers a relaxing atmosphere for an often-busy preserve. RVs and tenters enjoy the campground, though no hookups are available. Hot showers, flush toilets, and water spigots enhance the overnight experience.

Beyond the campground, begin a pattern of curving around a watery cove, then winding around or cutting across a wooded peninsula. The shoreline is dotted with small beaches that present superior views as well as waterplay locales for people and their dogs. By 1.5 miles you have turned into the Hicks Creek embayment and left the main body of Lake Norman. Continue snaking along the shoreline in this narrower part of the lake. Reach a noteworthy view at 2.3 miles, where the trail runs along the shore of a cove and opens onto the greater Hicks Creek embayment.

At 2.5 miles, meet the other end of the Short Turn Trail. Keep straight and go the whole way, crossing Boat Launch Drive at 3.0 miles. The hillsides are sharper as you continue up the Hicks Creek embayment, meeting the Group Camp Spur at 4.0 miles. Stay left with the Lake Shore Trail, leaving the water for a while to cross State Park Road at 4.3 miles. Descend in woods to see the lake's shimmer, and crisscross a powerline before crossing the swim beach access road at 5.2 miles. Hike just a little more through the woods, then you'll emerge back at the trailhead at 5.4 miles to conclude the fun hike.

Mileages	0.0	Lake Shore trailhead
	0.7	Spur to family campground
	2.5	Short Turn Trail
	3.0	Cross Boat Launch Drive
	4.0	Group Camp Spur
	5.4	Lake Shore trailhead

17 VIEWS FROM PILOT MOUNTAIN
■ Pilot Mountain State Park

This highlight-heavy hike packs a big punch in just a few miles. It starts at the top of Pilot Mountain and descends the Grindstone Trail toward bluffs. Next, cruise an incredible cliffline replete with views near and far along the Ledge Spring Trail. Finally, the Jomeokee Trail leads around Pilot Mountain itself: a wonderment of biodiversity, big bluffs, and bigger panoramas where geological wonders await.

Distance 2.7-mile balloon loop

Hiking time 1.5 hours

Difficulty Easy to moderate

Highlights Views, bluffs, rock climbers, biodiversity

Cautions Cliffs

Best seasons Whenever the skies are clear

Other trail users None

Hours December–January, 7 a.m.–6 p.m.; February, 7 a.m.–7 p.m.; March–April, 7 a.m.–9 p.m.; May–September, 7 a.m.–10 p.m.; October, 7 a.m.–9 p.m.; November, 7 a.m.–7 p.m.; closed Christmas Day

Trail contact Pilot Mountain State Park, 1792 Pilot Knob Park Road, Pinnacle, NC 27043, 336-325-2355, www.ncparks.gov/pilot-mountain-state-park

Finding the trailhead From Exit 131 on US 52 (the Pilot Mountain State Park exit), 16 miles north of Winston-Salem, drive a short distance on the access road to reach the state park entrance. Continue on the main park road past the visitor center, heading toward the summit area. Follow the main road 2.2 miles to dead-end at the summit parking area.

GPS trailhead coordinates 36.340548, –80.480192

North Carolina's state parks harbor many noteworthy peaks, but Pilot Mountain may top them all. Situated in the Sauratown Mountains rising above the Carolina Piedmont, Pilot Mountain, with its trademark conical

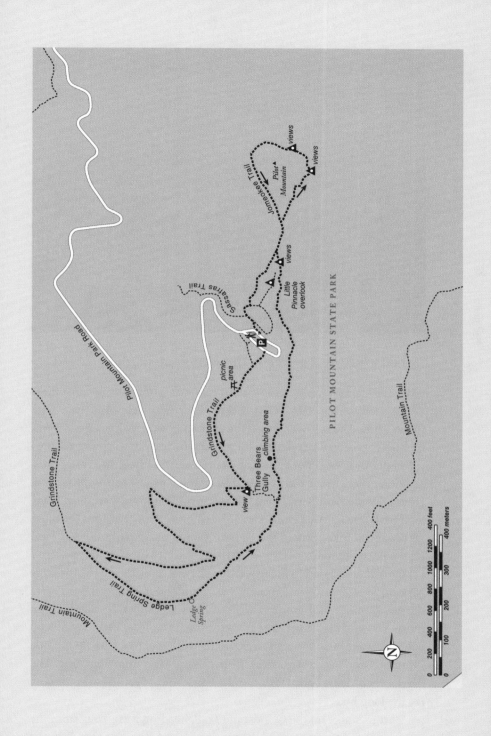

PILOT MOUNTAIN STATE PARK

Views aplenty await hikers here atop Pilot Mountain.

peak, vertical rock walls, and wooded cap, was named for its usefulness as a beacon to passersby, piloting them in their travels all the way back to the Saura Indians, who called the peak Jomeokee. (This hike features the Jomeokee Trail.) Some say the mountain resembles a cake set on a ridgeline. In 1968, Pilot Mountain State Park was established after preservation efforts by local citizenry. It had been a private tourist attraction. Later, additional property along the nearby Yadkin River was added to the total park acreage. Today the state-owned preserve is a beacon for those who want to hike, paddle the Yadkin, camp, and explore the Tar Heel State's great outdoors.

Pilot Mountain can be a busy, crowded park, as evidenced by the large parking area atop the mountain. I recommend avoiding the preserve during summer and autumn weekends. If you must do this hike on those weekend days, get here early to avoid the crowds. Before your loop you may want to do the short trek on the wide concrete path up to Little Pinnacle Overlook. It starts near the parking area restroom building. The overlook will deliver great vistas, and the trek will get your blood pumping for the loop hike.

Start this hike on the Grindstone Trail, heading west, away from the restroom building and toward the picnic area and climbing area. Pass the climbers registration area and descend to reach the picnic area at .1 mile, escaping the nest of trails and sidewalks encircling the upper parking lot. There the track becomes a pure hiking trail, working through widely spaced fire-managed oaks, hickories, and pines, along with blueberry bushes. At .3 mile, reach signed Three Bears Gully. Here climbers access a steep crack in the mountaintop bluff on a park-created shortcut trail, allowing quicker access to the climbing area at the bluff's base. Enjoy the Piedmont view from the nearby outcrops, then continue on a less-used portion of the Grindstone Trail.

The well-maintained gravel path switchbacks downhill. Avoid unofficial unmarked trails. At 1.0 mile, head left on the Ledge Spring Trail as the Grindstone Trail continues for lower terrain. The Ledge Spring Trail begins curving around the mountain on a nearly level gravel track. At 1.3 miles, reach Ledge Spring, which pours from a rock lip and then across the trail. Beyond here, the path becomes more primitive and rough, with stone stairs and irregular footing, as it works up the base of a majestic cliffline rising above. At 1.5 miles, the trail passes under a conspicuous stone overhang. A little beyond there, the trail through Three Bears Gully enters from your left and the signed climbing area begins. At this point you may see climbers along the trail and above, often suspended by ropes, with their peers standing above and below them. It's a sight!

At 1.8 miles, the official climbing area ends. You are still enjoying bluff views above and outward vistas down into the Piedmont from rocky areas mixed with pitch pines, Table Mountain pines, brush, and sourwood. More steps lead ever upward along cliffs and additional views. At 2.0 miles, a view opens of the circular cone of Pilot Mountain ahead. From here, the trail actually descends to quickly join the Jomeokee Trail, which circles Pilot Mountain. Designated a National Natural Landmark, Pilot Mountain is one of thirteen such landmarks in the Tar Heel State.

Ahead, steps lead to the circuit portion of the Jomeokee Trail. Head right. This portion of Pilot Mountain is called Big Pinnacle. When nearing the multihued bluffs of Big Pinnacle, you will see the stone walls fashion a mosaic of tan, black, and gray, rising higher than the bluffs you passed earlier. Atop the bluffs, a flat crown of pines adds a unique touch to Big Pinnacle. More panoramas open and the bluffs above you rise in stately splendor. Beyond Big Pinnacle, lands to the east spread wide and far, including the crags of Hanging Rock State Park. Take your time. A clear day will deliver views to the distant horizon, including Winston-Salem. Curve to the north side of the mountain, noting the spread of rhododendron in this cooler, moister locale. Complete the loop at 2.7 miles, considering that Pilot Mountain may indeed be North Carolina's most distinctive peak.

Mileages   **0.0** Parking area
              0.3 Trail through Three Bears Gully
              1.0 Left on Ledge Spring Trail
              2.0 View of Big Pinnacle; join Jomeokee Trail
              2.7 Parking area

18 MOUNTAIN TRAIL AT PILOT MOUNTAIN
Pilot Mountain State Park

This circuit hike circumnavigates Pilot Mountain, making a full loop along its lower slopes. The less-used track wanders into hollows, along ridges, and through boulder gardens, offering views of the Piedmont below. In other places, you may spot imprints of pre-park residents. The path also crosses several seasonal and perennial streams on the way.

Why does someone climb a mountain? The standard answer: Because it is there. And why does someone circumnavigate a mountain? Likewise: Because they can. And you too can do just that: walk completely around Pilot Mountain, or circumnavigate it, primarily using the Mountain Trail, along with the Grindstone Trail and a small portion of the Grassy Ridge Trail, which together create a 5-plus-mile circuit around the wooded slopes of Pilot Mountain. The hike has views, to be sure, but it also has miles of glorious forest hiking, much of it in the park's less-visited region.

Not only can you commune with nature, you can also escape the crowds that sometimes throng the crest of Pilot Mountain. This would be an excellent autumn-color hike in late October and early November. That is when the oaks, sourwoods, black gums, and other trees will be displaying their orange, yellow, and red hues against the backdrop of deep green pines and slate gray stone.

The trek begins at the park office parking lot, not the newer visitor center. Cross the main park road and reach a trail kiosk. Head left, joining

Distance 5.4-mile loop

Hiking time 2.7 hours

Difficulty Moderate

Highlights Views while circumnavigating Pilot Mountain

Cautions None

Best seasons September through May

Other trail users None

Hours December–January, 7 a.m.–6 p.m.; February, 7 a.m.–7 p.m.;
    March–April, 7 a.m.–9 p.m.; May–September, 7 a.m.–10 p.m.; October,
    7 a.m.–9 p.m.; November, 7 a.m.–7 p.m.; closed Christmas Day

Trail contact Pilot Mountain State Park, 1792 Pilot Knob Park Road, Pinnacle,
    NC 27043, 336-325-2355, www.ncparks.gov/pilot-mountain-state-park

Finding the trailhead From Exit 131 on US 52 (the Pilot Mountain State Park
    exit), 16 miles north of Winston-Salem, drive a short distance on the
    access road to reach the state park entrance. Continue on the main park
    road past the visitor center, heading toward the summit area. Follow the
    main road .2 mile to the state park office parking area on your right.

GPS trailhead coordinates 36.342180, –80.463641

the Grassy Ridge Trail on our clockwise circuit around Pilot Mountain. Enter oak-dominated hardwood forest, along with maple and hickory. You will quickly cross a stream course draining the upper reaches of Pilot Mountain. This pattern will repeat itself time and again—hillside, streambed, hillside, streambed. Though some of the streams are perennial, most run only in winter or during heavy rain periods in the summer. These watercourse micro-environments add an aquatic component to the park's biodiversity, stretching the range of life-forms to creatures like minnows and salamanders, as well as watering the park's four-legged critters, such as skunks, deer, and bobcats.

At .1 mile, head right on the Mountain Trail as the Grassy Ridge Trail heads left. Begin working along the east slope of Pilot Mountain. This area and the south slope were once parts of farms, mostly grazing land, and were the least sloped of the lands currently comprising the park. Note the locusts here, a pioneer species that often comes in to reclaim old fields. The park also uses prescribed fire to shape the forests. In

The Mountain Trail traverses some impressive and rugged terrain.

pre-Columbian days, low-level lightning-caused fires crawled across the Piedmont, shaping the forest makeup.

Ahead, look for faint old roadbeds, squared-off flat spots, and crumbled rock fences, vestiges of a forgotten past. You are cruising around 1,200 feet, continuing to bisect streambeds divided by drier lands. At 1.2 miles, the Corridor Trail splits left, tracing a literal corridor of park property down to the park tract on the banks of the Yadkin River. Our hike continues wandering the south slope of Pilot Mountain, climbing a bit. The slope steepens. At 1.8 miles, the trail makes a hard switchback to the right, followed by a switchback left at 2.0 miles. You are now at 1,500 feet, and the slopes are decidedly sharper and the terrain rockier. The trail runs just below the primary upward thrust of the mountain. In places between the trees, the rock bluffs of the mountaintop are visible, more so in winter. Reach the high point of the hike, 1,595 feet elevation, at 2.3 miles. Roll through woods, then turn north onto the mountain's west slope at 2.8 miles. At 2.9 miles, stone steps lead across a fern- and brush-bordered spring branch running directly down the mountain. Ahead, bisect an impressive boulder garden, opening the forest and providing distant westerly panoramas.

At 3.7 miles, the foot trail picks up and traces an obvious old roadbed.

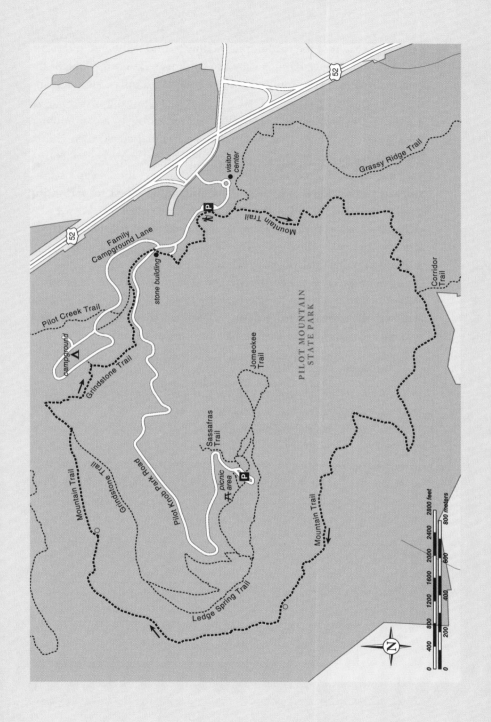

PILOT MOUNTAIN STATE PARK

Grassy Ridge Trail

Corridor Trail

Mountain Trail

visitor center

Family Campground Lane

stone building

Pilot Creek Trail

campground

Grindstone Trail

Mountain Trail

Grindstone Trail

Pilot Knob Park Road

Sassafras Trail

Jomeokee Trail

picnic area

Mountain Trail

Ledge Spring Trail

52

52

N

0   400   800   1200   1600   2000   2400   2800 feet
0   200   400   600   800 meters

Look to the right of the road in this vicinity to find a dug-out, moss-bordered spring. The walking is easy as you cruise the north slope of the mountain, coming to a multiway intersection at 4.2 miles. Head left and downhill on the Grindstone Trail, which at this point is a wide road. At 4.3 miles, the Grindstone Trail splits right, returning to a conventional hiking path that dives sharply to cross a perennial creek, then climbs back out just as steeply. At 4.5 miles, reach another intersection. Here a spur goes left and downhill to the park's fine campground. Keep straight, and at 4.7 miles you'll come near the mountaintop access road, running parallel to it. At 4.9 miles, the Pilot Creek Trail heads left, but we stay right, now tracing the crumbling old road used when the mountain was a private tourist destination. Cars were charged $2 for the privilege of motoring up this track down which you walk.

At 5.1 miles, cross the current park road, then pass by the old entrance station before returning to woods at the lower end of the old entrance station parking area. Here, cross one last stream, then return to the office parking area, completing the hiking adventure at 5.4 miles.

Mileages	0.0	Parking area
	1.2	Corridor Trail leaves left
	4.2	Join Grindstone Trail
	4.9	Pilot Creek Trail leaves left
	5.4	Parking area

YADKIN RIVER HIKE
▬ Pilot Mountain State Park

Savor the chance to trek along a major Carolina river at a
waterside parcel of Pilot Mountain State Park to view a historic
canal project from two centuries back. Start the trek by following
small, scenic Horne Creek to meet the Yadkin, then trace the big
waterway upstream to Bean Shoals, where long ago a canal project
sought to bypass cataracts. Return through wooded hills above the
Yadkin to complete the rewarding trek.

Distance 5.3-mile balloon loop

Hiking time 2.4 hours

Difficulty Moderate

Highlights Canal works, big river, Yadkin Islands

Cautions Crossings of Horne Creek

Best seasons March through November

Other trail users Equestrians in some places

Hours December–January, 7 a.m.–6 p.m.; February, 7 a.m.–7 p.m.;
   March–April, 7 a.m.–9 p.m.; May–September, 7 a.m.–10 p.m.; October,
   7 a.m.–9 p.m.; November, 7 a.m.–7 p.m.; closed Christmas Day

Trail contact Pilot Mountain State Park, 1792 Pilot Knob Park Road, Pinnacle,
   NC 27043, 336-325-2355, www.ncparks.gov/pilot-mountain-state-park

Finding the trailhead From Exit 129 (the Pinnacle exit) on US 52 north of
   Winston-Salem, take Perch Road westbound for 3.3 miles, then veer right
   on Hauser Road. Follow Hauser Road for 2.2 miles, then turn left again,
   still on Hauser Road, as the road you have been following becomes Caudle
   Road. Continue for .9 mile, then you will see the gravel entrance road to
   this segment of Pilot Mountain State Park. *Do not turn left here*; rather,
   continue .3 mile farther to the large, open Corridor Trail parking area.

GPS trailhead coordinates 36.267699, –80.495745

This is an underrated, rather unique hike in North Carolina's state park
trail system. Not only do you get to walk along the protected banks of a
big river, you also trek a contrastingly small creek and explore early North

Carolina transportation history. I recommend starting at the Hauser Road trailhead, because reaching the parking area inside the park requires a pair of auto fords of Horne Creek. Skip the auto fords and park safely. However, this hike requires that you ford Horne Creek and its tributaries three times on foot. If the water is excessively high and muddy, save it for another day. However, most of the time the fords will be easily doable. Additionally, you are near Horne Creek Living Historical Farm, an official North Carolina historic site, a farmstead frozen in time to the lifeways of the year 1900. Check it out before or after your hike.

Our hike leaves the Corridor Trail parking area, heading east on the Yadkin Islands Trail. Travel thickly wooded bottomlands of Horne Creek, flowing to your right. Sycamores, river birches, and ironwoods rise in ranks. At .2 mile, cross a tributary of Horne Creek, then join and turn right on the gravel main park road as it heads south through a mix of woods and fields. At .4 mile, reach the first crossing of Horne Creek. Also, this is where the Yadkin Islands Trail—your return route—leaves to the right. For now, after crossing Horne Creek, stay with the road to reach a picnic area with restroom at .6 mile. Here, head left on the Horne Creek Trail, a dedicated footpath winding under lush creek-bottom woods rich with beech trees. The path traces the gravelly, gurgling Horne Creek as it courses toward the Yadkin River under a rock-pocked hillside. Step over a pair of tributaries of Horne Creek at 1.0 miles. Return to Horne Creek at 1.4 miles, crossing it on stepping-stones. Continue downstream to reach and carefully cross the active Norfolk Southern railroad tracks, then enter a wooded, potentially wet flat, reaching the banks of the Yadkin at 1.6 miles.

The Yadkin River, over 200 miles long, courses off the east side of the Blue Ridge, flowing east nearly to Winston-Salem before turning south, joining the Uwharrie River to become the Pee Dee River, where the Pee Dee leaves the Tar Heel State for South Carolina, eventually ceding its waters to the Atlantic near Georgetown. An important source of municipal water, the Yadkin is dammed in several locations. North Carolina has established a 130-mile paddle trail along the Yadkin that passes this very locale.

Begin hiking upriver, gaining looks at the wide, rock-studded waterway. The banks drop off about 8–10 feet. Sandy areas are created by the convergence of side creeks and the Yadkin. Pawpaw trees are abundant. Wetlands form away from the river as you hike a berm between the wetlands and the river. At 2.7 miles, the Horne Creek Trail ends at a

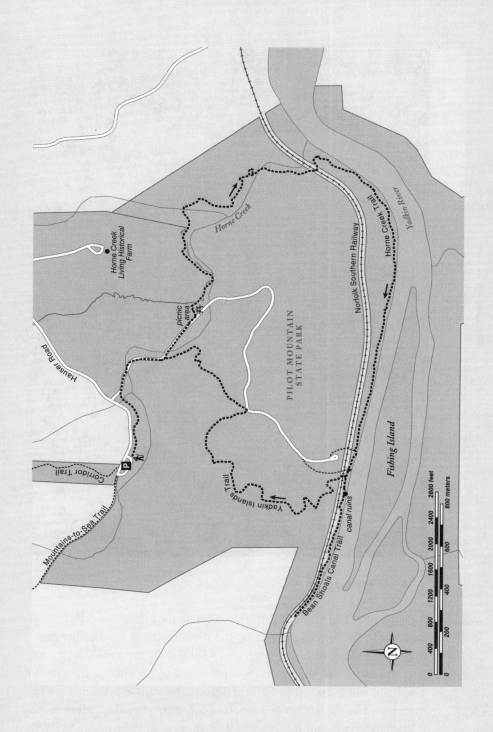

Horne Creek Living Historical Farm

picnic area

Horne Creek

PILOT MOUNTAIN STATE PARK

Hauser Road

Corridor Trail

Mountains-to-Sea Trail

Yadkin Islands Trail

Bean Shoals Canal Trail

canal ruins

Norfolk Southern Railway

Horne Creek Trail

Yadkin River

Fishing Island

N

N

0   400   800   1200   1600   2000   2400   2800 feet
0   200   400   600   800 meters

A field of flowers graces a field near Horne Creek.

trail junction. Here a short path leads right to the end of the gravel main park road. We keep straight along the river, reaching another intersection and sandbar. At low water levels, hikers cross the Yadkin here and head south for the Yadkin Islands, preserved as part of the state park. The main isle is known as Fishing Island. The trails are not marked or maintained on the islands and are accessible only when the Yadkin River is low enough to easily ford. Our route continues straight, passing a third path heading right. This is the other end of the Yadkin Islands Trail, your return route. For now keep straight, cruising along the river on the Bean Shoals Canal Trail, and come to the first of several stone berms that were part of the canal works, ostensibly built to enhance river commerce between Salisbury and Wilkesboro. From 1820 to 1825, locks and the canal were worked on but then abandoned, as costs were too high. Later the railroad used part of the canal route and the retaining wall you see. In places you walk on sandbars and directly along the Yadkin, gaining upstream views of Bean Shoals. The Bean Shoals Canal Trail dead-ends at 3.1 miles, near a little island. Backtrack, taking in river scenes as well as canal ruins, then cross the railroad line and join the Yadkin Islands Trail. The path rises to a bluff overlooking the river, then turns away, traversing fire-managed woods. At 4.2 miles, pass a gated road and curve right. At 4.5 miles, come to the main park road, then immediately curve left away from the gravel road, back on trail. Ahead, descend by switchbacks to the Horne Creek bottoms. Pop out on the main park road again at 4.9 miles. From here, backtrack .4 mile to the trailhead.

Mileages		
	0.0	Corridor Trail parking area
	0.6	Picnic area; join Horne Creek Trail
	1.6	Reach Yadkin River
	2.7	End of Horne Creek Trail
	3.1	Bean Shoals Canal Trail
	4.9	Complete loop portion of hike
	5.3	Corridor Trail parking area

20

HANGING ROCK HIGHLIGHT HIKE
▓▓ Hanging Rock State Park

*This triple adventure at Hanging Rock State Park takes you to
three sights on three short hikes, all from the same trailhead. First
make the stroll to Upper Cascades, then the little longer walk to
Window Falls, followed up by the trek to Hanging Rock, where
worthy views await atop the state park's namesake crag. These three
trails can all be executed as individual easy day hikes or collectively
as a moderate endeavor.*

Distance 0.6 mile, 1.4 miles, and 2.6 miles, respectively

Hiking time 2.8 hours

Difficulty Moderate

Highlights Three waterfalls, outcrop with stellar views

Cautions Sheer cliffs

Best seasons Year-round

Other trail users None

Hours December–January, 7 a.m.–6 p.m.; February, 7 a.m.–7 p.m.;
    March–April, 7 a.m.–9 p.m.; May–September, 7 a.m.–10 p.m.; October,
    7 a.m.–9 p.m.; November, 7 a.m.–7 p.m.; closed Christmas Day

Trail contact Hanging Rock State Park, 11005 Visitor Center Drive, Westfield,
    NC 27053, 336-593-8480, www.ncparks.gov/hanging-rock-state-park

Finding the trailhead From Winston-Salem, take US 52 North to Exit 110B.
    Follow US 311 North for 17 miles to NC 89 West. Keep going westbound
    on NC 89 for 9 miles to Hanging Rock Road. Turn left on Hanging Rock
    Road and follow it for 1 mile to enter the state park. Follow the park
    road uphill to reach an intersection. Make a left turn toward the visitor
    center into an outsized parking lot. As you face the visitor center, the
    Upper Cascades Falls Trail is to your left, the Window Falls Trail is to
    your right, and the Hanging Rock Trail is behind you to your right.

GPS trailhead coordinates 36.394846, –80.266251

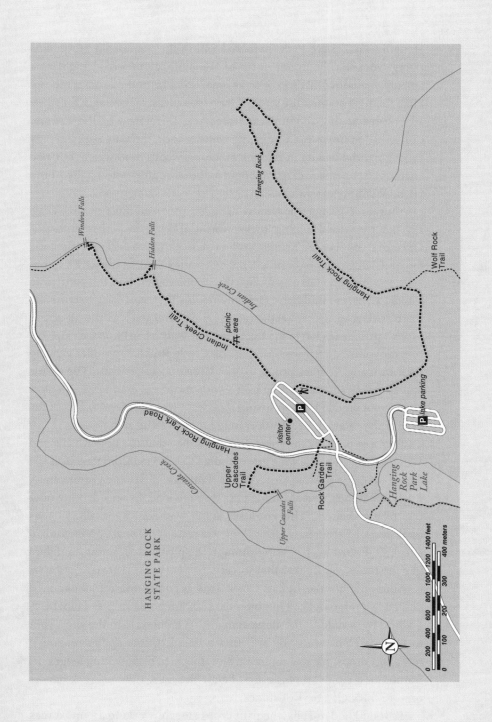

Hanging Rock State Park, harbored within the Sauratown Mountains rising from the Piedmont north of Winston-Salem, offers highlights aplenty, including this trio of treks emanating from the same trailhead. Hike them all at one time and it'll leave you pleased and eager for more adventures at this action-packed preserve. Developed by the Civilian Conservation Corps (CCC) nearly a century back, the state park not only exudes natural beauty in its rock outcrops, woods, and waters but also encompasses a historical component in the structures—and trails—built by those strapping young men.

Your three-pronged adventure includes three waterfalls and one view-rich outcrop—the Hanging Rock—worthy of being the park's namesake. Of course you'll enjoy North Carolina state park–level scenery all along the trails. Begin on the .3 mile Upper Cascades Trail, in the park's southwest sector, to the left as you face the visitor center. Join the path as an asphalt all-access trail curves left and rejoins the main track to cross the main park road. Here, keep straight on a gravel track as the all-access asphalt path heads left to the Rock Garden. Walk a level wooded ridge before dropping to a tributary of Cascade Creek. Reach a multitier viewing deck with a wide-open look at 25-foot Upper Cascades Falls. The scenic spiller makes an angled drop over a wide rock face, ending in a shallow sandy pool pinched in by a rising rock wall. Use the steps to access the base of the cataract. Backtrack .3 mile to the parking area.

Part 2 is perhaps the most popular walk—that to Hidden Falls and Window Falls. Join the wide gravel Indian Creek Trail from the northeast end of the large parking area, to your right as you face the visitor center. Enter oak woods, and at .1 mile pass through a picnic area that includes two picnic shelters. This confuses some would-be waterfallers—they don't know whether they are walking to a picnic area or are on the Indian Creek Trail. Just keep passing through the picnic area, acting confident like the trail-savvy trekker that you are.

Sure enough, the Indian Creek Trail becomes more trail-like as it descends a ridge cloaked in pines, oaks, mountain laurel, and blueberry bushes. By .4 mile, come along Indian Creek, then reach the short spur to Hidden Falls. Here you will find a tiered 16-foot spiller making a few short drops, narrowing into a dive, followed by widening ledges, all framed in a stone amphitheater. Below the falls, Indian Creek dances onward through a bevy of stones.

Beyond Hidden Falls, the path drops steeply, working around a rock face, then at .6 mile it comes to a bluff where you first find the Window,

A fog lifts, opening a view of and from Hanging Rock.

a natural hole (technically an arch) in a cliff. The fascinating feature is followed by steps leading to the base of 24-foot Window Falls, a classic curtain cataract that plummets from an overhung stone brow, then splashes down an angled ledge before flowing on, deep in a stone grotto. Ample sitting rocks provide spots for repose and relaxation.

Backtrack .6 mile to the parking lot, then make your way to the hike's denouement—Hanging Rock. The wide, well-constructed trail—initially concrete—drops to an evergreen copse and crosses the headwaters of Indian Creek. The path turns to gravel, beginning a 500-foot climb to Hanging Rock. Hardwoods shade the wide track. Rise into oak-heavy hardwoods, meeting the Wolf Rock Trail at .5 mile. Keep straight, climbing a bit more and then rolling along the ridge of Hanging Rock. By .8 mile the ridgeline narrows. Steps become frequent as you rise among rock outcrops and soil-starved, stunted pines. Climb more than not. Pass beneath a rock bluff as the ridge drops off.

At 1.1 miles, atop the knob of Hanging Rock, the path curves west. Note the imperiled Carolina hemlocks here. Ahead, traverse striated outcrops contrasting with pockets of trees and brush. Reach Hanging Rock at 1.2 miles. Here, make your way to a narrowing precipice extending outward from the body of the knob, a stone tongue: the Hanging Rock. Views extend west, south, and north to parklands below and the world beyond. Multiple vantages deliver panoramas near and far. Check out these outcrops and sit a spell, enjoying this true highlight.

Mileages

0.0	Visitor center parking area
0.3	Upper Cascades Falls
0.6	Visitor center parking area
0.0	Join Indian Creek Trail
0.4	Hidden Falls
0.6	Window; Window Falls
1.2	Visitor center parking area
0.0	Join Hanging Rock Trail
0.5	Wolf Rock Trail leaves right
1.2	Hanging Rock
2.4	Visitor center parking area

21   COOK'S WALL LOOP
■ Hanging Rock State Park

This scenic hike at Hanging Rock State Park cobbles together several trails that together lead you to three major overlooks in the Sauratown Mountains as well as adding an aquatic aspect, traveling along a stream and Park Lake. Go on a clear day and you will be well rewarded with vistas that give you renewed respect for hiking in the Piedmont.

Distance 5.8-mile loop including spur

Hiking time 3.2 hours

Difficulty Moderate, does have 1,200-foot aggregate elevation change

Highlights Panoramic vistas, stream, lake

Cautions Sheer cliffs

Best seasons Whenever the skies are clear; winter for solitude

Other trail users None

Hours December–January, 7 a.m.–6 p.m.; February, 7 a.m.–7 p.m.; March–April, 7 a.m.–9 p.m.; May–September, 7 a.m.–10 p.m.; October, 7 a.m.–9 p.m.; November, 7 a.m.–7 p.m.; closed Christmas Day

Trail contact Hanging Rock State Park, 11005 Visitor Center Drive, Westfield, NC 27053, 336-593-8480, www.ncparks.gov/hanging-rock-state-park

Finding the trailhead From Winston-Salem, take US 52 North to Exit 110B. Follow US 311 North for 17 miles to NC 89 West. Keep going westbound on NC 89 for 9 miles to Hanging Rock Road. Turn left on Hanging Rock Road and follow it for 1 mile to enter the state park. Follow the park road uphill to reach an intersection. Make a left turn toward the visitor center into an outsized parking lot. As you face the visitor center, the Hanging Rock Trail, your starting point, is behind you to your right.

GPS trailhead coordinates 36.394846, –80.266251

The Sauratown Mountains rise from the North Carolina Piedmont, monuments of rock and stone. These outcrops along the crest of ridges open onto the lowland below, allowing for numerous vista points. This

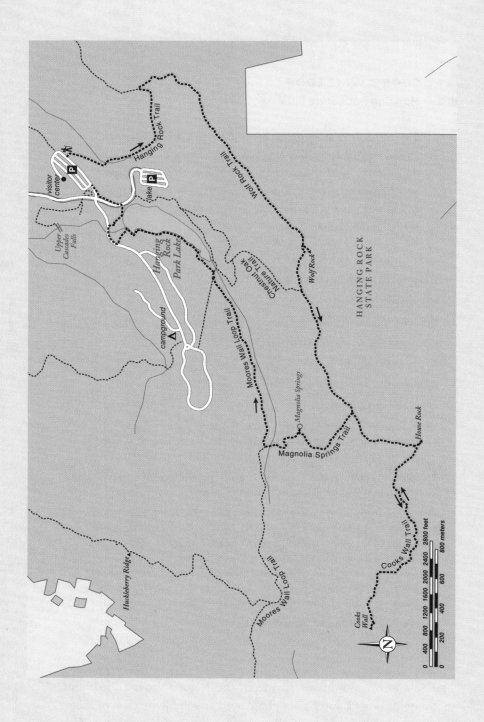

HANGING ROCK
STATE PARK

visitor center

Upper Cascades Falls

Hanging Rock

Hanging Rock Trail

Wolf Rock Trail

Wolf Rock

Park Lake

lake

campground

Moores Wall Loop Trail

Chestnut Oak Nature Trail

Magnolia Springs

Magnolia Springs Trail

House Rock

Huckleberry Ridge

Moores Wall Loop Trail

Cooks Wall Trail

Cooks Wall

N

0   400   800   1200 1600 2000 2400 2800 feet
0   200   400   600   800 meters

Looking southwest from Wolf Rock.

particular hike at Hanging Rock State Park leads you up, up, and away to three of these open crags—Wolf Rock, House Rock, and Cook's Wall, where your actual vista is from a point known as the Devil's Chimney. In addition, Cook's Wall is a popular climbing area in the park, as is Moore's Wall. The final part of the hike leads you down a cool, clear tributary of Cascade Creek, then passes the dammed portion of that tributary, where you can walk astride the 12-acre impoundment.

Start your loop on the busy Hanging Rock Trail, leaving the northeast corner of the large parking area at the visitor center. The wide path begins as a concrete track, descending to cross the evergreen-shaded headwaters of Indian Creek at .1 mile. The path then climbs away from the creek, now as a gravel track. Here it rises to reach a gap and trail intersection at .5 mile. Head right onto the less-used Wolf Rock Trail.

Ascend from the gap under oak, pines, and scads of sourwood. The trailbed is sandy in places, yet in other spots it can be extremely rocky. At 1.0 miles, user-created spur trails begin leaving left toward outcrops with southeasterly views into the Piedmont. At 1.4 miles, come to a signed spur for Wolf Rock. Here you open onto several jutting protuberances of stone, each offering a vista southward into a mosaic of forest, field, and habitation. Scramble around and find your favorite overlook among the many.

From Wolf Rock, continue southwest to reach an intersection at 1.6 miles. Here the Chestnut Oak Nature Trail descends right. We stay straight on the Wolf Rock Trail, traveling a nearly level ridgeline in rocky woods. At 2.0 miles, the Magnolia Springs Trail—your return route— leaves right. Our hike keeps straight, joining the Cook's Wall Trail at it climbs to the crest of Cook's Wall, still in chestnut oaks and pines. Come to the signed spur to House Rock at 2.3 miles. Here a nearly level stone outcrop delivers sceneries of the Piedmont, Hanging Rock, and other stone promontories. Beyond House Rock, climb more among black gum, mountain laurel, and witch hazel. The vegetation becomes tightly grown alongside the path before opening onto hickory woods with a grassy understory just before you rise to an outcrop in the vicinity of the Devil's Chimney at 3.1 miles. Here, gaze west to prominent Pilot Mountain, among other sights. The trail goes just a bit farther before dead-ending.

To continue the loop, backtrack 1.1 miles on the Cook's Wall Trail, then head left (i.e., northward) on the Magnolia Springs Trail. Descend through fire-managed woods, passing a couple of small spring branches before coming to the signed spur to Magnolia Springs at 4.4 miles. The upwelling emerges from a rock face, then follows gravity's orders, down, down, down. Continue hiking downhill in holly, fern, and rhododendron to bridge the main creek filling the park lake and reach the Moore's Wall Loop Trail. Here, head right along the stream on a trail that has acted as a fire break in the past. Boardwalks help you navigate wet areas and small creeklets. At 5.1 miles, the other end of the Moore's Wall Loop leads left toward the campground. We stay right, walk just a few feet, then split left on the Fishing Trail, a.k.a. the Lake Trail, a singletrack trail running the west side of the park lake. Pass shoreline fishing accesses where anglers vie for catfish, bream, and bass. Check out the rustic swim beach bathhouse across the water.

The trail leaves the lake, coming to the park campground road at 5.6 miles. Follow the road to the right, crossing the lake's outflow stream. Here, turn right, back on trail, returning to the water, and then stay left, crossing the lake access road before returning to the visitor center parking lot at 5.8 miles, completing another North Carolina state park adventure.

Mileages		
	0.0	Visitor center parking area
	0.5	Right on Wolf Rock Trail
	1.4	Wolf Rock
	2.3	House Rock
	3.1	Cook's Wall vista
	4.4	Magnolia Springs
	5.2	Come alongside park lake
	5.8	Visitor center parking area

22   MOORE'S KNOB TOWER HIKE
Hanging Rock State Park

This circuit hike at Hanging Rock State Park nears the park lake and the CCC-built historic bathhouse before trekking along a tributary of Cascade Creek, then climbing amid rocky woods to a stone observation tower atop Moore's Knob with 360-degree panoramas. While you're up there, also visit Balanced Rock, then drop back via the Endless Staircase to the tributary of Cascade Creek and the park lake, passing through the fine park campground along the way.

This state park was originally developed by the Civilian Conservation Corps (CCC). From 1935 through 1942, hundreds of young men lived and worked at Camp 3422, building roads, trails, and stone structures. Their handiwork is visible at the hike's beginning—the wood and stone bathhouse. It was placed on the National Register of Historic Places in

Distance 4.7-mile balloon loop

Hiking time 2.6 hours

Difficulty Moderate, does have 850-foot climb

Highlights 360-degree views from historic tower, stream, lake

Cautions None

Best seasons Year-round

Other trail users None

Hours December–January, 7 a.m.–6 p.m.; February, 7 a.m.–7 p.m.; March–April, 7 a.m.–9 p.m.; May–September, 7 a.m.–10 p.m.; October, 7 a.m.–9 p.m.; November, 7 a.m.–7 p.m.; closed Christmas Day

Trail contact Hanging Rock State Park, 11005 Visitor Center Drive, Westfield, NC 27053, 336-593-8480, www.ncparks.gov/hanging-rock-state-park

Finding the trailhead From Winston-Salem, take US 52 North to Exit 110B. Follow US 311 North for 17 miles to NC 89 West. Keep going westbound on NC 89 for 9 miles to Hanging Rock Road. Turn left on Hanging Rock Road and follow it for 1 mile to enter the state park. Follow the park road uphill to reach an intersection. The left turn goes to the visitor center, a right takes you to the campground. Keep straight, toward the park lake, to swimming, boating, and picnicking. Continue for .3 mile to dead-end in a large parking area. The trail starts near the lake bathhouse, in the southwest corner of the large parking lot.

GPS trailhead coordinates 36.390431, –80.267658

1991. Moore's Knob, your destination, rises beyond the serene park lake. A keen eye will spot the squat observation tower that rises slightly above the tree line.

Leave the southwest corner of the lake parking lot on a wide path, toward the picturesque bathhouse overlooking the 12-acre impoundment and swim area. Once at the bathhouse, climb a few steps and reach a trail kiosk. Start cruising along the park lake on the Lake Trail, passing a trail left to the picnic area, then to the singletrack Chestnut Oak Nature Trail. Continue along the water under a mantle of oaks, hickory, maple, and scads of rhododendron and mountain laurel. User-created water accesses split from the trail. Narrow boardwalks cross streamlets and wetlands.

At .3 mile, the other end of the Chestnut Oak Nature Trail leaves left. Keep straight, immediately bridging the clear tributary of Cascade Creek and then coming to another intersection. Here the Lake Trail leaves right,

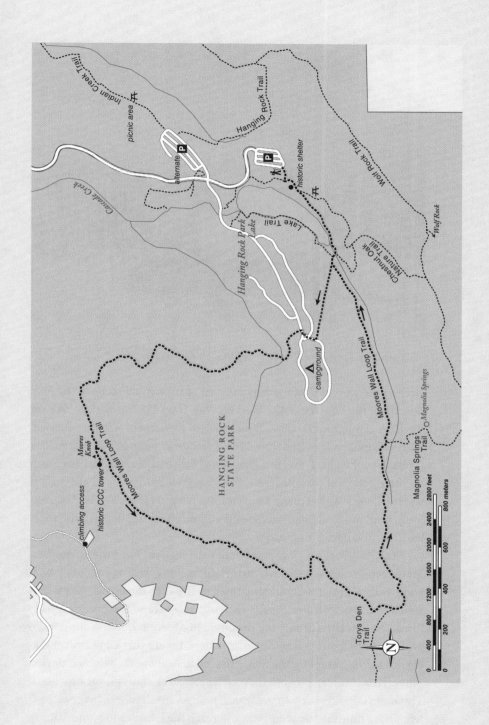

Panoramas open in all directions from Moore's Knob Tower.

circling the west side of the park lake. At .4 mile you'll come to the loop portion of the hike. Here the Moore's Wall Loop Trail goes right, toward the park campground, and left, upvalley of the stream you just crossed. Stay left, in a mix of moisture-loving woods to your left and drier oak forest to your right. Traverse a long boardwalk over a wetland, then reach an intersection at .9 mile. Here the Magnolia Springs Trail climbs left toward Cook's Wall, but we keep straight toward Moore's Wall. Interestingly, both bluffs are climbing destinations, attracting those of the rope, harness, and daring demeanor.

At 1.5 miles, rise to a gap and trail intersection. Here the Tory's Den Trail keeps straight while we turn right, staying with the Moore's Wall Loop Trail. Climb the now-rocky track in fire-managed oaks, pines, and sourwood. By 1.8 miles, larger rock outcrops show themselves in the forest. As you rise further, the drop-offs of Moore's Wall to your left are evident. Little paths go to outcrops where hikers just can't wait. Blueberries are yet another attraction, growing lush above the wind-contorted pines. At 2.1 miles, level off, then alternately trek through rock gardens. The main climb is over. At 2.7 miles, pass an overhanging ledge to your left, then a little farther ahead you will reach the left spur to Moore's Knob

Observation Tower and Balanced Rock. This spur itself splits, and you walk a short piece right to Balanced Rock, a large wheel-shaped stone perched atop a larger rock. The trail to the tower rises to an outcrop. And here you reach Moore's Knob, 2,497 feet above sea level. Climb the tower, where views extend in all directions. Pilot Mountain rises to the west, the Blue Ridge to the northwest, and the Piedmont to the southeast, and the park lake and visitor center lie below. Note the pilings of a former tower. The original, a steel tower topped with a 7-by-7-foot viewing box, was erected 1938 by the CCC. However, it was replaced with a two-story stone tower in 1951, and the viewing box was removed after storm damage. Now we have an open viewing platform atop the lower part of the stone tower.

From here, the Moore's Wall Loop Trail curves northeasterly and loses elevation, using the 684 stone steps known as the Endless Staircase. Pines and oaks partially shade the track. Cross Cascade Creek on stepping-stones at 3.9 miles. A short climb follows, and at 4.1 miles you'll reach the highly recommended park campground. Follow the signs directly through the camp, splitting left at 4.2 miles, between campsites 39 and 40. Head left, back on trail, descending toward the park lake, and complete the loop at 4.3 miles. From here, backtrack .4 mile to the trailhead.

Mileages 0.0 Lake parking area
0.4 Split left with Moore's Wall Loop Trail
1.5 Intersect Tory's Den Trail
2.8 Moore's Knob Observation Tower
4.1 Park campground
4.7 Lake parking area

23 HAW RIVER BOARDWALK
■ Haw River State Park

Take a walk through varied environments capped with a wetland trek on a long boardwalk at Haw River State Park, one of North Carolina's newer preserves. Start near the office and lodge, then work your way to the bucolic park lake. Walk its shores, then roll through hills to reach the aforementioned boardwalk, where you cross a wooded swamp to view the headwaters of the Haw River.

Piedmont

Distance 1.9-mile balloon loop

Hiking time 1.1 hours

Difficulty Easy

Highlights Lake-viewing deck, wetland boardwalk

Cautions None

Best seasons September through May

Other trail users Campers and event attendees

Hours Year-round 8 a.m.–5 p.m.; closed Christmas Day

Trail contact Haw River State Park—The Summit, 339 Conference Center Drive, Browns Summit, NC 27214, 336-342-6163, www.ncparks.gov/haw-river-state-park

Finding the trailhead From Exit 120 on I-73, north of Greensboro, take US 158 East for 11 miles, then turn right on Cunningham Mill Road. Follow it for 1.7 miles, then turn right on Spearman Road and follow it for 1.7 miles, then turn right on Conference Center Drive, stay with it for .5 mile, and park at the state park office / main lodge. The hike starts on the back side of the park office / main lodge.

GPS trailhead coordinates 36.250806, –79.756306

This hike takes place at one of North Carolina's newer preserves, Haw River State Park. Located along the south bank of the Haw River in the northern Piedmont north of Greensboro, the initial park parcel purchased was a former Episcopal retreat. Other tracts were added, and now

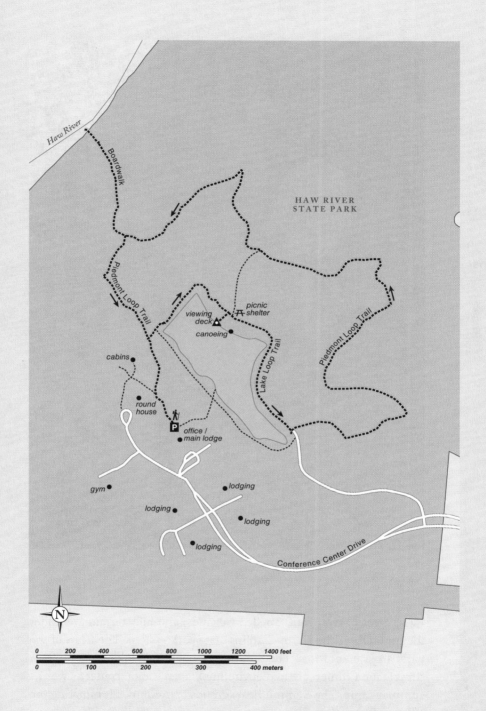

HAW RIVER
STATE PARK

Haw River

Boardwalk

Piedmont Loop Trail

Piedmont Loop Trail

viewing
deck

picnic
shelter

canoeing

Lake Loop Trail

cabins

round
house

office /
main lodge

gym

lodging

lodging

lodging

lodging

Conference Center Drive

N

| 0 | 200 | 400 | 600 | 800 | 1000 | 1200 | 1400 feet |
| 0 | | 100 | | 200 | | 300 | | 400 meters |

Hiker cruises the Haw River boardwalk.

1,429 acres of riverfront, wooded wetlands, and hilly terrain are under the umbrella of the North Carolina state park system. The heart of the park, a place known as The Summit, is where this hike takes place. A combination conference and environmental education center as well as summer camp, The Summit hosts groups and events, illuminating the whys and wherefores of nature.

To that end the park features a set on interconnected nature trails that make for a fun and rewarding hike that's doable by most trail trekkers on the hiking spectrum. Another parcel of the park known as the Iron Ore Belt access boasts its own 3.2-mile loop trail, which presents a fine woodland walk with glimpses of the Haw River wetlands.

This hike starts at the back of the park office / main lodge, where you will see a trail sign. Head straight toward the lake overlook on a concrete path, soon coming near the Round House, one of the many lodgings here at The Summit. Descend past the elevated cabins, then at .1 mile reach a trail intersection. Here, head right on the Lake Loop Trail. Cross the dam of the quaint 6-acre lake, where an unnamed tributary of the Haw River is dammed to provide an aquatic recreational opportunity for visitors. Begin circling around the lake, then walk to the shore and out onto the T-shaped lake overlook that extends into the water. This is one of my favorite relaxing spots at Haw River State Park.

Beyond the overlook, a spur leads left, shortcutting the Piedmont Loop Trail. Then you near a picnic shelter overlooking the lake, a fine spot for a little trail lunch. The Lake Loop Trail reaches the head of the tarn at .5 mile. Here, look left for the shaded Piedmont Loop Trail climbing away from the lake. This section climbs and dips through hilly woods, so it's more of a workout than you might expect. If you see a white deer in these parts, you aren't crazy. Deer in this area have a strain of albinism, so some of the deer in and around Haw River State Park are white.

At 1.1 miles, the shortcut to the Lake Loop leaves left. From there, descend toward the Haw River bottoms, coming to a gas line clearing and trail intersection at 1.4 miles. Turn right toward the boardwalk in floodplain forests, where pawpaws form an understory. They are often found together in groups, since they reproduce by root sprouts. Pawpaws have large leaves, 6–12 inches long, that droop like their tropical cousins farther south. Their yellow-green banana-like fruits are favored by wildlife, especially raccoons and possums. Early Carolina settlers made bread and puddings from pawpaw fruits. Attempts have been made to cultivate pawpaw as a fruit tree, with some success. The small tree/bush ranges throughout North Carolina south to Middle Georgia, west to East Texas, and north to lowermost Michigan.

The land gives way to the wetland boardwalk. This segment of the Haw is characterized by wide, swampy, wooded wetlands stretching on either side of a narrow river channel. Bird watchers will be seen overlooking these marshes. At the boardwalk's end, find the channel of the Haw, flowing just 10 feet wide. Much of the river courses through the swamps at this point. Backtrack from the boardwalk and continue looping back toward the trail, once again near the park lake, then climbing past facilities to hike's end at 1.9 miles.

<table>
<tr><td>Mileages</td><td>0.0</td><td>Park office/lodge</td></tr>
<tr><td></td><td>0.5</td><td>End of lake</td></tr>
<tr><td></td><td>1.4</td><td>Boardwalk</td></tr>
<tr><td></td><td>1.9</td><td>Park office/lodge</td></tr>
</table>

24 THREE RIVERS / FALL MOUNTAIN HIKE
▓▓ Morrow Mountain State Park

This double loop at Morrow Mountain State Park explores environments high and low. Start alongside Lake Tillery, then explore bottomland forest, gaining looks at the convergence of three rivers. Next, climb from the water, making your way past a pair of historic internments before looping to the top of Fall Mountain, where you gain extensive views of the Uwharrie Mountains and the Pee Dee River basin. Conclude the loop with a final waterside walk.

You will enjoy visual variety on this hike at Morrow Mountain State Park, located in the Piedmont's Uwharrie Mountains, a low but scenic range with a high point of just under 1,200 feet. Here at Morrow Mountain State Park, several wooded peaks rise from the mountain's base, where the Yadkin and Uwharrie Rivers converge to form the Pee Dee River, at this point dammed up as Lake Tillery. Views from the mountains often include both waters and hills, enhancing the park's beauty. It is also a historic area. The Uwharries were famed for being part of North Carolina's early 1800s gold boom. Morrow Mountain State Park in particular preserves the reconstructed Kron House, originally built in 1870 to be the home of the area's first doctor, Francis Kron. On this hike you will pass by the Kron Cemetery, as well as the gravesite of William McGregor, an early preacher who called these rocky hills home.

Leave the southwest corner of the parking lot, enter the woods, and stay left with the Three Rivers Trail as it crosses the paved park entry road. Soon come to the loop portion of the Three Rivers Trail, heading

Distance 5.0-mile figure-eight loop

Hiking time 2.5 hours

Difficulty Moderate, does have 400-foot climb

Highlights Aquatic and land views, history

Cautions Three Rivers Trail can be sloppy in late winter and spring

Best seasons Fall through spring

Other trail users None

Hours December–February, 7 a.m.–7 p.m.; March–April,
    7 a.m.–8 p.m.; May–September, 7 a.m.–10 p.m.; October,
    7 a.m.–9 p.m.; November, 7 a.m.–8 p.m.; closed Christmas Day

Trail contact Morrow Mountain State Park, 49104 Morrow Mountain
    Road, Albemarle, NC 28001, 704-982-4402, www.ncparks.gov
    /morrow-mountain-state-park

Finding the trailhead From the intersection of US 52 and NC 27 in Albemarle,
    take NC 27 East and stay with it for 4.3 miles. Turn left on Valley Drive
    and follow it for 3.3 miles, then turn right onto Morrow Mountain Road.
    Stay with Morrow Mountain Road for 4.4 miles, following the signs to the
    fishing and boating area on Lake Tillery. The road veers left into a lakeside
    parking lot. The Three Rivers / Fall Mountain trailhead is located in the
    southwest corner of the parking area, not at the adjacent boat ramp.

GPS trailhead coordinates 35.380759, –80.062462

left under a wildflower-rich flood plain of river birch and sycamore, using
boardwalks to span old drainage canals. Soon come alongside the water,
dammed as Lake Tillery, and the confluence of the Yadkin and Uwharrie
Rivers, blending to create the Pee Dee River. Tree-clad hills rise from
the water. Later you will see just how rocky these hills can be. For now,
enjoy paralleling the shoreline before climbing into the hills above the
floodplain, where pines and oaks rise forth. The Three Rivers Trail soon
drops back to the floodplain, and by .7 mile you have completed this loop.
Now, cross the park road and join the Fall Mountain Trail, stopping by
the parking area to retrieve anything you forgot.

The Fall Mountain Trail enjoys a little floodplain too before crossing
the gated group camp gravel access road and then rising into hardwoods
dominated by oaks, along with pine and holly. The park uses prescribed
fire to maintain the park in its pre-Columbian state, leaving the woods
looking a bit ragged, with rising grasses, brush and younger trees, and

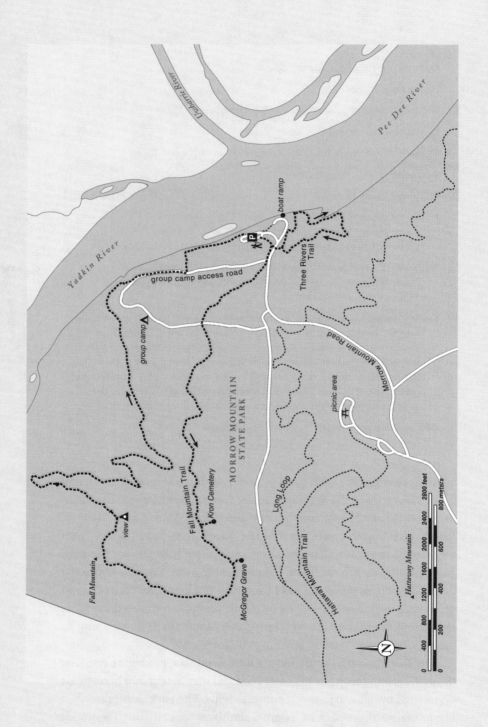

Forest encircles the grave of the Reverend William McGregor.

blackened, scarred trunks among the bigger specimens. A non-fire-managed forest would eventually grow in and thicken with beech and other shade-loving trees. These frequent burns also expose the rocky ground of the Uwharries, most notably the white and bright quartz rocks.

Cross the gravel group camp access road a second time at 1.1 miles. Descend to come alongside an unnamed tributary of the Yadkin River. Notice the thicker forest in the moist valleys. At 1.6 miles, leave the watercourse, climbing lower Fall Mountain. Keep an eye peeled for the unmarked left spur to the Kron Cemetery at 1.8 miles. This cemetery purportedly contains around fifty graves, but you will see far fewer markers than that: there are just a few inscribed stones and one taller monument left defaced by disrespectful visitors. A path on the far side of the cemetery leads to the Kron House. Continuing down the Fall Mountain Trail, pass the unsigned spur to the McGregor grave at 2.0 miles. This lone tomb is marked with a hand-carved gray stone surrounded by native rocks and complemented with a marble marker added in 2004. Born in Scotland in 1734, the Christian pastor emigrated to North Carolina and ministered to a new United States before passing away in 1804.

The climbing starts in earnest beyond the McGregor grave. Rise sharply on a wide stony track. Ahead, an old fire road comes in to your left. Climb more, cruising by the crest, then descend a bit to come along-side a rocky, partly wooded brow opening to the south, where you can enjoy views of Lake Tillery and adjacent hills at 2.7 miles. Run along-side the brow, then begin switchbacking down the mountain in brushy, fire-managed, rocky woods to reach Lake Tillery in tulip tree–rich flats at 4.5 miles. Turn right, running parallel to the water. Dip to bridge a stream just before it meets Lake Tillery, then join the group camp access road. At 4.8 miles, the Fall Mountain Trail turns left away from the gravel road and returns to shore. Make one last waterside walk among beard cane on a sometimes sandy path, then emerge at the large trailhead parking area, concluding your hike at 5.0 miles.

Mileages   0.0 Three Rivers / Fall Mountain trailhead
0.7 Complete Three Rivers Trail loop
1.8 Spur to Kron Cemetery
2.7 Views from Fall Mountain
4.5 Lake Tillery
5.0 Three Rivers / Fall Mountain trailhead

25 MORROW MOUNTAIN HIKE
Morrow Mountain State Park

This stimulating trek tops two mountains amid attractive woodlands of Morrow Mountain State Park. Views can be had on Sugarloaf Mountain but especially on Morrow Mountain, the highest point in the preserve, with designated overlooks as well as natural panoramas that reveal waves of wooded mounts and Lake Tillery. Start by looping over Sugarloaf Mountain, then take the spur to the top of Morrow Mountain, where you circle the peak before backtracking to complete the Sugarloaf Mountain Trail.

This rewarding hike entails almost 1,500 feet of elevation gain/loss, a good bit of up-and-down for a Piedmont pathway. You will be climb-ing two rocky mountains on well-maintained trails. The top of Morrow Mountain is accessible to autos, but greater rewards await those who undertake greater effort to get there. Atop the mountain you can take a

Distance 5.6-mile loop with spur

Hiking time 3.0 hours

Difficulty Moderate to difficult

Highlights Views, high point in state park

Cautions None

Best seasons Fall through spring

Other trail users None

Hours December–February, 7 a.m.–7 p.m.; March–April,
7 a.m.–8 p.m.; May–September, 7 a.m.–10 p.m.; October,
7 a.m.–9 p.m.; November, 7 a.m.–8 p.m.; closed Christmas Day

Trail contact Morrow Mountain State Park, 49104 Morrow
Mountain Road, Albemarle, NC 28001, 704-982-4402,
www.ncparks.gov/morrow-mountain-state-park

Finding the trailhead From the intersection of US 52 and NC 27 in
Albemarle, take NC 27 East and stay with it for 4.3 miles. Turn left on
Valley Drive and follow it for 3.3 miles, then turn right onto Morrow
Mountain Road. Stay with Morrow Mountain Road for 2.0 miles, then
turn acutely right on a gravel road toward the Sugarloaf Mountain Trail
and equestrian trailhead and descend to a large gravel parking area. The
signed Sugarloaf Trail starts in the northeast corner of the large lot.

GPS trailhead coordinates 35.365468, –80.091989

break at a historic stone picnic shelter constructed in the 1930s by the
CCC, which developed this state park nearly a century back.

The hike traverses fire-managed woods on ridgetops and moist forests
along streams, adding to the biodiversity. You will also pass the spur to
the park's backcountry camping area. Consider turning this hike into
an overnight adventure. A fee and reservation are required. Note: Even
though this hike starts at Morrow Mountain State Park's equestrian trailhead and crosses a bridle trail, the paths it uses—Sugarloaf Mountain
Trail and the Morrow Mountain Trail—are for hikers only.

Leave the large parking area on the signed Sugarloaf Mountain Trail.
Hike through a flat and shortly reach a trail split. Stay left here, beginning a clockwise circuit. Cross little tributaries of Mountain Creek. Some
crossings have wooden bridges. Undulate through rocky wooded terrain heavy with oaks and sourwood. At .4 mile, cross the paved Morrow
Mountain access road, then begin a steepish ascent up the west flank of

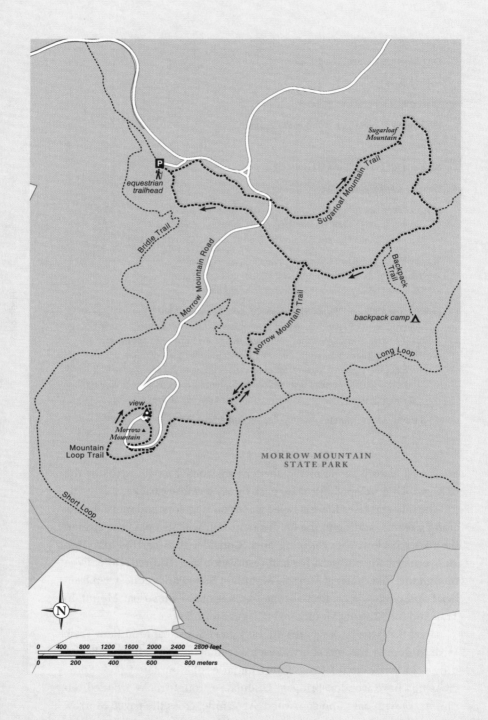

equestrian
trailhead

Sugarloaf
Mountain

Sugarloaf Mountain Trail

Bridle Trail

Morrow Mountain Road

Backpack Trail

backpack camp

Morrow Mountain Trail

Long Loop

view

*Morrow
Mountain*

Mountain
Loop Trail

MORROW MOUNTAIN
STATE PARK

Short Loop

N

| 0 | 400 | 800 | 1200 | 1600 | 2000 | 2400 | 2800 feet |

| 0 | 200 | 400 | 600 | 800 meters |

Gazing into the Pee Dee River valley from atop Morrow Mountain.

Sugarloaf Mountain on a wide rocky track. By .6 mile, enjoy partial views of Lake Tillery and the Uwharries.

Join the crest of the ridge and keep working uphill on a more modest grade. Views improve as you top out on the nearly level, partly grassy crown of Sugarloaf Mountain at 1.0 mile. Drop sharply on a rocky, mountain laurel–bordered singletrack path. Angle down the side slope of the mountain in sparse woods, with low brushy areas that enable more-distant looks. Parts of this trail segment are very steep.

Meet the Backpack Trail at 1.6 miles. You are lower than when you started. Stay right with the Sugarloaf Mountain Trail / Backpack Trail, rolling across drainages flowing off Sugarloaf Mountain in thick woods of oak and pine. At 1.8 miles, the Backpack Trail splits left .3 mile to the backpack campsites. There are fire rings and a pit toilet on site, but you must bring your own water. Continue the Sugarloaf Mountain Trail. Look for brightly blooming dogwoods here in the spring.

At 2.1 miles, head left on the Morrow Mountain Trail. You are probably expecting to climb, but instead cross a couple of creeks in rich but rocky forest. At 2.6 miles, dip to a stream and reach yet another intersection. Here, cross the Bridle Trail. You are now at the base of Morrow

Mountain. Rise a bit, then at 2.8 miles get your mojo on for a stony, steep uptick. The path is very wide here. By 3.1 miles, curve left around the south side of Morrow Mountain. The park access road, where people in vehicles climb up the easy way, is within sight.

At 3.2 miles, come to another intersection and the Mountain Loop Trail. It does what its name implies, making a circuit around Morrow Mountain. Stay left for a clockwise loop. Bridge a steep gully. Ahead, grand vistas open to the south of Lake Tillery and the arched NC 24 / NC 27 Bridge crossing the dammed waters of the Pee Dee River, along with a host of hills. In the near, exposed rhyolite rubble is leftover from Indigenous peoples quarrying the stone for making tools. By 3.6 miles you are on the north side of the peak. Stay right and shortly make your way to a cleared wooden observation deck. Here vistas open north up the Yadkin River valley and into the Uwharries. Restrooms, picnic tables, and a historic picnic shelter can also be found here.

Continue the Mountain Loop Trail, reaching the Morrow Mountain access road at 3.8 miles. Here, stay left and cross the road at an auto pullout. Enjoy more views, then complete the Mountain Loop Trail at 3.9 miles. Begin backtracking toward Sugarloaf Mountain Trail, reaching it at 5.0 miles. Here, head left on the woodsy Sugarloaf Mountain Trail, rising to a gap between two mounts. Dip to cross the Morrow Mountain access road. Step over a clear tributary of Mountain Creek. These creek bottoms are a good place to spot a deer. A final easy walk returns you to the trailhead at 5.6 miles, completing the hike that climbs two mountains.

Mileages	
0.0	Sugarloaf Mountain and equestrian trailhead
1.0	Crown of Sugarloaf Mountain
1.6	Right at Backpack Trail
1.8	Backpack Trail leaves left
2.1	Left on Morrow Mountain Trail
3.2	Begin Mountain Loop Trail
3.9	Finish Mountain Loop Trail
5.0	Resume Sugarloaf Mountain Trail
5.6	Sugarloaf Mountain and equestrian trailhead

26 OCCONEECHEE MOUNTAIN HIKE

Occoneechee Mountain State Natural Area

Hike to a rewarding view from the highest point between nearby Hillsborough and the Atlantic Ocean at this preserve. The trek circles around the attractively wooded mountain, then comes along the Eno River at some scenic bluffs. Next, visit an old rock quarry before rising on the north slope of the mountain to a surprisingly distant vista.

Distance 2.8-mile loop

Hiking time 1.3 hours

Difficulty Easy to moderate

Highlights Distant views, bluffs, quarry

Cautions None

Best seasons Year-round; summer can be hot

Other trail users None

Hours November–February, 8 a.m.–6 p.m.; March–April, 8 a.m.–8 p.m.; May–August, 8 a.m.–9 p.m.; September–October, 8 a.m.–8 p.m.; closed Christmas Day

Trail contact Occoneechee Mountain State Natural Area, 625 Virginia Cates Road, Hillsborough, NC 27278, 919-383-1686, www.ncparks.gov/occoneechee-mountain-state-natural-area

Finding the trailhead From Exit 164 on I-85, near Hillsborough, head north on Churton Street and follow it for .1 mile to turn left at a traffic light on Mayo Street. Follow Mayo Street for .3 mile, then turn left onto Orange Grove Road and follow it for .3 mile. Turn right on Virginia Cates Road. Follow it into the state natural area, then turn left into the trailhead parking area at .3 mile.

GPS trailhead coordinates 36.060833, –79.116889

Occoneechee Mountain, 867 feet high, not only offers views but also harbors several plant and animal species more commonly found in Carolina's mountains rather than the Piedmont, including the brown elfin

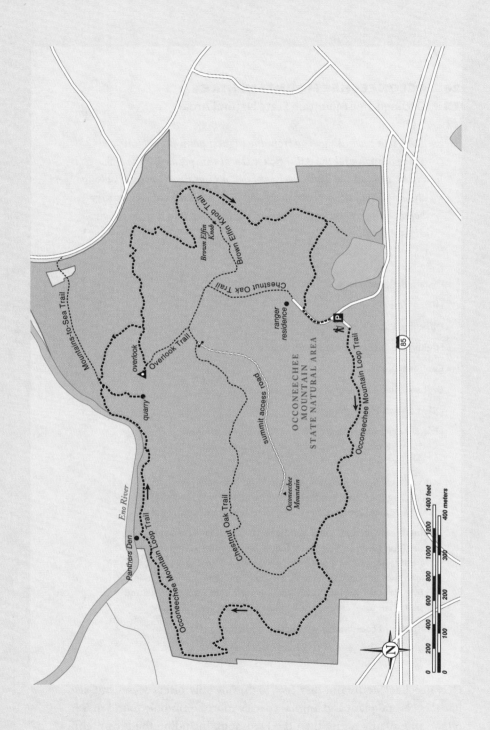

Brown Elfin Knob Trail

Brown Elfin Knob

Chestnut Oak Trail

Mountains-to-Sea Trail

overlook

Overlook Trail

quarry

ranger residence

OCCONEECHEE MOUNTAIN STATE NATURAL AREA

summit access road

Chestnut Oak Trail

Occoneechee Mountain

Eno River

Panthers Den

Occoneechee Mountain Loop Trail

Occoneechee Mountain Loop Trail

P

85

N

0   200   400   600   800   1000   1200   1400 feet
0   100   200   300   400 meters

Gazing down on the Eno River from atop Occoneechee Mountain.

butterfly. Now, one butterfly might not sound like a big deal, but this healthy population is more than 100 miles distant from other brown elfin butterflies. Always a landmark for peoples of the Piedmont, today Occoneechee Mountain is topped with communication towers. The state natural area was established in 1997, a by-product of the movement to establish nearby Eno River State Park. Previously, the mountain had also been quarried for a silica known as pyrophyllite, used in the making of ceramics, insecticides, and rubber production, among other things. You can visit the quarry on this hike, and it is above the quarry where the primary mountaintop vista opens.

Hemmed in on the north by the Eno River and on the south by I-85, Occoneechee Mountain rises more than 350 feet from the water, allowing panoramas of the Eno River valley and of nearby Hillsborough. Start your hike to the overlook from the parking/picnic area. I-85 roars to your south, the only downer of this rewarding hike used by locals for daily exercise and hikers like us who love North Carolina's state parks.

Hike along the south slope of Occoneechee Mountain in rocky woods of shortleaf pine, chestnut oak, and hickory. Wildlife such as deer don't seem to mind the auto noise. They are prevalent in the state natural area. At .4 mile, the Chestnut Oak Trail leaves right, while we stay left on the gravelly Occoneechee Mountain Loop Trail, curving around the west slope of the peak, passing rock outcrops.

Descend to the Eno River, reaching it at .9 mile. Hike ferny bottoms, coming to a squeeze between the river and a tall bluff at 1.1 miles, labeled "Panthers Den" on official USGS quadrangle maps. Mountain laurel, ironwood, and beech grow on these north-facing slopes. At 1.4 miles, take the spur right to the old pyrophyllite quarry. A nest of user-created trails makes this area confusing, but you soon reach a view of the quarry itself and the high bluffs above. Pines are taking hold here. Resume the loop, passing a leg of the Mountains-to-Sea Trail, then head up a powerline clearing before reentering woods at 1.6 miles. At 1.7 miles, head right on the Overlook Trail and soon reach the cliff above the diggings. Here the Eno River valley stretches into the distance, flanked by wooded hills. Part of Hillsborough can also be seen below. What a rewarding Piedmont panorama!

Backtrack to the Occoneechee Mountain Loop Trail, dipping to a hollow and climbing to meet the Brown Elfin Knob Trail at 2.2 miles. Drift downhill, then reach a spur to the state natural area fishing ponds at 2.5 miles. Here largemouth bass and bream are sought by anglers. Look to the right of the trail in this vicinity for evidence of an old homesite. At 2.7 miles, the Occoneechee Mountain Loop Trail meets the wide Chestnut Oak Trail near a ranger residence. Head left on the wide Chestnut Oak Trail before returning to the trailhead, concluding the hike at 2.8 miles.

Mileages	0.0	Parking area
	0.9	Eno River
	1.8	Overlook
	2.5	Ponds
	2.8	Parking area

Piedmont

27 BUCKQUARTER CREEK LOOP
Eno River State Park

This highly recommended hike takes you along the rocks and rapids of the Eno River, then to the site of Holden Mill, before heading to a remote part of Eno River State Park, up the vale of Buckquarter Creek. Pass a pair of pre-park dwellings before finally returning on steep hills above the river.

Distance 4.9-mile loop

Hiking time 2.6 hours

Difficulty Moderate

Highlights Geology, historic mill and home ruins

Cautions Use care around old structures

Best seasons Year-round; mornings in summer

Other trail users None

Hours Fews Ford access: December–February, 7 a.m.–7 p.m.; March–April, 7 a.m.–9 p.m.; May–September, 7 a.m.–10 p.m.; October, 7 a.m.–9 p.m.; November, 7 a.m.–8 p.m.; closed Christmas Day

Trail contact Eno River State Park—Fews Ford access, 6101 Cole Mill Road, Durham, NC 27705, 919-383-1686, www.ncparks.gov/eno-river-state-park

Finding the trailhead From Exit 173 on I-85, west of downtown Durham, join Cole Mill Road northbound. Follow it 5.1 miles to enter the Fews Ford area of Eno River State Park. Continue past the ranger station and take the first right, shortly reaching the Piper-Cox House and a parking area.

GPS trailhead coordinates 36.078115, –79.007085

You can check out no less than five historic structures and sites on this hike that traverses naturally eye-pleasing terrain. The preserved Piper-Cox House, a combination log cabin / clapboard house, can be seen from the trailhead. The house has been restored to its appearance in the 1870s, when a man named Cox added on to the original 1700s Piper Cabin. You will also see the site of Fews Mill, the stone remains of Holden Mill, as well as a pair of wooden structures that pre-park residents called home.

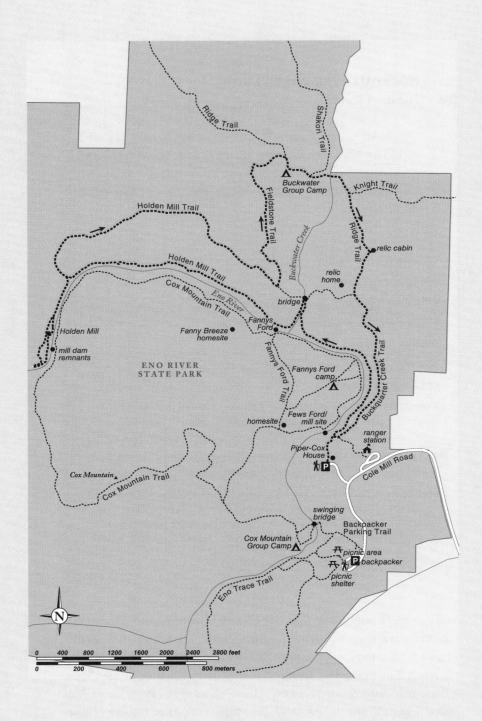

Ridge Trail

Shakori Trail

Buckwater Group Camp

Knight Trail

Holden Mill Trail

Fieldstone Trail

Buckwater Creek

relic cabin

Holden Mill Trail

Cox Mountain Trail

Eno River

relic home

bridge

Ridge Trail

Holden Mill

mill dam remnants

Fanny Breeze homesite

Fannys Ford

ENO RIVER STATE PARK

Fannys Ford Trail

Fannys Ford camp

Buckquarter Creek Trail

homesite

Fews Ford/ mill site

Cox Mountain

Cox Mountain Trail

ranger station

Piper-Cox House

P

Cole Mill Road

swinging bridge

Backpacker Parking Trail

Cox Mountain Group Camp

picnic area

backpacker

P

Eno Trace Trail

picnic shelter

N

0	400	800	1200	1600	2000	2400	2800 feet		

0	200	400	600	800 meters

Rocks, water, and vegetation conspire to create eye-pleasing scenery on this hike.

From the Piper-Cox House parking area, descend the paddler access path down to the Eno River and Fews Ford, where a mill was built in 1758 below the shallow crossing. Most remains of the combination sawmill/gristmill have long since washed away. Turn right onto the Buckquarter Creek Trail, running along the splashy Eno River, then hike up and over a riverside rock outcrop. Enjoy some of the most inspiring scenery in the greater Triangle—a sublime composite of rocks, water, elevation, and vegetation.

Bluffs give way to flats, and you turn to reach a bridge and clear Buckquarter Creek at .7 mile. Cross the bridge constructed in 2019, joining the Holden Mill Trail and returning to the Eno River, soaking up more everywhere-you-look beauty, from rocky rapids to colorful wildflowers to stone outcrops over which you hike. River birch, ironwood, sycamore, and beech thrive in the valley. Scan across the water for the Cox Mountain Trail, which at this point also runs along the Eno River.

At 1.6 miles, stay left, heading for Holden Mill, then soon loop around the stone remains of the mill structure, millrace, and dam. Holden Mill was constructed in 1811. Over the years the mill ground flour, cut timber, pressed seeds for oil, and even ginned cotton. The mill stayed in operation for nearly a century, and a community sprang up around it.

Nowadays the trees have reclaimed the lands around the mill site. Make the loop around the mill, going both above and below it, giving the historic site close inspection before returning to the main part of the Holden Mill Trail at 2.2 miles. Here, head up a tributary of the Eno River, then make a 230-foot climb to a hill rising above the water. Up here the forest has morphed to hickory, oak, maple, and pine. Your hard-earned elevation is quickly lost, and at 3.1 miles you reach another intersection. Head left on the less-used Fieldstone Trail, so named for the rock piles and stone walls made to clear land for crops. Now that the fields have returned to woods, the stone piles seem out of place.

Roll through the upper valley of Buckquarter Creek, joining the Ridge Trail at 3.6 miles. Quickly pass Buckquarter Group Camp, then the Shakori Trail. Descend to a bridgeless crossing of Buckquarter Creek at 3.8 miles. Heavy stepping-stones aid your passage. Rise past the Knight Trail, then dip to a hollow at 4.1 miles. Look left for a deteriorating log cabin, ensconced in the hollow and worth a look. Continuing downtrail, look for a still-standing clapboard house in the bottomland woods to your right, just before rejoining the Buckquarter Creek at 4.2 miles. Head left, ascending a rugged steep bluff rising above the Eno. The water sings below as you travel amid scads of mountain laurel. Drop back to the river, passing a spur leading to the park office. Ahead, backtrack on the paddler access path, rising to the Piper-Cox House and the parking lot, completing the historic hike at 4.9 miles.

Mileages		
	0.0	Piper-Cox House
	1.8	Holden Mill
	3.8	Buckquarter Creek crossing
	4.1	Old log cabin
	4.9	Piper-Cox House

28   FANNYS FORD LOOP
■   Eno River State Park

Enjoy a riverside and mountaintop trek at Eno River State Park's largest parcel. First, descend to the famous swinging bridge over the Eno, then walk along the river's edge, reveling in everywhere-you-look splendor. Make a 260-foot climb to the top of wooded Cox Mountain before returning to cross the swinging bridge one more time. Note: This hike also has backpack camping possibilities.

Distance 4.5-mile loop

Hiking time 2.4 hours

Difficulty Moderate, does have some hills

Highlights Swinging bridge, riverside rapids, backpack camping

Cautions None

Best seasons Year-round; mornings in summer

Other trail users None

Hours Fews Ford access: December–February, 7 a.m.–7 p.m.; March–April, 7 a.m.–9 p.m.; May–September, 7 a.m.–10 p.m.; October, 7 a.m.–9 p.m.; November, 7 a.m.–8 p.m.; closed Christmas Day

Trail contact Eno River State Park—Fews Ford access, 6101 Cole Mill Road, Durham, NC 27705, 919-383-1686, www.ncparks.gov/eno-river-state-park

Finding the trailhead From Exit 173 on I-85, west of downtown Durham, join Cole Mill Road northbound. Follow it 5.1 miles to enter the Fews Ford area of Eno River State Park. Continue past the ranger station and follow the main road to dead-end at the trailhead at .5 mile.

GPS trailhead coordinates 36.073808, –79.006263

Two centuries back, the Eno River valley thrived in its own way, populated mostly by scattered farmers and other residents, most of them centered around the 30-plus mills that once operated by the waterpower provided by the Eno River. This hike passes two such mill sites—Fews Ford and Holden Mill. Perhaps more importantly, though, the story of

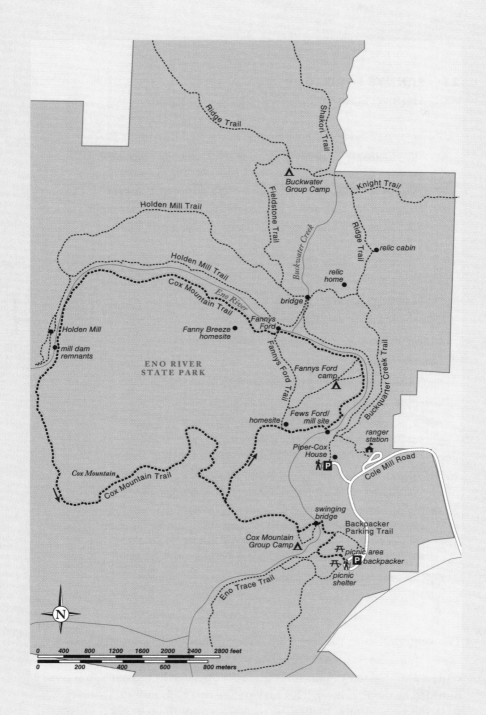

Ridge Trail

Shakori Trail

Knight Trail

Buckwater Group Camp

Fieldstone Trail

Holden Mill Trail

relic cabin

relic home

Holden Mill Trail

Buckwater Creek

Cox Mountain Trail

Eno River

bridge

Ridge Trail

Holden Mill

Fannys Ford

Fanny Breeze homesite

mill dam remnants

ENO RIVER STATE PARK

Fannys Ford Trail

Fannys Ford camp

Buckquarter Creek Trail

homesite

Fews Ford/ mill site

ranger station

Piper-Cox House

Cox Mountain

Cole Mill Road

Cox Mountain Trail

Cox Mountain Trail

swinging bridge

Backpacker Parking Trail

Cox Mountain Group Camp

picnic area

backpacker

Eno Trace Trail

picnic shelter

N

0   400   800   1200   1600   2000   2400   2800 feet

0   200   400   600   800 meters

This pretty swinging bridge leads to the loop over Cox Mountain.

the Eno River valley involves people. One such person was Fannie Breeze, a Black enslaved woman whose name still reverberates down the Eno. See, Fannie was a midwife, helping birth babies up and down the river. There weren't hospitals all over the place then. Fannie would stay with the expectant mothers until they delivered. Her homesite is now part of the state park. The shallow river crossing just upstream with the Eno River's confluence with Buckquarter Creek was named after her, since she used the ford in her traveling duties as a midwife. The current names *Fannys Ford* and *Fannys Ford Trail* are misspellings that have taken root over time, a common occurrence in mapmaking.

This hike takes you by Fannys Ford, among other places. Start the adventure at the Fews Ford access picnic area of Eno River State Park. This is the largest tract of mostly linear Eno River State Park, creating a sizable natural, wild area for wildlife—and you—to enjoy. Take the Cox Mountain Trail as it winds through the picnic area and then passes the Eno Trace Trail, leaving left before dropping to the Eno River proper and the fabled swinging bridge that crosses the waterway here. This is a popular waterplay area for kids young and old.

After crossing the long wooden span, drop to the west bank of the Eno River. Here a spur leads left to the Cox Mountain Group Camp. Keep straight. At .6 mile you'll come to another intersection. Turn right and begin your circuit, still on the Cox Mountain Trail. Walk between rising Cox Mountain to your left and river bottoms to your right, crossing a couple of streambeds flowing off Cox Mountain. At 1.0 miles, split right with the Fannys Ford Trail, passing the crumbled chimney of a homesite to your left. At 1.1 miles, drop to the Eno River at shallow Fews Ford and a mill site just downstream. The Piper-Cox Home access is just across the river. Head up along the left bank of the Eno River, nearing big rapids. The Buckquarter Creek Trail is visible across the river from these rapids.

At 1.3 miles, meet the first spur leading left to the Fannys Ford backpacker campground. Overnight camping with preregistration is allowed at six designated sites. Each site has a tent pad and fire ring with a central privy. Bring your own water. Continue upriver, as the waters alternate in gurgling shallows and slower silent pools. River birch, beech, and sycamore shade the track. At 1.6 miles, you are across from the mouth of Buckquarter Creek. Just upstream from here is Fannys Ford. At 1.7 miles, come to a trail intersection. Stay right with the Cox Mountain Trail as it continues close to the Eno River. Formerly, the Cox Mountain Trail followed the historic road to the homesite of Fannie Breeze and on to Holden Mill. Continue up the valley, passing old rock piles and stone fences.

At 2.3 miles, the newer trail merges with the older road/trail and leads you right beside the river. At 2.5 miles, squeeze past the dam remnants of Holden Mill. The actual mill was on the far side of the river, but the dam once stretched across this locale. At 2.6 miles, the hike leads away from the watercourse and up a hollow, gently but steadily climbing Cox Mountain. This reroute is much gentler than the old trail. Enter rocky hickory-oak woods, topping out at 3.3 miles. Descend in wide, loping switchbacks, completing the loop at 3.9 miles. From here it is .6 mile back to the trailhead. Enjoy that swinging bridge once more time, taking pictures or shooting video on the second go-round.

Mileages		
	0.0	Picnic area parking
	0.3	Swinging bridge
	1.0	Fannys Ford Trail
	2.5	Holden Mill
	3.3	Cox Mountain
	3.9	Complete loop
	4.5	Picnic area parking

29 ENO QUARRY / CABELANDS HIKE
■ Eno River State Park

This nifty hike explores a variety of scenes at Eno River State Park. First it travels attractive bluffs above the Eno River to reach Eno Quarry, where you can see three bodies of water at once. From there, make your way to the Cabelands, looping by the Eno River again to visit the old Cabe Mill before working your way back to the trailhead.

Distance 5.1-mile double balloon loop

Hiking time 2.5 hours

Difficulty Moderate

Highlights Eno River, Eno Quarry, Cabe Mill site

Cautions Beware swimming in quarry

Best seasons Year-round, any day but Saturday

Other trail users Swimmers, anglers

Hours Pleasant Green access: December–February, 8:30 a.m.–5:30 p.m.; March–April, 8:30 a.m.–7:30 p.m.; May–September, 8:30 a.m.–8:30 p.m.; October, 8:30 a.m.–7:30 p.m.; November, 8:30 a.m.–6:30 p.m.; closed Christmas Day

Trail contact Eno River State Park—Pleasant Green access, 4770 Pleasant Green Road, Durham, NC 27705, 919-383-1686, www.ncparks.gov/eno-river-state-park

Finding the trailhead From Exit 170 on I-85, west of downtown Durham, take US 70 West a short distance to Pleasant Green Road. Turn right and follow Pleasant Green Road .4 mile to the trailhead on your left, just before the bridge over the Eno River.

GPS trailhead coordinates 36.046688, –79.011120

Eno River State Park, set in the busy Triangle, clutches a lot of history within its bounds. And in 2004 a vital tract of the park was acquired that included Eno Quarry as well as 1.3 miles of riverbank on the south side

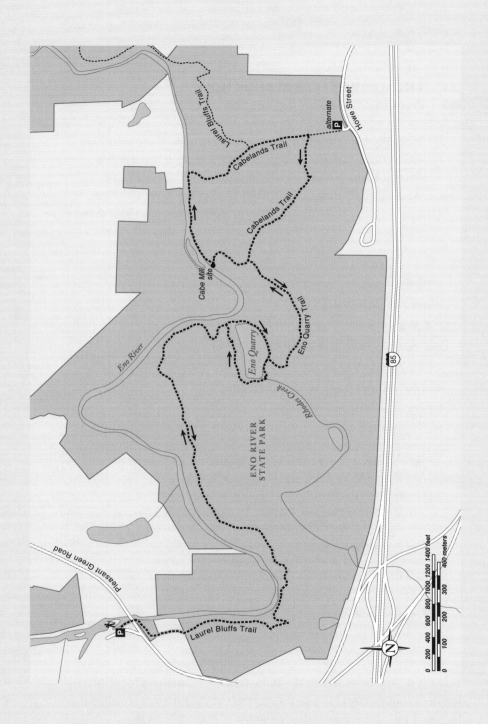

Laurel Bluffs Trail

Cabelands Trail

Cabelands Trail

alternate

Howe Street

P

Cabe Mill site

Eno River

Eno Quarry

Eno Quarry Trail

Rhodes Creek

ENO RIVER STATE PARK

Pleasant Green Road

P

Laurel Bluffs Trail

85

N

0   200   400   600   800 1000 1200 1400 feet

0   100   200   300   400 meters

of the Eno, creating a contiguous corridor of parkland from Pleasant Green Road to the Cabelands, making this hike possible. Back in the early 1960s, when Raleigh, Durham, and Chapel Hill were transforming from sleepy southern towns to a massive booming metropolitan area, Interstate 85 was being built. Stone was needed for the project, and the Coile family leased a tract of their property that was worked by Superior Stone Company. In 1964, the quarry was abandoned, then slowly filled with water, resulting in a 4-acre, 60-foot-deep pond. And in 2004 this tract was added to the park. The quarry has been a huge attraction, and swimmers flock to it during the warm season, resulting in inevitable drownings. Park rangers have created a rescue road to access the accidents that regularly occur here. However, with a little caution you can enjoy this quarry and the Cabelands beyond.

The hike leaves the Pleasant Green access, also used by paddlers plying the Eno River, on the Laurel Bluffs Trail, also part of the greater Mountains-to-Sea Trail. Pass under Pleasant Green Road heading eastbound. Look for old bridge pilings in the river here. Soon enter woods and curve into a small but rocky pair of feeder branches that form little cascades when boldly flowing, a mini-slice of mountain scenery. Climb to bluffs above the river, where the Laurel Bluffs Trail, a path enveloped in mountain laurel, lives up to its name. Hike near a house from the days of the Coile estate, now home for a park ranger. Ahead, shortcut a bend in the Eno, hiking amid planted pines.

Return to the river bottoms at 1.3 miles, where maple, river birch, ironwood, and sycamore spread their limbs. Come to a line of big boulders and Eno Quarry at 1.5 miles. At this point, the Eno River is to your left, Eno Quarry to your right, and Rhodes Creek flows just ahead. It is not often you can see three distinctly different bodies of water at once. For now, keep straight on the Laurel Bluffs Trail, enjoying views of the quarry, where park visitors may be fishing or swimming in the warm season. Since the quarry is 60 feet deep, it is often colder than people expect.

The trail turns up Rhodes Creek along the man-made berm dividing the creek from the quarry. At 1.7 miles, cross Rhodes Creek, climbing through pine/oak/hickory woods for the Cabelands. Ahead, you'll twice cross a sunken road, originally an Occoneechee Indian path that linked their villages with aboriginals encamped on the Neuse River. It later became Fish Dam Road, though this segment was abandoned. Contemplate all those who passed this way on a sunken forgotten passage . . .

At 2.0 miles, head left on the Cabelands Trail. Descend, returning

Admiring the still waters of Eno Quarry.

to the Eno River at 2.1 miles. Here in the 1700s, Barnaby Cabe built a mill, and a community sprang up around it and became known as the Cabelands. Barnaby almost singlehandedly grew the community with his three wives and nine daughters.

When you reach the river, look for the mill tailrace to the right, pushing water to a long-gone wheel. The dam has also disappeared. Cabe Mill was in operation during the late 1700s through early 1800s. Also savor natural beauty on the rocky track beside a rocky stretch of river. Picturesque bottomlands stretch to your right. Bridge a pair of tributaries of the Eno at 2.4 miles. Turn right just after these bridges, disregarding a user-created trail continuing downriver. At 2.5 miles, the Laurel Bluffs Trail heads left, downriver, but we keep straight, rising to meet another intersection at 2.6 miles (if you reach the Howe Street trailhead, you have gone too far). Head right, still on the Cabelands Trail, rolling through woods to complete the Cabelands loop at 3.0 miles. Now, backtrack to Eno Quarry, turning left when you reach the Rhodes Creek crossing at 3.4 miles. Walk the perimeter of the quarry, checking it out from different angles, passing the ranger rescue road along the way. At 3.6 miles, you have completed the Eno Quarry circuit. From here, backtrack 1.5 miles to the Pleasant Green access.

30 BOBBITT HOLE LOOP
Eno River State Park

Hike along the Eno River to the Bobbitt Hole, a swimming hole and historic spot with a mysterious past. From there, climb into hills, passing the Piper Creek backcountry campground, which provides camping possibilities. Rise into piney hills before returning to the trailhead. You can also add another loop to this hike from the same trailhead.

This is one of the most scenic of all hikes in Eno River State Park. And that is saying a lot. Plus a hint of mystery always adds to an adventure. You will near the site of the McCown/Cole Mill, one of many mills located along the Eno River in the pre-electricity days, when waterpower was used to operate machinery. A little settlement grew up around the mill, but the area has returned to nature, and now only a keen eye is able to spot evidence of the past. More relics are across the Eno on the Laurel Bluffs Trail.

The river has kept its flowing splendor throughout the past and into the present. The adventure travels a formerly well-settled portion of the Eno River valley.

Try to get here early or late in the day—the parking area can fill quickly with hikers, paddlers using the canoe/kayak launch, and backpackers overnighting at the Piper Creek backcountry campground. Then add a busy picnic area, and you can easily see how the parking area often fills to capacity.

Additionally, you can add mileage to this hike by making a 3-mile loop using the Pea Creek and the Dunnagan Trail. It leaves the same parking area, heads downstream along the Eno, then heads into the hills, coming by the Dunnagan Place and cemetery on the way back.

Distance 2.7-mile loop

Hiking time 1.4 hours

Difficulty Easy

Highlights Eno River, Bobbitt Hole, backcountry campground

Cautions Beware swimming in river

Best seasons Year-round

Other trail users Backpackers

Hours Pleasant Green access: December–February, 7:30 a.m.–6:30 p.m.;
March–April, 7:30 a.m.–8:30 p.m.; May–September, 7:30 a.m.–9:30 p.m.;
October, 7:30 a.m.–8:30 p.m.; November, 7:30 a.m.–7:30 p.m.; closed
Christmas Day

Trail contact Eno River State Park—Cole Mill access, 4390 Old Cole
Mill Road, Durham, NC 27712, 919-383-1686, www.ncparks.gov
/eno-river-state-park

Finding the trailhead From Exit 173 on I-85, west of downtown Durham, join
Cole Mill Road northbound. Follow it 3.4 miles to reach a traffic light
just after bridging the Eno River. Turn left at the traffic light onto Old
Cole Mill Road and follow it to enter the park. Drive to the lowermost
part of the parking area and start the Cole Mill Trail down there.

GPS trailhead coordinates 36.056481, –78.979489

The Bobbitt Hole hike starts at the lower end of Old Cole Mill Road, itself a relic of the past, dead-ending now at the Eno River where a bridge once crossed it. Join the Cole Mill Trail, passing the canoe/kayak launch and turning upstream. The Eno runs about 60 feet wide, flowing over a rocky course. Here, when Cole Mill was in operation from 1813 to 1908, water was backed behind the dam. As was almost always the fate of the historic mills on the Eno, a flood came and washed the mill away.

Continue upriver, passing the shaded picnic area to your right. Iron-wood, walnut, and tulip trees shade the trail, along with beech. The trail's proximity to the river allows for superior aquatic views but also sometimes forces you to walk amid high-water stream braids. The trail can be rooty in places. Ahead, bisect the marked county line dividing Orange and Durham Counties. Squeeze past some riverside rocks. At .7 mile, reach a trail intersection. Here, stay left and join the Bobbitt Hole Trail. Cruise riparian flats, then bridge a little tributary. Just beyond there, look for an unusual triple-trunked tulip tree. (Say that three times fast.)

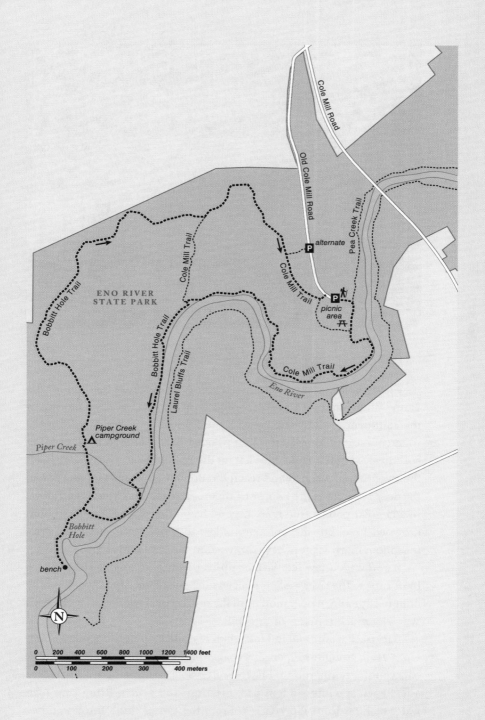

Hiker points to a turtle sunning at the Bobbitt Hole.

The riverside scenery remains inviting. Scan across the Eno for the Laurel Bluffs Trail. At 1.1 miles, bridge larger Piper Creek, sauntering by the confluence of this stream with the Eno River. Turn away from the watercourse and journey through wooded flats. Come to another intersection at 1.2 miles. Here, hike left for the Bobbitt Hole. Curve along with the river to find a bench and reach the Bobbitt Hole, purportedly one of the deepest spots in the Eno, at 1.3 miles. Here the Eno widens and slows in a circular pool, a true hole. Legend has it that a man named Bobbitt drowned here, but the full story is lost to time. Since the state park's inception, many visitors have drowned in the river and at Eno Quarry.

If you walk a few feet farther upriver from the Bobbitt Hole, a rock bluff runs to the river's edge. This was the site of the Alpha Woolen Mill, built in 1852 and in operation until the mill owners were slain in the Civil War. Not much remains of this mill.

Backtrack from Bobbitt Hole, then resume looping along the Bobbitt Hole Trail, bridging Piper Creek again and reaching the Piper Creek backcountry campground. The five reservable campsites are available for a fee. Each site offers a tent pad, fire ring, and bench. Bring your own water or filter from Piper Creek. From the camp, climb through piney woods to pass under a powerline. Reenter the woods and roll through them 150 feet above the Eno. At 2.3 miles, stay left with the Cole Mill Trail, then return to signed Durham County. Descend from the hills, making a second powerline crossing. Ahead, you will trundle alongside the upper end of the parking area, then complete the loop hike at 2.7 miles.

Mileages   0.0 Cole Mill access
             0.7 Bobbitt Hole Trail
             1.3 Bobbitt Hole
             2.3 Cole Mill Trail
             2.7 Cole Mill access

31 PUMP STATION WALK
Eno River State Park

This circuit hike at Eno River State Park is great for families and for spring wildflowers. It follows a hillside down to Eno River bottomlands, where you walk riverside to discover the ruins of a former water pump station built by the city of Durham over a century ago. You will also see the remains of a high dam on Nancy Rhodes Creek, a tributary of the Eno River. Work your way up Nancy Rhodes Creek, then loop back through forests of pine.

Residents of what is now the Triangle have always looked to the Eno River for waterpower and water itself to sustain their farms and later the towns and cities that sprang up around this waterway. When Durham was officially founded in the late 1860s, it needed a reliable water source and distribution point. Enter A. H. Howland. In 1886, he won a contract to build a gravity-fed reservoir atop a spot called Huckleberry Hill. He would build a high dam on Nancy Rhodes Creek to create a lake, a reliable water source through flood and drought. The water from Nancy Rhodes Creek would be pumped to Huckleberry Hill using waterpower garnered from a dam on the Eno River, built just a short distance from the lake on Nancy Rhodes Creek. Once the water was on Huckleberry Hill, gravity would distribute it to homes and businesses throughout Durham.

By 1888 Mr. Howland's plan was in operation, albeit with a few flaws. First, water pressure was low and inconsistent. And then there was the matter of the water being muddy and sometimes containing fish.

Distance 1.7-mile loop

Hiking time 1.0 hours

Difficulty Easy

Highlights Pump station ruins, dam ruins, Eno River

Cautions None

Best seasons Year-round

Other trail users Runners

Hours Pump Station access: December–February, 7:30 a.m.–6:30 p.m.; March–April, 7:30 a.m.–8:30 p.m.; May–September, 7:30 a.m.–9:30 p.m.; October, 7:30 a.m.–8:30 p.m.; November, 7:30 a.m.–7:30 p.m.; closed Christmas Day

Trail contact Eno River State Park, 6101 Cole Mill Road, Durham, NC 27705, 919-383-1686, www.ncparks.gov/eno-river-state-park

Finding the trailhead From Exit 173 on I-85, west of downtown Durham, join Cole Mill Road northbound. Follow it 2.5 miles to turn right on Rivermont Road. Follow Rivermont Road for .3 mile to the trailhead on your left, just after Rivermont Road turns to gravel. Parking is on the shoulder.

GPS trailhead coordinates 36.058556, –78.969245

A filtration system cleared the water of mud and fish, but the lack of pressure proved devastating when fires broke out in the city and the inadequate pressure prevented firefighters from quickly putting out these blazes.

Durham moved on to bigger and better solutions for reliable water delivery. The pump station on the Eno and the dam on Nancy Rhodes Creek were kept in operation for backup but were eventually discontinued, left to time and the elements. The forests regrew where the lake once stood, and trees now shade the pump station in what today is state park property.

These relics are highlights of this fun family hike, a great excuse to enjoy the great outdoors on a great day. You will be surprised at the height of the dam on narrow Nancy Rhodes Creek. Look for the circular pond gouged out from the dam's overflow channel. Down by the Eno you will find the pump-house foundation on the Eno River, as well as the dam and adjacent filtration plant on the Eno. It is a lot to explore. Imagine life back then. Times change. A lot of growing North Carolina's past gets knocked

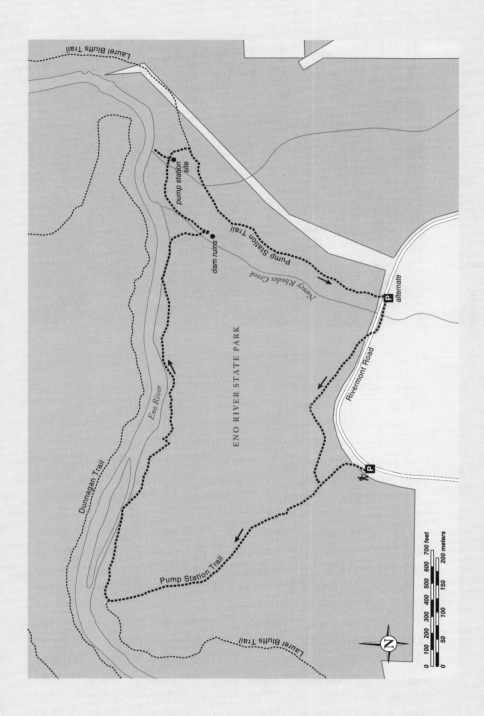

Laurel Bluffs Trail

pump station site

Pump Station Trail

dam ruins

Nancy Rhodes Creek

alternate

Eno River

ENO RIVER STATE PARK

Dunnagan Trail

Rivermont Road

Pump Station Trail

Laurel Bluffs Trail

N

0   100 200 300 400 500 600 700 feet
0   50   100   150   200 meters

Come see remnants of yesteryear on this walk.

down and paved over, especially in quickly expanding metropolitan areas like the Triangle. Come see a parcel of yesteryear on this walk.

Start your trek on the Pump Station Trail. There is nothing difficult about this path. It is wide, well-marked, and not steep, yet scenic throughout. The wide road-like track leaves Rivermont Road in beech, maple, and tulip trees, along with ever-present pine. At .1 mile, the loop portion of the trail enters on your right. Keep straight, passing under a powerline and gently descending to the Eno.

Reach the river at .4 mile. Head right, downstream in gorgeous flats dominated by beech trees. The Eno is flowing around an island at this point. Down in the bottoms during spring you may see trillium, jack-in-the-pulpit, and even yellow lady's slipper. Use a guidebook or a smartphone app to identify more blooms.

At .9 mile, reach a bridge on Nancy Rhodes Creek. The dam rises to your right. Check it out now or later, then continue down to explore the pump station and dam ruins that you reach at 1.0 mile. From there, ascend away from the Eno, passing the Laurel Bluffs Trail as it splits left, along with a ranger access road. Hike parallel to Nancy Rhodes Creek, then emerge on Rivermont Road at 1.4 miles. Cross the creek on the road bridge, then pick up the trail as it reenters forestland. Roll through these woods before completing the Pump Station Trail, making a final backtrack to reach the parking area at 1.7 miles.

Mileages	0.0	Rivermont Road
	0.4	Eno River
	1.0	Pump station
	1.7	Rivermont Road

32 SALS BRANCH TRAIL
William B. Umstead State Park

151

Piedmont

Great for families, this fun little loop hike at Umstead State Park explores two bodies of water as it makes a circuit often used by locals for daily exercise. Start at the park visitor center to cross winding Sals Branch, then reach Big Lake, a still impoundment of Sycamore Creek. From there the path rolls through hills, visits an old picnic area, and then passes near the recommended campground before winding along Sals Branch en route back to the trailhead.

The Triangle area of Raleigh, Durham, and Chapel Hill (along with Cary and other suburbs) continues to grow exponentially. In fact, when Umstead State Park was developed back in the 1930s as a Civilian Conservation Corps (CCC) works project, the area was an agricultural backwater. Fast-forward almost a century: the cities have grown together into one pulsing megalopolis, leaving this state park a valuable island of nature.

Back when it was developed, the park was first known as Crabtree Recreation Area; then, after being purchased by North Carolina, it became Crabtree State Park, named for Crabtree Creek, which flows through the south end of the 5,579-acre preserve. Later the state renamed the park to honor conservationist and North Carolina governor William B. Umstead. Today you can see not only the handiwork of the CCC but also a wooded wildland that will surprise you with its scenic value, including the park campground. I have spent many a night here and highly recommend it for tent campers who like a casual wooded atmosphere. The camp is convenient for local residents and also handy for accessing the numerous

Distance 2.6-mile loop

Hiking time 1.2 hours

Difficulty Easy

Highlights Sals Branch, Big Lake, good exercise trail

Cautions None

Best seasons Year-round; mornings in summer

Other trail users None

Hours November–February, 8 a.m.–6 p.m.; March–April, 8 a.m.–8 p.m.;
May–August, 8 a.m.–9 p.m.; September–October, 8 a.m.–8 p.m.;
closed Christmas Day

Trail contact William B. Umstead State Park, 8801 Glenwood Avenue, Raleigh,
NC 27617, 919-218-4170, www.ncparks.gov/william-b-umstead-state-park

Finding the trailhead From Exit 4A on I-540, northwest of downtown
Raleigh and southeast of Durham, take US 70 East/Glenwood
Avenue for 1.3 miles to turn right into Umstead State Park. Stay
straight on Umstead Parkway and follow it .8 mile to the visitor
center and trailhead on your right.

GPS trailhead coordinates 35.880933, –78.758483

amenities of Umstead State Park, including miles and miles of hiking, bicycling, and bridle paths (20 miles of trails are for hikers only); multiple picnic areas; and three lakes and several attractive creeks, which add aquatic scenery. The only downside of the park is its proximity to the Raleigh-Durham International Airport. You will hear airplane noise. But if you need to catch a flight, you are in good stead.

The Sals Branch Trail is popular with hiking families. Its 2.6-mile length is perfect for that. The circuit is not too far and not too steep and has highlights enough to keep kids engaged. Older hikers will enjoy it as well.

The Sals Branch Trail starts at the park visitor center. Facing the visitor center, walk around the right side of the building and pick up the trail. Head left, making a clockwise loop. Drift through piney woods, then emerge at the overflow parking lot. Walk a few steps right and reenter a forest of white oak, beech, tulip trees, and pine. These shady woods make it a viable summertime hike.

You'll bridge gravelly Sals Branch at .2 mile. The small winding

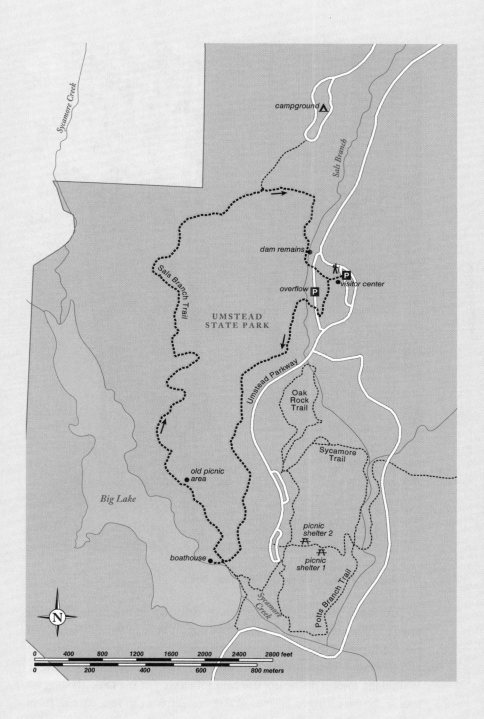

Sycamore Creek

campground ▲

Sals Branch

dam remains •

UMSTEAD
STATE PARK

P
overflow P visitor center

Sals Branch Trail

Oak
Rock
Trail

Sycamore
Trail

old picnic
area

Umstead Parkway

Big Lake

picnic
shelter 2

picnic
shelter 1

boathouse •

Potts Branch Trail

Sycamore
Creek

N

0   400   800   1200   1600   2000   2400   2800 feet

0   200   400   600   800 meters

Piney woods cloak much of Umstead State Park.

stream, bordered by sycamore, nearly dries up in autumn. The path rises to hills and crosses a park service road at .5 mile. The woodland floor is carpeted with ferns during the warm season. At .9 mile, emerge at a powerline clearing and Big Lake. A paved trail goes left and right. Walk right, toward the boathouse, and gain a view of Big Lake, the biggest lake in the park, ringed in trees. Water enthusiasts can rent park boats in season to paddle the impoundment.

Continue the loop, reentering woods from the powerline. Ahead, wander through an old picnic area, now returned to woods. Rock-enclosed grills are still standing among the new saplings that have sprung up. Cross the park service road a second time at 1.5 miles. The trail undulates between hill and hollow. Some of these hollows are former gullied areas where cotton was grown, depleting an already exhausted soil. At 2.3 miles, a level spur trail leads left .2 mile to the park campground. Take this side path to check out the camping area, where twenty-eight sites are strung out on a loop with a central bathhouse. Each site has picnic table, fire ring, tent pad, and lantern post. Water spigots are situated throughout the camps.

Descend to Sals Branch, a beech-bordered stream running roughly parallel to the main park road. Hike along the stream, passing the remains of an old dam before bridging Sals Branch and emerging at the overflow parking area. Climb a bit and you are back at the visitor center, a fine family hike completed.

Mileages		
	0.0	Visitor center
	0.9	Big Lake
	2.3	Spur to campground
	2.6	Visitor center

33 SYCAMORE LOOP
William B. Umstead State Park

*If you like hiking along beautiful wooded streams, this hike at
William B. Umstead State Park is for you. It begins in a popular
picnic area, then works across and along Potts Branch for warm-up
stream scenery. Next, drop into lower Sycamore Creek, where
you can follow this stream through eye-pleasing wooded valley for
miles, past rocky rapids and translucent pools under deep forests,
seemingly a world away from the busy Triangle. Complete a loop,
then backtrack to the picnic area.*

Anybody who admires a moving woodland waterway should enjoy this
hike. It is one of my favorites. The streamside hiking is first rate. The

Distance 7.2-mile balloon loop

Hiking time 3.8 hours

Difficulty Moderate to difficult

Highlights Streamside hiking, homesites

Cautions None

Best seasons Year-round; mornings in summer

Other trail users None

Hours November–February, 8 a.m.–6 p.m.; March–April, 8 a.m.–8 p.m.;
    May–August, 8 a.m.–9 p.m.; September–October, 8 a.m.–8 p.m.;
    closed Christmas Day

Trail contact William B. Umstead State Park, 8801 Glenwood Avenue, Raleigh,
    NC 27617, 919-218-4170, www.ncparks.gov/william-b-umstead-state-park

Finding the trailhead From Exit 4A on I-540, northwest of downtown
    Raleigh and southeast of Durham, take US 70 East / Glenwood
    Avenue for 1.3 miles to turn right into Umstead State Park.
    Stay straight on Umstead Parkway and follow it 1.6 miles
    to the picnic area at the dead end of the parkway.

GPS trailhead coordinates 35.872357, –78.760787

Piedmont

hardest part of the Sycamore Trail is not the distance but navigating the maze of asphalt and natural-surface paths at the picnic area where it starts. Speaking of which, the picnic area at the trailhead presents sunny and shaded tables as well as a pair of picnic shelters where you can enjoy a pre- or post-hike meal.

Keep an eye on those picnic shelters, as they'll help you get to the trail part of the Sycamore Trail. From the parking area, take steps up to a circular asphalt trail. Go left or right, aiming for signed Picnic Shelter 2, then signed Picnic Shelter 1. From Picnic Shelter 1 you've got it made. Here the signed Sycamore Trail morphs into a natural-surface track. Start switchbacking downhill in rocky woods on a rocky trail. At .3 mile, cross Potts Branch Trail at an angle, then descend to span Potts Branch on a trail bridge. Turn up the 10- to 12-foot-wide tributary of Sycamore Creek, overhung with trees. The Potts Branch Trail runs along the other side of the scenic rock-strewn stream. Savor a dose of waterside walking.

At .6 mile, cross Group Camp Road and rise into prototypical Piedmont pine/oak woods flavored with sweetgum, maple, and hickory. The

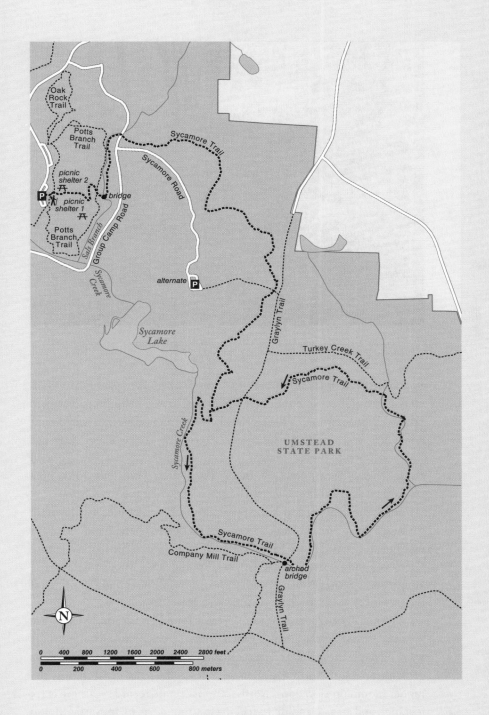

Oak
Rock
Trail

Potts
Branch
Trail

picnic
shelter 2

P

P

Salt Branch

picnic
shelter 1

bridge

Potts
Branch
Trail

Group Camp Road

Sycamore Creek

alternate

P

Sycamore Trail

Sycamore Road

Sycamore
Lake

Sycamore Creek

Graylyn Trail

Turkey Creek Trail

Sycamore Trail

UMSTEAD
STATE PARK

Sycamore Trail

Company Mill Trail

arched
bridge

Graylyn Trail

N

0   400   800   1200 1600 2000 2400 2800 feet

0   200   400   600   800 meters

The Sycamore Loop provides first-rate streamside hiking.

Sycamore Trail turns south, rolling through uplands to pass near a cemetery at 1.6 miles. Note the huge old-growth trees, including a very impressive white oak in this flat locale, likely a former homesite. Here a spur heads left, connecting to the multiuse Graylyn Trails. These multiuse trails are open to hikers, cyclists, and equestrians. We stay straight with the hiker-only Sycamore Trail. Begin descending a hillslope, bridging a streambed at 2.0 miles. Sycamore Lake is visible in the trees below.

Reach the loop portion of the Sycamore Trail at 2.2 miles. Go downhill to the attractive 20-foot-wide stream, not far below where the watercourse emerges from Sycamore Lake. It doesn't take long to see that Sycamore Creek is a sightly stream as it dances through richly wooded flats of sycamore and beech, garnished with ferns galore, with sunlight glinting off the stream as it swirls above a stone and gravel bottom.

As you might expect, many of the trees found on Sycamore Creek are sycamores, rising from its deep, rich, moist streamside soils, their roots weaving along the water's edge, stabilizing the stream's banks. Sycamores grow throughout North Carolina, except on the salty coast and in the higher mountain elevations. North Carolina's state-record sycamore is 115 feet high and an astounding 19 feet in circumference, up in Northampton

County toward the Virginia state line. Sycamores range from New England to Iowa to East Texas and south to the Florida panhandle.

Sycamores are easy to identify. Their tan bark is mottled on its trunk and even peeling in places, giving rise to the helpful hint that "sycamores look sick." Larger sycamores do have plated bark trunks, but even on those trees the upper trunk and branches are mottled. Sycamores have large five-pointed leaves that emerge late in the spring and turn gold during early autumn. Spot sycamores and other trees. In places you will see rock piles created when this area was cultivated. Walk out to the water's edge and grab a seat on a rock, just watching the stream flow by.

At 3.2 miles, the Sycamore Trail crosses the Graylyn Trail near where the Graylyn Trail spans Sycamore Creek on a picturesque arched bridge that begs a photograph. Continue following Sycamore Creek as it bumps into a big hill, forcing a curve. Pass under a powerline clearing at 3.3 miles. The woods remain rich and heavy with ferns in summertime. At 3.5 miles, the trail climbs a bluff above the stream. Dip back to bottoms, then at 4.0 miles the Sycamore Trail turns up a tributary of Sycamore Creek. Crisscross the small, clear feeder stream before leaving it at 4.4 miles. Rise to a wooded hilltop, crossing the Graylyn Trail at 4.9 miles. Continue hiking to complete the loop portion of the trek at 5.0 miles. From here, backtrack 2.2 miles to the trailhead, visiting Potts Branch one last time before returning to the picnic area / trailhead at 7.2 miles.

Mileages	0.0	Picnic area parking
	0.6	Cross Group Camp Road
	2.2	Begin loop portion of hike
	3.2	Come near arched bridge
	5.0	Complete loop portion of hike
	7.2	Picnic area parking

This balloon loop hike at Umstead State Park starts at busy Reedy Creek trailhead, then drops to big and beautiful Crabtree Creek, where you will find the site of a large mill with its breached dam. Hike along the creek, then rise to a less-visited eye-pleasing woodland of the park, coming near Sycamore Creek. Climb bluffs above Sycamore Creek, then cross a forested ridge, returning to Crabtree Creek, where you can enjoy more stream scenes before backtracking to the trailhead.

Distance 5.8-mile balloon loop

Hiking time 3.0 hours

Difficulty Moderate

Highlights Mill site, Crabtree Creek, less-visited woods

Cautions None

Best seasons Year-round; mornings in summer

Other trail users None

Hours November–February, 8 a.m.–6 p.m.; March–April, 8 a.m.–8 p.m.; May–August, 8 a.m.–9 p.m.; September–October, 8 a.m.–8 p.m.; closed Christmas Day

Trail contact William B. Umstead State Park, 8801 Glenwood Avenue, Raleigh, NC 27617, 919-218-4170, www.ncparks.gov/william-b-umstead-state-park

Finding the trailhead From Exit 287 on I-40 west of downtown Raleigh and southeast of Durham, take Harrison Road just a short distance east to the Reedy Creek entrance of Umstead State Park. Follow the main road to a large parking area at its end. The Company Mill Trail starts in the northwest corner of the large parking area.

GPS trailhead coordinates 35.836504, –78.75992

This is a tale of two parts of one trail. The first mile of the Company Mill Trail receives heavy use to where the path reaches Crabtree Creek and the old Company Mill site. Here you have the remnants of a stone

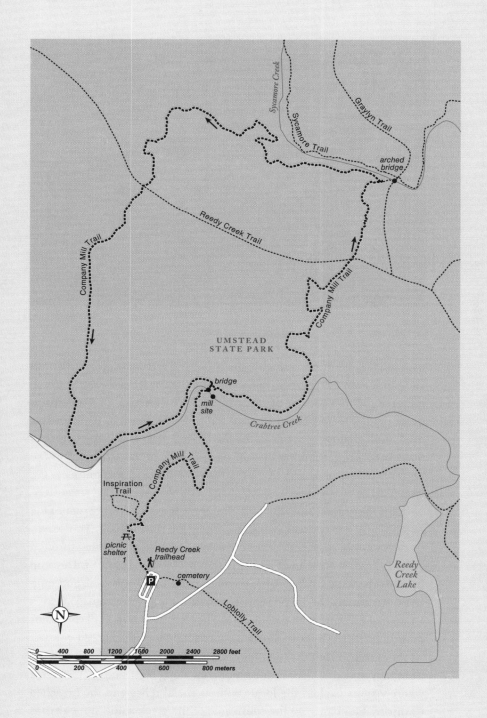

Sycamore Creek

Sycamore Trail

Graylyn Trail

arched
bridge

Reedy Creek Trail

Company Mill Trail

Company Mill Trail

UMSTEAD
STATE PARK

bridge

mill
site

Crabtree Creek

Company Mill Trail

Inspiration
Trail

picnic
shelter
1

Reedy Creek
trailhead

P

cemetery

Loblolly Trail

Reedy
Creek
Lake

N

| 0 | 400 | 800 | 1200 | 1600 | 2000 | 2400 | 2800 feet |

| 0 | 200 | 400 | 600 | 800 meters |

This very millstone was used at Company Mill.

dam, rocks aplenty for rest and relaxation, and rapids below the old mill site—and even a huge relic millstone from the day when Crabtree Creek powered the mill back in the 1800s. (For an easier hike, just trek down to this mill site and back.) Beyond the mill site, the trail is much less used, even qualifying as one of the least-hiked trails at popular Umstead State Park. Enjoy roaming the hilly forests here in the "back 40" of the preserve before returning to the Company Mill site as you complete the loop portion of the hike.

Start the gravel Company Mill Trail from the northwest corner of the big and busy Reedy Creek entrance parking lot. (The Loblolly Trail leaves from the northeast corner of the same lot.) Enter woods, hiking through a shaded picnic area, and follow the trail past Picnic Shelter 1. Descend by switchbacks, crossing a streambed under pines, sourwood, and tulip trees. At .2 mile, the Inspiration Trail, with interpretive signage, leaves left to make a .4-mile loop of its own. The Company Mill Trail continues downhill toward Crabtree Creek in woods lighted with exposed quartz.

At .9 mile, reach the long hiker bridge over Crabtree Creek and the Company Mill site. User-created trails run along both sides of the creek, where visitors explore the locale with its metal relics and the breached Company Mill dam. On the south side of the creek some stonework is still intact. The official trail bridges Crabtree Creek. After crossing the span, head right and begin the circuit downstream along Crabtree Creek. On busy days, park visitors will be perched on rock outcrops around the mill site and old dam, with kids playing in the water.

Soon you'll come to the huge millstone and plaque marking where Company Mill stood. Originally the land was the homesite for Anderson Page, and beginning in 1810 the Page family operated a mill using waterpower to grind products brought to them by nearby residents. The dam was washed away in a big flood in the early 1930s and never opened again. Company Mill gave way to what became Umstead State Park. However, looking around you can still spot other pre-park relics of metal and concrete.

Continue in streamside flats along Crabtree Creek, where fields have regrown into shady woodlands from which tree-clad hills rise. You would never know by the scenery of Crabtree Creek inside Umstead State Park that beyond its boundaries Crabtree Creek is an often-dammed urban stream, subject to floods that have cursed Raleigh time and again. However, multiple dams, parks, and greenways around Crabtree Creek have eased the flood danger while enhancing the beauty of the creek and the corridor through which it travels.

At 1.4 miles, turn up a tributary, then climb away from Crabtree Creek, rising through quartz-rich hills on switchbacks. At 2.1 miles, meet the Reedy Creek Trail, a road-like multiuse track. This is the old Reedy Creek Road. Once across the trail, look for a homesite. Here you will find tin roofing, scattered bricks, and flowers that keep rising every spring. Here, as in the rest of Umstead State Park, the past is being engulfed by the relentless growth of forest. From the homesite the Company Mill Trail switchbacks downhill. Pass a short spur leading right, to the Graylyn Trail, at 2.4 miles. You are now along Sycamore Creek, and the Sycamore Trail runs on the other side of the stream. Stay left with the Company Mill Trail as Sycamore Creek displays its natural beauty. Rise above the stream on bluffs and finally turn away from Sycamore Creek. Cross Reedy Creek Trail again at 3.6 miles.

The path wanders through woods, then picks up an old roadbed on a level, easy segment before descending back down to Crabtree Creek. Return to the wide waterway at 4.4 miles. Enjoy more riparian regality in a less-visited portion of the creek. Small branches flow over the trail, and you bridge them. At 4.9 miles, return to the hiker bridge over Crabtree

Creek, then backtrack up to the trailhead, completing the hike at 5.8 miles.

Mileages 0.0 Reedy Creek parking
0.9 Company Mill site
2.4 Sycamore Creek
4.4 Return to Crabtree Creek
4.9 Complete loop portion of hike
5.8 Reedy Creek parking

Piedmont

35 VISTA POINT HIKE
Jordan Lake State Recreation Area

Delight in lake views, deep woods, and a little history at the Vista Point unit of Jordan Lake State Recreation Area. Start on the Blue Trail, descending along a shallow drainage before looping by an old tobacco barn. From there, aim for Jordan Lake, passing through the group tent campground. Next, join the Red Trail and hike through rich forestlands out a peninsula affording excellent lake views. Curve along the shore before ending up near the boat ramp. A little road walking leads you back to the Blue Trail, more path hiking, and the trailhead.

Vista Point is one of nine units that comprise Jordan Lake State Recreation Area, all situated on the shores of big Jordan Lake, a little south of Chapel Hill. Mostly short trails are scattered among the nine units. Camping is a big draw—Jordan Lake State Recreation Area offers over 1,000 campsites! Boating, sailing, and swimming are naturally popular as well. Massive, destructive flooding on the Cape Fear River led the US Army Corps of Engineers to erect flood control dams along the Cape Fear and its tributaries, in this case the Haw River. Thus, the Haw River and New Hope Creek were backed up to create 14,000-acre Jordan Lake, and in 1973 the floodgates were closed. The state of North Carolina then established Jordan Lake State Recreation Area. It has become wildly popular, especially when a torrid Tar Heel summer rolls over the Piedmont.

Vista Point offers camping, but only group camping, with a group tent campground and an unusual group RV campground. Nevertheless,

Distance 4.8-mile loop

Hiking time 2.2 hours

Difficulty Easy to moderate, level trails

Highlights Vistas of Jordan Lake, old tobacco barn

Cautions Seasonal entrance fee in summer

Best seasons Mid-September through mid-May

Other trail users None

Hours November–February, 8 a.m.–8 p.m.; March–April, 8 a.m.–9 p.m.; May–
September, 8 a.m.–10 p.m.; October, 8 a.m.–9 p.m.; closed Christmas Day

Trail contact Jordan Lake State Recreation Area—Vista Point,
2498 N. Pea Ridge Road, Pittsboro, NC 27312, 919-362-0586,
www.ncparks.gov/jordan-lake-state-recreation-area

Finding the trailhead From Chapel Hill, take the southbound US 15/501
Bypass to Jack Bennett Road and a traffic light. Turn left on Jack
Bennett Road and follow it for 2.4 miles, then turn right on Big
Woods Road. Follow Big Woods Road south to US 64. Keep straight
here, joining Seaforth Road. Follow Seaforth Road for 1.9 miles
to turn left on Pea Ridge Road. Follow Pea Ridge Road .7 miles
to reach the park and entrance station. Parking is on the right in
a small gravel lot just before reaching the entrance station.

GPS trailhead coordinates 35.709146, –79.058960

the place is hopping in summer, with its large day-use boat ramp and picnicking facilities, so I recommend avoiding this hike then. Boat noise on the lake can drive some hikers crazy. Autumn can be colorful, while winter will be very quiet. Spring is good, too, with wildflowers and budding dogwoods. However, most of the woods are flat and can be moist in spring, with vernal pools in low spots. The park service has installed boardwalks in these locales. Finally, these two trails can be split into separate easy family walks if you want.

Our hike maximizes the trail mileage at Vista Point. Start near the park entrance station at a small trailhead. Here the Blue Trail, also known as the Tobacco Barn Trail, leaves west, dipping across a low drainage that could be wet in season. Aforementioned boardwalks aid in help with dry passage. Loblolly pine, oak, and scads of holly form a tree canopy. At .2 mile, the lightly used trail splits. Head right toward the tobacco barn, mostly in pines on gently sloping land. It is easy to visualize this

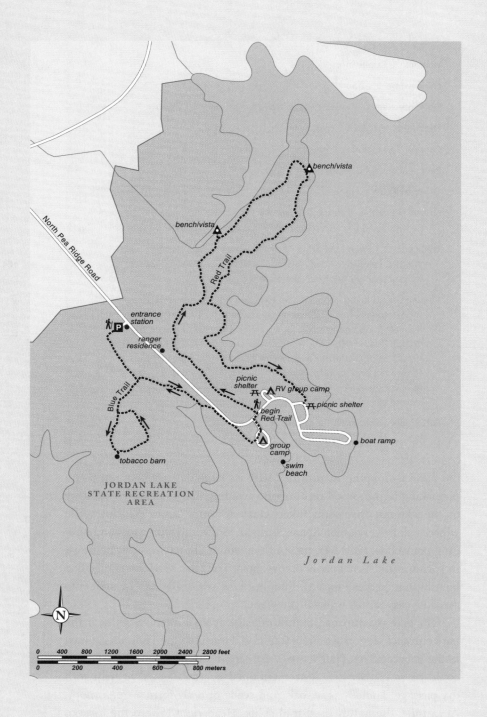

North Pea Ridge Road

bench/vista

bench/vista

Red Trail

entrance
station

ranger
residence

picnic
shelter

RV group camp

picnic shelter

begin
Red Trail

boat ramp

Blue Trail

group
camp

tobacco barn

swim
beach

JORDAN LAKE
STATE RECREATION
AREA

Jordan Lake

N

| 0 | 400 | 800 | 1200 | 1600 | 2000 | 2400 | 2800 feet |

| 0 | 200 | 400 | 600 | 800 meters |

This preserved tobacco barn harks back to Piedmont days gone by.

terrain being farmed a century or more back. At .4 mile, curve right as the trail splits, and by .5 mile you are at the preserved tobacco barn. This gives you an idea of what was grown here in the New Hope Creek valley when there was no Triangle and traffic and subdivisions and shopping centers, mainly just farmers extracting what they could from the good ol' Piedmont red clay.

Complete the loop, then backtrack to resume the Blue Trail, now heading toward Jordan Lake. An embayment comes into view. Open onto a field near the park road before reaching the group tent campground at 1.4 miles. Here, head left and return to the main park road, where you pick up the Red Trail, also known as the Vista Point Trail. This less-used but well-blazed singletrack path heads north in thick woods, coming near the park ranger residence at 1.8 miles. Beyond there, the path heads out a wooded peninsula, reaching a bench and viewpoint at 2.3 miles. Gaze out over a slender bay. Cross over to the east side of the peninsula in mixed pine-oak flatwoods dotted with ephemeral wetlands. Open onto a small beach and extensive view at 2.7 miles, a true vista far into the impoundment's 180 miles of shoreline. Turn south and curve with the small inlets of the shore, crossing intermittent drainages. Emerge at the picnic shelter near the boat ramp at 3.9 miles. From here, head out to

the main park road and pick up the Blue Trail near the group tent campground, backtracking on the footpath to reach the trailhead at 4.8 miles,
completing the two-pronged hike.

Mileages   **0.0** Trailhead parking
              0.5 Tobacco barn
              1.4 Group camp
              2.7 Vista
              3.9 Picnic shelter
              4.8 Trailhead parking

36 NEW HOPE CIRCUIT
Jordan Lake State Recreation Area

*Arguably the best hike at Jordan Lake State Recreation Area, this
loop travels a hilly peninsula along the shores of Jordan Lake,
melding the sights and sounds of woods and waters. The path
takes you north to a peninsula and a rewarding panorama before
turning south and following the shoreline, passing two hike-in
campgrounds before climbing away from the lake to Merry Oaks
Mountain. From here it leads back to the trailhead, a rewarding
experience completed.*

The New Hope Overlook unit is one of my favorite parcels of Jordan Lake
State Recreation Area. The hilly terrain stretches out on a peninsula and
is thus surrounded by water on three sides, creating a scenic setting. The
two primitive walk-in camping areas keep it rustic. You should avoid this
hike during the summertime, when the boat ramp is hopping. But the
shoulder seasons are great—the primitive walk-in campsites are open,
yet the lake is not overloaded with Triangle boaters trying to find their
slice of aquatic paradise.

Leave the large trailhead parking area, entering a dense growth of
sweetgum, pine, and tulip trees. Pine needles carpet the forest floor.
Travel just a short distance and come to a trail split. Head right on the
Blue Trail. (At this point the Red Trail is blazed conjunctively with the
Blue Trail.) Shortly come to the crumbled chimney of an old homesite.
Notice the periwinkle still growing at the spot that has now returned to

Distance 5.1-mile loop

Hiking time 2.7 hours

Difficulty Moderate, does have hills

Highlights Jordan Lake views, walk-in camping

Cautions Seasonal entrance fee in summer

Best seasons Mid-September through mid-May

Other trail users None

Hours November–February, 8 a.m.–8 p.m.; March–April, 8 a.m.–9 p.m.; May–September, 8 a.m.–10 p.m.; October, 8 a.m.–9 p.m.; closed Christmas Day

Trail contact Jordan Lake State Recreation Area—New Hope Overlook, 339 W. H. Jones Road, New Hill, NC 27562, 919-362-0586, www.ncparks.gov/jordan-lake-state-recreation-area

Finding the trailhead From Exit 59 on I-540 west of Raleigh, take US 64 West for 5.9 miles to Beaver Creek Road. Turn left on Beaver Creek Road and follow it 3.2 miles, then turn right on Pea Ridge Road. Follow Pea Ridge Road for 2.0 miles, to W. H. Jones Road. Turn right on W. H. Jones Road; after .5 mile you will reach New Hope Overlook entrance station. Turn right at the entrance station and follow it .2 mile toward the boat ramp. After entering the boat ramp parking area, look left for the trailhead.

GPS trailhead coordinates 35.682539, –79.048166

woods. Also look for old rock fences and piles of stones, created when a subsistence farmer cleared the land to plant crops and a garden, graze some cattle, and raise chickens and pigs to feed his family. Tobacco was the money crop used to pay property taxes and purchase items that couldn't be grown.

Continue north and curve near a cove of Jordan Lake, passing through a mix of deciduous trees mixed with cedar, holly, and ever-present pine. At .8 mile, come to an intersection. Here, split right toward the New Hope Overlook. Open onto a fine panorama, where New Hope Creek valley stretches forth. Look north at a natural, tree-lined shoreline. Scan northeast for the swim beach at the Ebenezer Church unit of the recreation area. On the far horizon, US 64 bridges Jordan Lake. This is a fine place to stop and drink it all in.

Backtrack from the overlook and continue the circuit, rolling through wooded hills. Cross the Camping Area A access road at 1.1 miles. Camping Areas A and B have walk-in campsites strung out along respective

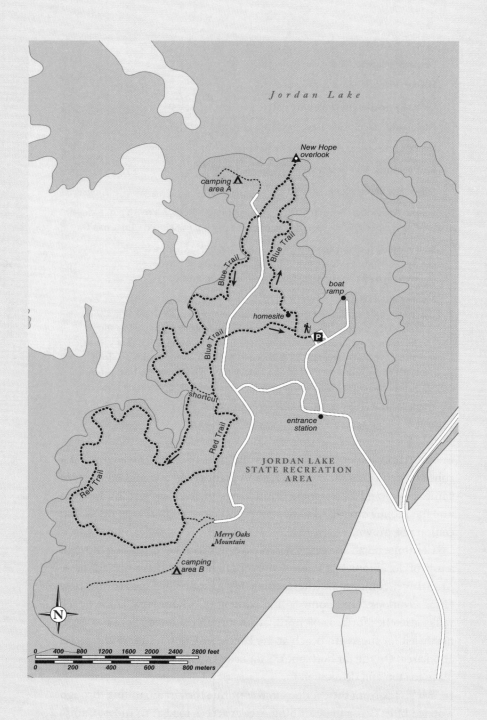

Jordan Lake

New Hope
overlook

camping
area A

Blue Trail

Blue Trail

boat
ramp

homesite

Blue Trail

shortcut

Red Trail

entrance
station

Red Trail

JORDAN LAKE
STATE RECREATION
AREA

Merry Oaks
Mountain

camping
area B

N

| 0 | 400 | 800 | 1200 | 1600 | 2000 | 2400 | 2800 feet |
| 0 | | 200 | | 400 | | 600 | | 800 meters |

Gravel beaches like this one are easily accessed from the trail.

trails. Therefore, you tote your gear from the parking area to the camp-site. Individual campsites have a lantern post, fire ring, and picnic table. Bring your own water. Reservations are required. I enjoyed pitching my tent here at Camping Area A after my hike. You can even turn the hike into a backpacking experience by starting at the day hiker trailhead.

Beyond the access road, the trail comes alongside the New Hope Creek channel of Jordan Lake. This part of the channel is narrow. Con-tinue along the shoreline, then around little coves, alternating between watery and woodsy views. Pass more fieldstone piles. At 2.3 miles, reach a trail intersection. Head left if you want to shortcut the loop, making it a 2.7-mile endeavor. Otherwise, head right and stay with the Red Trail, continuing to play tag with the shoreline in sloped woods, occasionally bridging intermittent streambeds.

At 3.5 miles, turn away from the lake, climbing ambitiously named Merry Oaks Mountain. The trail is steep in places but doesn't go to the top of Merry Oaks. At 4.1 miles, a spur trail leads right up to Camping Area B. The Red Trail keeps straight, crosses a gravel maintenance road, then rolls though mixed woods to reach the shortcut at 4.6 miles. From here the Red Trail keeps undulating to cross the Camping Area A access road again at 4.9 miles. After that, climb a bit, then make a long descent, returning to the trailhead and concluding the hike at 5.1 miles.

Mileages	**0.0**	Hiker trailhead
	0.9	New Hope Overlook
	2.3	Shortcut
	4.1	Spur to Camping Area B
	5.1	Hiker trailhead

37 CAMPBELL CREEK LOOP
Raven Rock State Park

Enjoy a classic circuit hike at fine Raven Rock State Park. Follow the Campbell Creek Loop Trail from the park visitor center to cross Campbell Creek and roll through wooded and rocky hills to find the park backcountry campground. From there, take the spur to Lanier Falls, a rapid on the brawling Cape Fear River. Grab a second view of the river before hiking up the wildflower-rich valley of Campbell Creek, with its rock outcrops, rapids, and deep woods.

Raven Rock State Park has grown from just a few hundred acres at its 1969 inception to 4,684 acres, protecting not only *the* Raven Rock but also other features along the Cape Fear River and hills that rise above it, such as Lanier Falls, a feature you will see on this hike. Pretty Campbell Creek also flows through the preserve. You will cross that waterway and hike along its length and through its wooded bottoms.

The park also boasts a first-rate visitor center, mountain biking, and equestrian-specific trails as well as a quality auto-accessible campground, picnic areas, a backcountry campground for hikers, and riverside camp-sites for paddlers accessing the park via the Cape Fear River. In fact, what became the park was originally recognized as a waymark for boat travelers on the Cape Fear River, an important mode of travel when North Carolina was a young state and much of the land was trackless woods. During those days, residents used the waterways for commerce and travel. Raven Rock, originally named Patterson's Rock, was a distinct point of passage. Later, locks were built to get around rapids such as those found in the

Distance 5.1-mile loop

Hiking time 2.7 hours

Difficulty Moderate

Highlights Lanier Falls, Campbell Creek

Cautions None

Best seasons September through May

Other trail users Backpackers

Hours November–February, 7 a.m.–7 p.m.; March–May, 7 a.m.–9 p.m.;
June–August, 7 a.m.–10 p.m.; September–October, 7 a.m.–9 p.m.;
closed Christmas Day

Trail contact Raven Rock State Park, 3009 Raven Rock Road, Lillington,
NC 27546, 910-893-4888, www.ncparks.gov/raven-rock-state-park

Finding the trailhead From the intersection of US 421 and US 401 in
Lillington, take US 421 North for 6.2 miles, then turn right on Raven
Rock Road. Follow it for 3.3 miles to reach the park's visitor center.

GPS trailhead coordinates 35.464003, –78.913885

vicinity of Raven Rock. Evidence of these locks still remains. And other rapids, such as Lanier Falls, gained a reputation as being challenging to navigate either up- or downstream. Lanier Falls is actually a river rapid and is marked on official USGS topo maps. Interestingly, Campbell Creek is marked as Camels Creek on those same government maps.

Name aside, we start our hike by picking up the Campbell Creek Loop Trail, leaving west from the visitor center. Quickly enter woods as a connector path goes left toward the main picnic area. Keep west with the gravelly Campbell Creek Loop Trail in hickory- and oak-dominated woodlands with a scattering of sparkleberry. Keep a continuous downgrade, dropping 200 feet before meeting Campbell Creek and a trail bridge at .5 mile. Cross the span, enjoying looks at the dancing stream below, to immediately reach a trail intersection. Stay left here, beginning the actual loop portion of the hike. The path rolls through hill and hollow, undulating more than you may expect. Quartz sparkles on the forest floor. Pass a stream at 1.3 miles that features a little cascade of 3 feet or so, dropping off a ledge. Ahead, watch for a huge beech tree beside the trail.

At 1.9 miles, the trail turns abruptly right where it meets a park service road. An easy walk will bring you near the backcountry campground

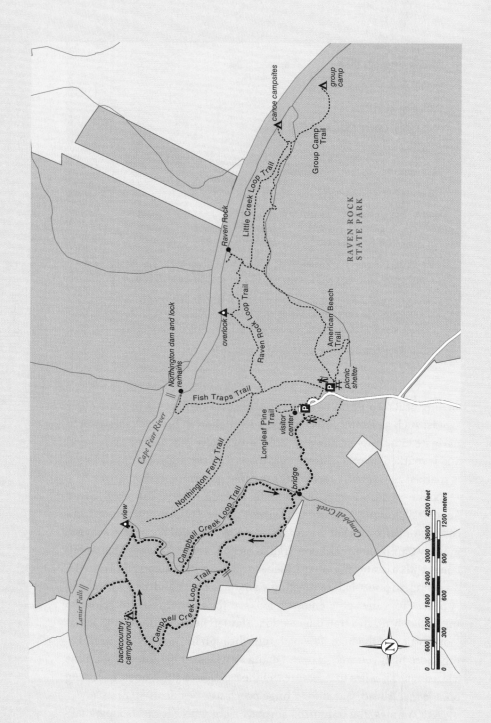

canoe campsites

group camp

Group Camp Trail

Little Creek Loop Trail

Raven Rock

RAVEN ROCK STATE PARK

overlook

Northington dam and lock remains

Cape Fear River

Raven Rock Loop Trail

American Beech Trail

picnic shelter

Fish Traps Trail

Longleaf Pine Trail

visitor center

Northington Ferry Trail

bridge

Campbell Creek

Campbell Creek Loop Trail

view

Campbell Creek Loop Trail

Lanier Falls

backcountry campground

N

0   300   600   900   1200 meters

0   600   1200   1800   2400   3000   3600   4200 feet

Part of Lanier Falls on the Cape Fear River.

and a restroom at 2.2 miles. Each of the five backcountry sites offers a bench, fire ring, and tent site. Bring your own water. Camping reservations must be made in advance. Continue downhill to turn left toward Lanier Falls. Drop fast on wood and earth steps. The din of Lanier Falls roars back at you. Reach the water's edge at 2.5 miles. Peer through the trees—the frothy rapid would present obstacles to self-propelled watercraft of yesteryear.

Continue the Campbell Creek Loop Trail after leaving Lanier Falls, and at 3.1 miles, follow a spur left toward the confluence of Campbell Creek and the Cape Fear River, where you'll get a second close-up view of the big river and its smaller tributary. From there, backtrack and begin heading upstream along 15-foot-wide Campbell Creek, rolling and splashing over rocks as it winds between hills, slowing in still pools and dividing around islands. The beard cane–scattered bottomlands here are richly forested with sycamore, loblolly pine, and ironwood that overhang the creek. Waterside rock outcrops call you to sit in contemplation beside the gurgling stream. Boardwalks offer dry passage over spring seeps flowing into Campbell Creek. Complete the loop portion of the hike at 4.6 miles after passing through floodplain woodlands. From here, make the half-mile uphill trek to return to the visitor center at 5.1 miles.

38   RAVEN ROCK LOOP
■■ Raven Rock State Park

This highlight reel of a hike explores woods and waters deep in the Cape Fear River valley at Raven Rock State Park. Start at the preserve's fine picnic shelter, then descend into the everywhere-you-look-is-beautiful valley of cascading Little Creek. Emerge along the Cape Fear River and make your way to the long overhanging bluff that is Raven Rock. Climb to an overlook of the river valley before dropping to explore the Fish Traps rapids and the remains of old Northington Lock and Dam before returning to the trailhead.

The Cape Fear River is one of North Carolina's most important waterways, so it is fitting that a North Carolina state park would be located on it. Situated near Lillington, this preserve harbors a mile-long riverside outcrop known as Raven Rock. The historic waterway splits Raven Rock State Park in two, above the town of Lillington. Most park facilities and trails are on the south side of the preserve, where this hike takes place. And what a hike it is, truly one of the best in the state park system. You will not only see (and walk atop) the mile-long bluff of Raven Rock but also take in great upstream views of the Cape Fear River as well as the Northington Lock and Dam remains. The Cape Fear River has always been a key shipping conduit from the Atlantic Ocean into the Piedmont. (Even today, locks and dams enable shipping on the Cape Fear River from the coast to Fayetteville.)

The park's situation along the fall line, where the hard rocks of the Piedmont give way to Atlantic Coastal Plain, is evident on this hike as you walk along the rocky stream of Little Creek and especially along the Cape Fear River, with stone bluffs and surprisingly rugged rapids around which boats navigated, necessitating the Northington Lock and Dam.

Piedmont

Distance 5.2-mile loop

Hiking time 2.8 hours

Difficulty Moderate

Highlights Little Creek, Raven Rock, overlook, lock remains

Cautions None

Best seasons September through May

Other trail users None

Hours November–February, 7 a.m.–7 p.m.; March–May, 7 a.m.–9 p.m.;
June–August, 7 a.m.–10 p.m.; September–October, 7 a.m.–9 p.m.;
closed Christmas Day

Trail contact Raven Rock State Park, 3009 Raven Rock Road, Lillington,
NC 27546, 910-893-4888, www.ncparks.gov/raven-rock-state-park

Finding the trailhead From the intersection of US 421 and US 401 in
Lillington, take US 421 North for 6.2 miles, then turn right on Raven
Rock Road. Follow it for 3.2 miles, and turn right into the park
picnic shelter parking lot just before reaching the visitor center.

GPS trailhead coordinates 35.461895, –78.911722

This weir was overwhelmed by storm flow in 1859 and never rebuilt:
dam reconstruction was too expensive to compete with the emerging
railroads.

Begin this hike by joining the Raven Rock Loop Trail near the attractive park picnic shelter. Pass the short American Beech Trail (a nature
trail), then the picnic area bathrooms. Hike through upland flatwoods of
oak and hickory. By .3 mile you are descending to reach Little Creek at .6
mile, winding through thickets of mountain laurel. Little Creek cascades
over stone shoals and slides, reflecting light in the dim, dense streamside
forest littered in pine needles dropped by moisture-loving loblolly pines
looming overhead. Bridge the 6-foot-wide brook twice at .6 mile.

At .8 mile, split right to follow the Little Creek Loop Trail, enjoying
more of this intimate ferny valley bordered by sheer stone bluffs in places,
with Little Creek making stream-wide drops that form almost-waterfalls.
At 1.6 miles, a spur trail leads right, bridging Little Creek for the park's
group camp. Leave Little Creek, then pass a spur leading right down to
the canoe campsites, set on the Cape Fear River. These reservable sites

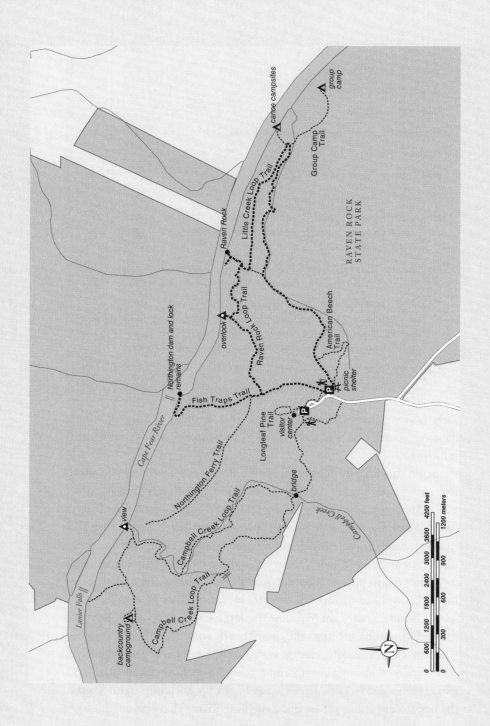

canoe campsites

group camp

Group Camp Trail

RAVEN ROCK STATE PARK

Little Creek Loop Trail

Raven Rock

overlook

Raven Rock Loop Trail

American Beech Trail

Northington dam and lock remains

Fish Traps Trail

picnic shelter

Cape Fear River

Longleaf Pine Trail

visitor center

bridge

Northington Ferry Trail

Campbell Creek

Campbell Creek Loop Trail

view

Campbell Creek Loop Trail

Lanier Falls

backcountry campground

0   600   1200 1800 2400 3000 3600 4200 feet
0   300   600   900   1200 meters

N

Raven Rock rises from riverside flats along the Cape Fear River.

are accessible by river paddlers and backpackers. They offer a fire pit and tent site. You can check out the river from here, too.

The hike continues on the Little Creek Loop Trail as it climbs the bluff of Raven Rock in mostly pine woods. Rejoin the Raven Rock Loop Trail at 2.3 miles and head right. Just ahead, you'll reach another junction. Drop right toward Raven Rock on a steep wooden staircase with ninety-nine steps. You are then below the overhung bluff. The scenery here will surprise, as the rock cliff overhangs the land below, forming long rockhouses along a flood-prone strip of land between the bluff and river. Explore the bluff up- and downstream. The locale recalls the Carolina mountains rather than the Piedmont.

Leave the bluff, climbing the ninety-nine steps and continuing the Raven Rock Loop Trail. Reach a spur right to a bluff-top overlook at 3.1 miles. Peer upstream toward rapids and pools of the wide waterway cutting a swath through wooded lands. The depth of this view is an unexpected surprise in this neck of North Carolina. Resume the loop and meet the Fish Traps Trail at 3.6 miles. Descend right on a wide, easy track, passing the Northington Ferry Trail as it traces a historic route to a river crossing. We continue dropping to meet the Cape Fear River again at 4.1 miles, at the noisy Fish Traps rapids. Continue downstream to trail's end at a rock outcrop. Below you can see the former Northington Dam, along with parts of the locks that lifted and lowered boats, allowing them to get around the dam.

Climb from the lock and dam remains, backtracking to the Raven Rock Loop Trail. Resume the loop hike on an easy, wide track in flatwoods, emerging at the picnic area parking lot at 5.2 miles, completing the highlight reel of a hike.

Mileages	0.0	Picnic area parking
	0.8	Little Creek Loop Trail
	2.4	Raven Rock
	3.1	Overlook
	4.2	Lock and dam remains
	5.2	Picnic area parking

39 WEYMOUTH WOODS SANDHILLS LOOP
Weymouth Woods Sandhills Nature Preserve

Enjoy this rewarding hike at North Carolina's first designated nature preserve, harboring old-growth longleaf pines and attendant species of a fast-disappearing ecosystem. Travel amid towering evergreens and down into richly wooded thickets along James Creek and its tributaries.

Distance 3.8-mile loop

Hiking time 2.1 hours

Difficulty Easy to moderate, sandy trails in spots

Highlights Old-growth pines, swamp thickets, red-cockaded woodpecker habitat

Cautions Heat in summer

Best seasons Mid-September through mid-May

Other trail users None

Hours November–February, 8 a.m.–6 p.m.; March–October, 8 a.m.–8 p.m.; closed Christmas Day

Trail contact Weymouth Woods Sandhills Nature Preserve, 1024 Fort Bragg Road, Southern Pines, NC 28387, 910-692-2167, www.ncparks.gov/weymouth-woods-sandhills-nature-preserve

Finding the trailhead From the intersection of US 1 and US 501 in Southern Pines, head north on US 1 / Sandhills Boulevard for .7 mile, then turn right on Saunders Boulevard. Follow it for 1.2 miles, then turn left on Bethesda Road and drive a total of 1.6 miles as Bethesda Road becomes Fort Bragg Road, then turn left into the preserve. Follow the park road for .2 mile to dead-end at the visitor center / trailhead.

GPS trailhead coordinates 35.146835, –79.368917

When North Carolina was an English colony, it became an important source for naval stores—products used to build ships, such as masts, rosin, pitch, turpentine, and tar. These naval stores were obtained from

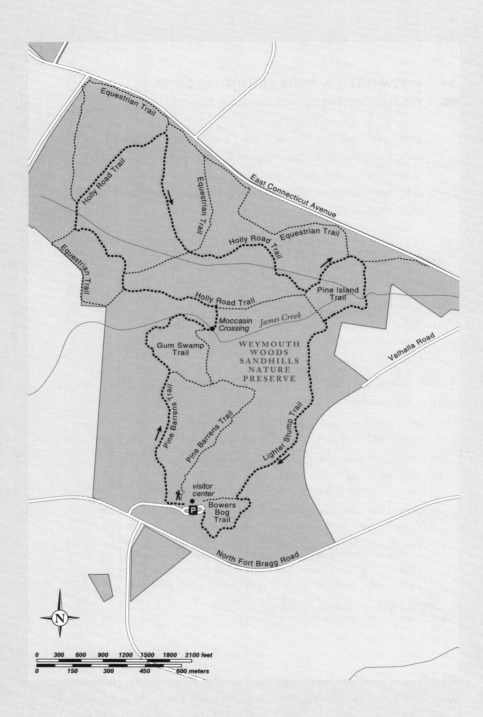

Equestrian Trail

Holly Road Trail

Equestrian Trail

East Connecticut Avenue

Holly Road Trail

Equestrian Trail

Equestrian Trail

Holly Road Trail

Pine Island Trail

Moccasin Crossing

James Creek

Gum Swamp Trail

WEYMOUTH WOODS SANDHILLS NATURE PRESERVE

Valhalla Road

Pine Barrens Trail

Pine Barrens Trail

Lighter Stump Trail

visitor center

P

Bowers Bog Trail

North Fort Bragg Road

N

| 0 | 300 | 600 | 900 | 1200 | 1500 | 1800 | 2100 feet |

| 0 | 150 | 300 | 450 | 600 meters |

Pines like these were important for the naval stores industry in the early days of North Carolina.

the vast old-growth longleaf pine forests that once reached across the land. The pines were cut down, and sap was distilled from standing evergreens. At one point, one-third of the world's naval stores were coming from North Carolina, and that's one reason it was nicknamed the Tar Heel State.

The railroads came to the Carolina sandhills after the Civil War, and the giant pines came down in alarming numbers. By 1900, a Mr. Boyd from nearby Southern Pines bought a tract of old-growth forest, and this 400-acre parcel eventually became the NC State Parks nature preserve we can visit today.

On this hike you travel underneath ancient tall evergreens, on sloped mixed woods, and across clear swamp streams flowing between the piney hills. It is unlikely you will see the rare pine barrens tree frog, but knowing that this amphibian and lots of other flora and fauna are protected in this preserve enhances the overall experience. Additionally, the world's oldest-known longleaf pine is in part of the preserve, dating back to the mid-1500s.

You will see the nesting trees for the endangered red-cockaded woodpecker, marked with a band of white paint. Start your natural North

Carolina adventure on the Pine Barrens Trail, leaving left as you face the visitor center. Early pioneers named these longleaf pine forests "barrens" because the wide spacing of the trees and minimal understory led them to believe the soils were poor. (Recurring fire plays a role in shaping pine barrens.) You will soon see the majestic longleaf pines towering above the forest floor. Ahead, cross a park service road, one of many you will encounter. Don't worry about getting turned around: the official trails are signed and blazed. Cruise rolling hills dropping off to tributaries of James Creek. (Its official USGS name is Mill Creek, but that name was lost over time.) You will see local residents and as well as soldiers from Fort Bragg jogging the trails.

At .4 mile, head left on the Gum Swamp Trail, entering thick woods of bay, gum, and maple contrasting with the open pines atop the sandhills. At .8 mile, head left on the Moccasin Crossing, a boardwalk/bridge running above sandy, clear James Creek. Ahead, split left with the Holly Road Trail, running the margin between swamp woods and piney forest. The walking is easy and you roll northwest, crossing both the signed Equestrian Trail and service roads. The way is clear, and by 1.7 miles you are very near East Connecticut Avenue. Turn south there, and at 2.3 miles, bridge a tributary of James Creek, then meet the Pine Island Trail at 2.5 miles. Head left on the path, traversing thick, ferny, cane-filled bottomlands using multiple boardwalks. Look for gum trees in the swamps. During autumn the James Creek bottomland hardwoods will display a cornucopia of color.

At 2.9 miles, turn left on the Lighter Stump Trail. The name is a nod to resin-filled pine stumps, chopped into chips and used to start fires. Climb from James Creek back into longleaf pine barrens, heading left on the Bowers Bog Trail at 3.5 miles. Here, circle by some low, brushy wetlands, where you might be able to spy pitcher plants. By 3.8 miles you are back at the visitor center parking lot, concluding the hike.

Mileages		
	0.0	Visitor center
	0.8	Moccasin Crossing
	2.5	Pine Island Trail
	3.8	Visitor center

40 · MEDOC MOUNTAIN CIRCUIT
▰ Medoc Mountain State Park

This hike explores the highs and lows of underappreciated Medoc Mountain State Park. First cross Bear Swamp Creek, then climb to the crest of wooded Medoc Mountain. Next, loop down to the banks of Little Fishing Creek, a charming stream. Cruise the rich bottomlands and enjoy a view from a trail bridge crossing the creek before returning to the trailhead.

Distance 4.6-mile loop

Hiking time 2.2 hours

Difficulty Moderate

Highlights Medoc Mountain, creek bottoms

Cautions First .6 mile of hike is shared with mountain bikers

Best seasons September through May

Other trail users Mountain bikers first .6 mile

Hours November–February, 8 a.m.–6 p.m.; March–May, 8 a.m.–8 p.m.; June–August, 8 a.m.–9 p.m.; September–October, 8 a.m.–8 p.m.; closed Christmas Day

Trail contact Medoc Mountain State Park, 1541 Medoc State Park Road, Hollister, NC 27844, 252-586-6588, www.ncparks.gov/medoc-mountain-state-park

Finding the trailhead From Exit 150 on I-95 near Whitakers, take NC 33 West for .4 mile, then turn right onto NC 4 North / NC 48 North and follow it for 11.1 miles, then turn left onto NC 561 West and follow it for 2.3 miles. Turn left onto Medoc Mountain State Park Road and follow it for 1 mile to reach the park office / visitor center on your right.

GPS trailhead coordinates 36.263889, –77.888306

Looking at a map of North Carolina, you will see no other state parks near Medoc Mountain State Park, located on the eastern edge of the Piedmont, not far from the Virginia state line. Back in the 1970s, before the preserve at Medoc Mountain existed, state officials sought to

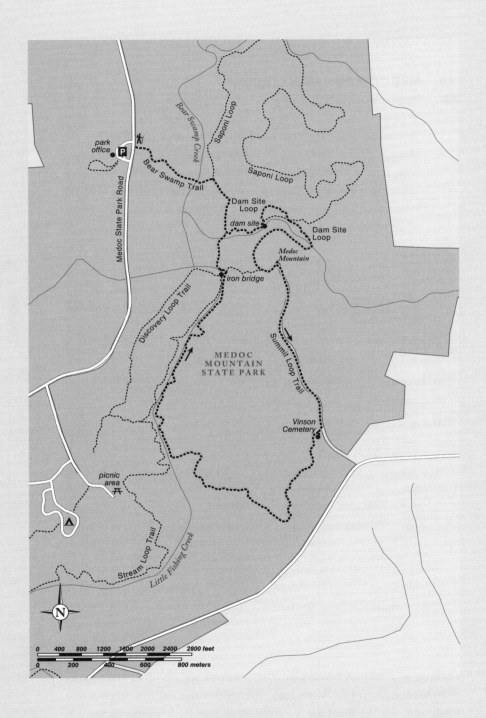

park office

P

Bear Swamp Creek

Medoc State Park Road

Bear Swamp Trail

Saponi Loop

Saponi Loop

Dam Site Loop

dam site

Dam Site Loop

Medoc Mountain

iron bridge

Discovery Loop Trail

MEDOC MOUNTAIN STATE PARK

Summit Loop Trail

Vinson Cemetery

picnic area

Stream Loop Trail

Little Fishing Creek

N

| 0 | 400 | 800 | 1200 | 1600 | 2000 | 2400 | 2800 feet |
| 0 | | 200 | | 400 | | 600 | | 800 meters |

View from the bridge over Little Fishing Creek.

establish a state park hereabouts, scouring a five-county region of the northern Piedmont. After officials examined the area's natural assets, Medoc Mountain literally and figuratively stood above the other candidates, with its namesake peak rising to an elevation of 325 feet amid the surrounding lands. Little Fishing Creek—one of the area's cleanest, clearest streams—flows through those lands in this 3,800-plus-acre park, which opened in 1973. Since then, former farmlands have continued to grow over to forests, while park personnel have developed facilities to make the natural assets more enjoyable. This includes separate trails for hikers like us as well as mountain bikers and equestrians. The park also includes a fine thirty-four-site campground for tenters and RVers as well as picnic spots and paddling accesses. I think you will be pleasantly surprised at this less-heralded preserve.

You will also like this hike. It explores the Little Fishing Creek valley after making the "must-do" ascent of Medoc Mountain. Start your trek at the park office, crossing east over the paved park road and officially joining the Bear Swamp Trail in regrowing woods. Relics reveal its pre-park status as a farm. Much of the current park was cultivated in grapes. Note the huge trailside white oak. Descend a hill to cross Bear Swamp Creek on a bridge; the creek flows more stream-like than swamp-like at this juncture.

Reach an intersection at .3 mile. Head right on the Saponi Loop, shared with mountain bikers. At .6 mile, come to another intersection. Head left, still on the Saponi Loop, as your return route enters on the right. At .7 mile, climb left on the hiker-only Dam Site Loop Trail. The path actually takes you through a concrete floodgate of a small abandoned dam. Curve over a hill, then descend, crossing the Saponi Loop, and shortly coming to a second, older dam site at 1.0 mile. Note the concreted rocks here that once slowed a tributary of Bear Swamp Creek. These were once small agricultural weirs, used to water crops and critters.

Beyond the second dam site, begin ascending Medoc Mountain on an oak- and hickory-heavy slope. At 1.4 miles, head left on the Summit Loop Trail. You've already climbed most of the way. Soon level off and roll atop the ridge on a wide track, a former road. The tree canopy rises high here, majestically shading the trail. At 2.1 miles, the Summit Loop Trail curves right and reaches the Vinson Cemetery, the graveyard for just one of many families that farmed this part of the Piedmont back when agriculture was a lifeway for most Tar Heel State residents.

Descend beyond the cemetery, reaching moist bottomland forest at 2.9 miles. Soon you'll come along Little Fishing Creek; turn upstream along the wide watercourse, paddled by kayakers and canoers when the waters are favorable. The 30-foot-wide stream is pocked with occasional tree snags and sonorant rocky shoals. Walk a level, woodsy track along the stream to reach a trail junction and iron bridge at 3.9 miles. The bridge offers a good stream-vista point and also connects to the Discovery Loop Trail and other hiker paths on the far side of Little Fishing Creek.

Keep straight, and soon you'll reach the Dam Site Loop. Stay left here, leaving Little Fishing Creek, tracing a tributary. Cross a small bridge, then complete the loop portion of the hike at 4.2 miles. From here, backtrack .6 mile to the park office.

Mileages		
	0.0	Park office
	0.6	Dam Site Loop Trail
	2.1	Vinson Cemetery
	3.9	Iron bridge
	4.7	Park office

Duck moss blankets a section of Merchants Millpond.

■ Coast and Coastal Plain

Cypress and tupelo trees await a weak winter sun.

41 MERCHANTS MILLPOND LOOP
■ Merchants Millpond State Park

Make a loop at stellar Merchants Millpond State Park, exploring the richly wooded hills and waters. The hike takes you along Merchants Millpond over knolls and into scenic vales before coming along Lassiter Swamp. Stop by a backcountry camp and cruise flatwoods before rolling through more hills that will challenge your perceptions of eastern North Carolina.

Distance 5.7-mile balloon loop

Hiking time 2.9 hours

Difficulty Moderate

Highlights Merchants Millpond, Lassiter Swamp, alluring woods

Cautions None

Best seasons Early fall through early summer

Other trail users None

Hours November–February, 8 a.m.–6 p.m.; March, October, 8 a.m.–8 p.m.; April–May, September, 8 a.m.–8 p.m.; June–August, 8 a.m.–9 p.m.; closed Christmas Day

Trail contact Merchants Millpond State Park, 176 Millpond Road, Gatesville, NC 27938, 252-357-1191, www.ncparks.gov/merchants-millpond-state-park

Finding the trailhead From the intersection of US 158 and NC 32 in Sunbury, head west on US 158 for 5.1 miles to turn left on Millpond Road. Drive southbound on Millpond Road for .9 mile, then turn left into the park. Pass the visitor center / park office and continue to where the road ends, at the picnic shelter parking area at .5 mile.

GPS trailhead coordinates 36.438118, –76.694288

Coast and Coastal Plain

Although it's two centuries old, Merchants Millpond is not natural. Formed when Bennetts Creek was dammed to provide waterpower for a sawmill, the unintended result is a gorgeous wooded wetland and lake. Now we have 760 watery acres scattered with regal bald cypress and tupelo trees as well as aquatic plants that create a scenic body of water

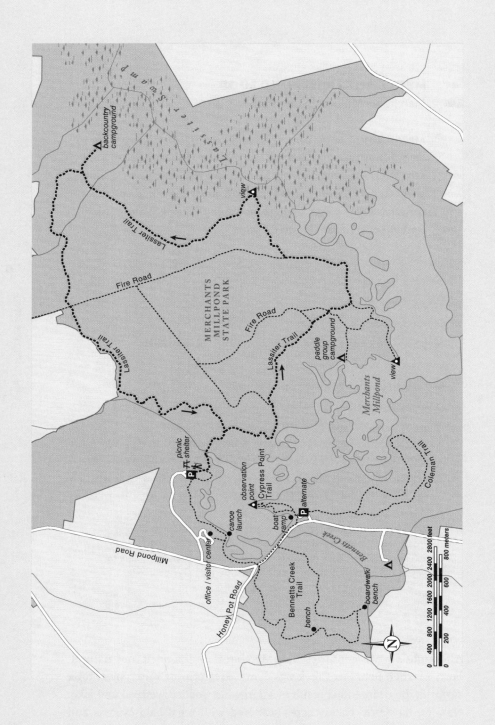

MERCHANTS MILLPOND STATE PARK

Lassiter Swamp

backcountry campground

view

Lassiter Trail

Fire Road

Fire Road

Lassiter Trail

Lassiter Trail

paddle group campground

view

Merchants Millpond

Coleman Trail

picnic shelter

P

observation point

Cypress Point Trail

alternate

P

canoe launch

boat ramp

office / visitor center

Millpond Road

Honey Pot Road

Bennetts Creek Trail

Bennetts Creek

bench

boardwalk / bench

bench

N

0   400   800   1200   1600   2000   2400   2800 feet
0   200   400   600   800 meters

where we can hike, paddle, fish, and camp. Additionally, over 3,000 wild acres surround Merchants Millpond, providing habitat for wildlife from birds to beavers, from bears to waterfowl, from snakes to alligators. And the park's diverse woodlands are a treat to hike through. You'll undoubtedly note the plethora of trailside beech trees, with their signature gray smooth trunks.

I highly recommend incorporating other activities into your hike. Merchants Millpond State Park is fun for paddlers, with marked trails winding through the tarn. Cyclists have still other trails to travel, and yet more pathways await hikers. And the camping is superb. Not only can you backpack-camp on this hike, but you can also paddle into a campsite or pitch your tent or park your rig at the auto-accessible campground. No matter your style, overnighting here is a real outdoors treat.

Yet this hike will stand on its own. From the back of the picnic shelter parking area, join the Lassiter Trail, blazed in white, and trace the gravel path downhill. You'll soon meet a trail that leads right to the park visitor center. The Lassiter Trail turns left here, descending to Merchants Millpond, now as a singletrack, natural-surface trail. Enjoy pounding a long boardwalk that crosses a cove of Merchants Millpond. Look out on tupelo and cypress trees rising from the duck-moss-covered pond.

Our particular hike traces the Lassiter Trail as it cruises near and above Merchants Millpond before turning away and coming near Lassiter Swamp, another wet wildland. The trail rolls underneath more impressive stands of beech before coming to the designated backcountry camping area found along the path. Here those wishing an overnight stay can pitch their tent in woods lording over Lassiter Swamp. The balance of the hike then works back toward the trailhead, aiming west in flatwoods before resuming hilly terrain. At .2 mile, come to the boardwalk's end, then get your first taste of the wooded hills and hollows surrounding Merchants Millpond. Beech, sweetgum, and tulip trees populate the forest, with an understory of beard cane. Keep your eyes peeled for an impressive old-growth tulip tree on trail right immediately after climbing from the boardwalk. At .3 mile, come to a trail junction. Here you turn right, southbound, to begin the loop portion of the Lassiter Trail, winding along wooded slopes where small streams flow into Merchants Millpond. By .6 mile, you are back along the millpond itself, enjoying more distant looks at the body of water from the hills above. At .7 mile, you will come near a trailside restroom beside a fire road. Tread eastward, using boardwalks to cross streams in hollows where beech trees dominate. This is a scenic section of trail. At 1.2 miles, come to another trail intersection. Here a fire road / bicycle trail crosses the Lassiter Trail. Keep straight here to come to a second intersection at 1.3 miles. Continue straight with the white-blazed Lassiter Trail and come to yet another intersection at 1.4 miles. Here a fire road leads right to a point on a peninsula and a rewarding panorama of Merchants Millpond. Consider a detour out to the point here.

The Lassiter Trail is now a doubletrack, traveling first east, then north. At 1.6 miles, cross a wooded swamp stream on a bridge. Here you can look east toward Lassiter Swamp, a huge wetland surrounding Bennetts Creek. Continue hiking northbound on a doubletrack. At 1.8 miles, leave the doubletrack as the easily missed Lassiter Trail splits right. The fire road / bicycle trail continues straight, northbound. Follow the now-single-track Lassiter Trail under majestic forest dipping into hollows and rising among hills with wooded Lassiter Swamp to your right. At 2.2 miles, the path leads by a bluff and vista down into Lassiter Swamp. From here the trail turns away from the wetland and makes a level, easy track in flatwoods. At 3.1 miles, the Lassiter Trail drops to cross a stream, then climbs out.

At 3.2 miles, reach the marked side trail leading to the backcountry camp, set on a peninsula between two hollows. A 500-foot walk leads to five dispersed campsites, each with a fire ring, yet with a common privy. From here the Lassiter Trail turns west in flatwoods. At 3.9 miles, the trail dips into a hollow and crosses the same stream you crossed at 3.1 miles. Rise from the waterway and enjoy more flatwoods walking. At 4.2 miles, the Lassiter Trail bisects the fire road / bicycle trail. Leave the flatwoods behind, cutting into deep hollows, bridging occasional streams cutting through the hollows. At 5.4 miles, complete the loop portion of the hike. From here, backtrack toward the trailhead, completing the adventure at 5.7 miles.

Mileages	0.0	Picnic shelter parking area trailhead
	0.3	Begin loop
	1.8	Lassiter Trail splits right
	3.2	Spur to backcountry camp
	5.4	Complete loop
	5.7	Picnic area trailhead

Coast and Coastal Plain

42 BENNETTS CREEK HIKE
███ Merchants Millpond State Park

Explore the waters and woods of picturesque Merchants Mill State Park on this triple-loop circuit. First, hike the sloped banks above striking Merchants Millpond, then walk forests along Bennetts Creek, enjoying a boardwalk to the stream itself. Next, stroll the easy Cypress Point Trail for more millpond panoramas. Finally, trek the Coleman Trail in one of the more remote stretches of this fine state park.

Distance 5.6-mile triple loop

Hiking time 2.8 hours

Difficulty Moderate

Highlights Swamp scenes, Bennetts Creek, pond spillway

Cautions Use caution during short road walk

Best seasons September through May

Other trail users None

Hours November–February, 8 a.m.–6 p.m.; March–October, 8 a.m.–8 p.m.; April–May, September, 8 a.m.–8 p.m.; June–August, 8 a.m.–9 p.m.; closed Christmas Day

Trail contact Merchants Millpond State Park, 176 Millpond Road, Gatesville, NC 27938, 252-357-1191, www.ncparks.gov/merchants-millpond-state-park

Finding the trailhead From the intersection of US 158 and NC 32 in Sunbury, head west on US 158 for 5.1 miles to turn left on Millpond Road. Drive southbound on Millpond Road for .9 mile, then turn left into the park. Pass the visitor center / park office and continue to where the road ends, at the park picnic area at .5 mile.

GPS trailhead coordinates 36.438118, –76.694288

The scenery at Merchants Millpond State Park is worthy of North Carolina state park designation. Here a cypress- and gum-tree-ringed pond is bordered by attractively wooded hillocks broken by spring-fed streamlets. It is where Bennetts Creek flows through wooded wetlands. It is where

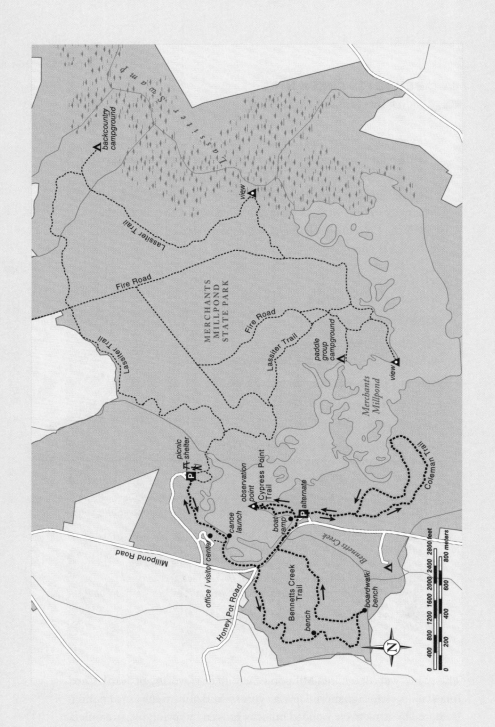

Water flowing over this dam feeds Bennetts Creek.

upland hardwood and evergreen forests create a naturally eye-pleasing habitat to walk through.

This hike highlights many of the above features as it traverses the western side of Merchants Millpond State Park, passing waters both still and moving, under a canopy of diverse forestlands. Start your hike at the picnic shelter parking area. Walk to the back of the shelter and head right, toward the visitor center, on an arm of the Lassiter Trail leading through woods dominated by pine, along with beech and holly. Cruise the sloped shore above 760-acre Merchants Millpond, created two-plus centuries back, when Bennetts Creek was dammed to provide waterpower to operate a mill. Later, storekeepers set up near this community gathering spot, leading to the *Merchants* in the millpond's name. Moss-draped cypress and gum dot the shore and pond proper.

At .3 mile, near a canoe launch, a spur trail leads right to the visitor center. Keep straight here, joining the Bennetts Creek Trail. Reach and carefully cross paved Millpond Road near its intersection with Honey Pot Road. Keep straight, still on the Bennetts Creek Trail in rich woods. At 1.0 mile, the trail drops into bottomland. Wax myrtle, cedar, and pine add an evergreen touch. Wind amid wetlands, bridging a swamp strand at 1.2 miles. Curve east, and at 1.6 miles take a boardwalk running to the edge of Bennetts Creek, flowing dark and under rich swamp woods. When I think of beautiful places in North Carolina's state parks, this spot comes to mind.

The Bennetts Creek Trail stays along the margin between swamp and hill, passing an old homesite before emerging back at Millpond Road at 2.3 miles. Here, head right, crossing Bennetts Creek on Millpond Road. While on the bridge, look down and admire the dam spillway and the duckweed-covered pond. Ahead, walk left into the boat launch parking area to pick up the universal access Cypress Point Trail. This pea gravel track loops through woods on a peninsula that juts into Merchants Millpond, proffering panoramas of the millpond from multiple viewpoints. Curve past a bench at the tip, then return to the parking area at 2.9 miles. Now, begin your third and final loop on the Coleman Trail, named for A. B. Coleman, the man who purchased the millpond and adjacent acreage and donated it to the state of North Carolina. His gift forms the heart of today's state park, which comes in at 3,250 acres.

The Coleman Trail leads you along the pond and through some of the scenic preserve that wildlife such as deer, beaver, water moccasins, otters, and songbirds call home. It is a true slice of Carolina paradise. At 3.2 miles, begin the loop portion of the Coleman Trail. Work over small hills and into densely wooded drainages. Come alongside Merchants Millpond at 3.9 miles. Enjoy yet another perspective of the impoundment before turning away and completing the loop at 4.5 miles. Now you'll backtrack from here to the trailhead, first returning to the canoe launch parking area, then walking along Millpond Road, and finally turning right and taking the Bennetts Creek Trail and Lassiter Trail to the picnic shelter parking area. While here, why not have a picnic, or paddle the pond, or camp in the auto-accessible campground, or at the backcountry site on the Lassiter Trail, or at the paddle-in campsite on Merchants Millpond or on Bennetts Creek? Come to think of it, maybe you should reserve a few days for your hiking visit here.

Mileages		
	0.0	Picnic shelter parking area
	0.6	Cross Millpond Road
	2.3	Finish Bennetts Creek Trail
	4.5	Complete loop of Coleman Trail
	5.6	Picnic shelter parking area

43 JOCKEYS RIDGE HIKE
Jockeys Ridge State Park

Make a pair of hikes at this unique Outer Banks state park
preserving the biggest dunes on the Atlantic coast. First, leave
the park visitor center on a boardwalk that leads you to massive
windswept dunes over which you clamber to visit Roanoke Sound
before ascending the heights of Jockeys Ridge, where you'll have
360-degree views of the Atlantic Ocean and nearby lands and waters.
Next, make a short drive to hike a loop on the Soundside Trail,
where you visit more dunes as well as beaches along Roanoke Sound.

Distance 1.3- and .8-mile loops

Hiking time 1.0 and .6 hour each

Difficulty Moderate due to dune climbs

Highlights Giant dunes, views, beach

Cautions Excessive sun possible

Best seasons Fall through spring

Other trail users None

Hours November–February, 8 a.m.–6 p.m.; March–April, 8 a.m.–8 p.m.; May–
September, 8 a.m.–9 p.m.; October, 8 a.m.–8 p.m.; closed Christmas Day

Trail contact Jockeys Ridge State Park, 300 W. Carolista Drive, Nags Head,
NC 27959, 252-441-7132, www.ncparks.gov/jockeys-ridge-state-park

Finding the trailhead From the intersection of NC 345, US 64 Bypass, and US
64 in Manteo, take US 64 East to join US 158 West on the Outer Banks.
Once on US 158 West, drive for 4.5 miles to turn left on Carolista Drive
and the state park. Follow it to dead-end at the visitor center after .3 mile.
The boardwalk leading to the dunes starts at the rear of the visitor center.

GPS trailhead coordinates 35.963953, –75.632407

Jockeys Ridge State Park offers the most unique hiking in the North
Carolina state park system. See, the 400-acre preserve on the Outer
Banks near Nags Head is home to the largest sand dunes on the Atlantic
coast, and it's bordered on one side by the Atlantic Ocean and the other

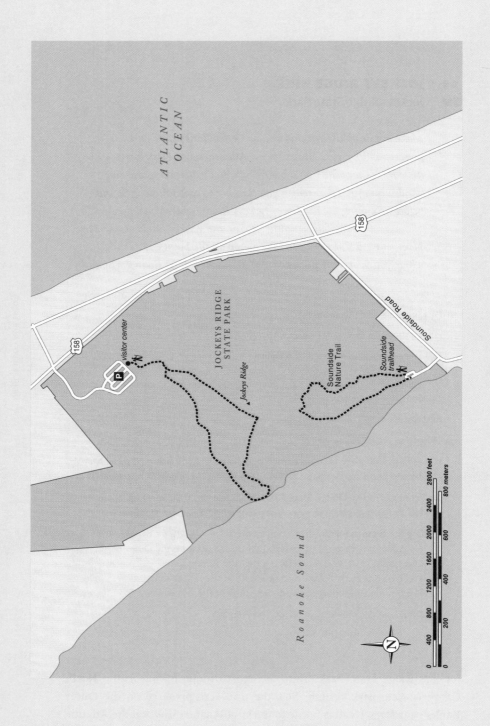

ATLANTIC OCEAN

158

Soundside Road

158

visitor center

P

JOCKEYS RIDGE
STATE PARK

Jockeys Ridge

Soundside
Nature Trail

Soundside
trailhead

Roanoke Sound

N

0   400   800   1200   1600   2000   2400   2800 feet
0   200   400   600   800 meters

This hike leads through the incredible dunes of Jockeys Ridge State Park.

by Roanoke Sound. Tall, shifting, vegetation-free dunes such as this, scientifically labeled *medano*, once were more prevalent along the Outer Banks but fell to development. Such was almost the case here, save for one Carolista Baum, who in 1973 stared down the bulldozers fixing to flatten Jockeys Ridge. The demolition stopped that day, and a group known as People to Preserve Jockey's Ridge was organized. An appeal was made to the state to perhaps create a park. Subsequently the National Park Service declared the dunes a National Natural Landmark, and two years later Jockeys Ridge officially joined the state park system. It is now a natural oasis amid the man-made Outer Banks attractions stretching along Bodie Island. The dunes of Jockeys Ridge are protected, and so are the estuarine coast and maritime forests along Roanoke Sound. Fascinatingly, the dunes of Jockeys Ridge are constantly shifting: they're an active dune system altered by northeast winds of winter and southwest winds of summer. Intermittent tropical cyclones foster faster alterations.

Coastal visitors are normally discouraged from walking on dunes, but these dunes are the exception. The park encourages not only hikers but also hang gliders, model plane operators, and kite fliers to exercise their passions on the sand mountains. The sand in your shoes after this adventure will mark you as someone fondly familiar with the dunes. (And shoes of some sort are necessary here at least on sunny summer days: the dune sand gets very hot.) Start the hike at the park visitor center, joining a boardwalk that leads you through maritime woods back to the dune system. At .1 mile, you'll reach an observation deck with viewing scope. Scan for hikers and others traipsing over the dunes before dropping off the deck and following wooden posts westward, passing partly vegetated dunes before climbing the medano. At .5 mile, crest out on Jockeys Ridge. Continue tracing the wooden posts west, looking out on the waters of Roanoke Sound, backed by historic Roanoke Island.

At .6 mile, descend to Roanoke Sound. At this point the waters force you south, skirting flats between Roanoke Sound to your right and partly vegetated dunes to your left. Enter maritime forest where cedar, oak, and pine find purchase. At .8 mile, turn away from the sound to ascend the heights of Jockeys Ridge. Here, find the tallest dune and go for it, first working through steep, partly wooded dunes. Depending on recent rains, the sands may be firm or loose. You can go straight up the mount of grains or angle up making switchbacks.

At 1.0 miles, reach the peak of Jockeys Ridge. The sand mount falls away in every direction, revealing distant vistas north, south, east, and west. The Atlantic Ocean extends to the curvature of the earth to the east. Bodie Island forms a barrier between the Atlantic Ocean and Roanoke Sound. Roanoke Island fashions a low barrier on the western horizon. Who says all the great views are in the western half of the Tar Heel State? From this magnificent perch, aim northeast for the boardwalk and visitor center, reaching the first hike's end at 1.3 miles.

Now to enjoy some oceanside trekking. From the visitor center, drive to the next hike, returning to US 158, and turn right, southbound, and follow it for .8 mile to Soundside Road and a traffic light. Turn right on Soundside Road and follow it .4 mile to the signed trailhead on your right. Leave the rear of the parking area on the Soundside Nature Trail. Come near a small interdunal wetland, a rare natural community on the Outer Banks these days. Take in the trailside interpretive information as you traverse older, partly wooded dunes. At .4 mile (of the second hike), come to the base of the huge dunes of Jockeys Ridge, then turn left toward Roanoke Sound, coming to a wide, sandy doubletrack. Here the marked trail is wide open to the sun, keeping the sand dry and often loose, slowing your progress. Roanoke Sound lies to your right as you turn south. Watch for trail posts to keep you on track, as spur trails lead right to isolated beaches fronting the sound. By .8 mile you are back at the trailhead. Grab your beach lounger, your cold drink, and this hiking guide, then find your waterside beach spot and relax, dreaming about more great hikes in North Carolina's state parks.

Mileages	
0.0	Visitor center trailhead
0.6	Roanoke Sound
1.0	Top of Jockeys Ridge
1.3	Visitor center trailhead
0.0	Soundside Road trailhead
0.4	Turn toward Roanoke Sound
0.8	Soundside Road trailhead

44   PETTIGREW DOUBLE HIKE
Pettigrew State Park

Enjoy two hikes from the same trailhead here at historic Pettigrew State Park, overlooking scenic Phelps Lake, a Carolina bay lake. First, hike the Moccasin Trail on a strip of park land nestled between Phelps Lake and adjacent farms to reach Moccasin Overlook, offering splendid vistas of Phelps Lake. After returning to the trailhead, trace a swamp boardwalk leading to the restored plantation known as Somerset Place. Explore the history and structures found there. Hike on past big trees to stop by Pettigrew Cemetery, then grab a final vista at Bee Tree Overlook.

Interestingly, Pettigrew State Park is used as a way-stop for visitors heading to the Outer Banks. A ranger here told me he's seen "people from all over the world" enjoying this state park set in far eastern North Carolina, on the shores of big Phelps Lake, yet another of the mysterious Carolina bay lakes. Touted as North Carolina's second-largest natural lake at 35 square miles of shallow waters, Phelps Lake forms the oval shape characteristic of bay lakes, and this double hike takes place along its shores.

Before the United States became a country, Algonquin Indians plied Phelps Lake in canoes. Their dugouts have been found on the lake bottom, where they were sunk and hidden between uses, but one day the Algonquins didn't come back. Over two dozen canoes have been discovered by archaeologists here. When America came to be, settlers pushed

Distance 5.6- and 4.4-mile out-and-backs

Hiking time 2.8 and 2.2 hours, respectively

Difficulty Moderate to difficult

Highlights Phelps Lake views, Somerset Place, big trees

Cautions None

Best seasons Early fall through late spring

Other trail users Mountain bikers

Hours November–February, 8 a.m.–6 p.m.; March–May, September–October, 8 a.m.–8 p.m.; June–August, 8 a.m.–9 p.m.; closed Christmas Day

Trail contact Pettigrew State Park, 2252 Lake Shore Road, Creswell, NC 27928, 252-797-4475, www.ncparks.gov/pettigrew-state-park; https://historicsites.nc.gov/all-sites/somerset-place

Finding the trailhead From Exit 558 on US 64 near Creswell, head south on Sixth Street and follow it .4 mile to turn left onto E. Main Street. Follow it for 1.9 miles, then turn right onto Thirty Foot Canal Road and follow it for 4.5 miles. Turn left onto Lake Shore Road, then right into Pettigrew State Park. Curve right past the park office, then keep straight for the boat ramp: there you'll see the trailhead on the left.

GPS trailhead coordinates 35.791545, –76.410073

west from the coast, and one Josiah Collins built a plantation, farming the rich soils along Phelps Lake. He named his parcel Somerset Place, and it grew for fourscore years, becoming its own self-sufficient village. More than fifty buildings rose up, including a laundry, church, stables, and mills. Over a thousand people, including 850 enslaved people, called Somerset Place home by the time the Civil War found its way to eastern North Carolina.

The Civil War freed the enslaved individuals of Somerset Place, and the 100,000-acre plantation subsequently fell to ruin decade after decade, until in 1939 it became part of newly established Pettigrew State Park. Today the restored site is a highlight of this hike. Make sure to build in time to explore the place. In addition, interpreter-led tours and living history demonstrations are conducted regularly. Interestingly, though Somerset Plantation was huge, the park was named for its next-door neighbors, the Pettigrews, who owned a farm dubbed Bonarva. All that remains of their place is the family cemetery you will see on this hike.

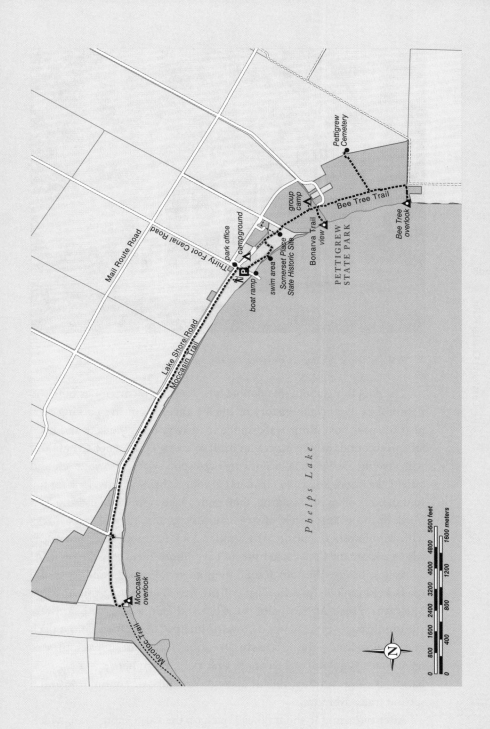

Mail Route Road

Thirty Foot Canal Road

park office

campground

boat ramp

swim area

Somerset Place
State Historic Site

group
camp

Bonarva Trail
view

Bee Tree Trail

Pettigrew
Cemetery

Bee Tree
overlook

PETTIGREW
STATE PARK

Lake Shore Road

Moccasin Trail

Moccasin
overlook

Moloac Trail

Phelps Lake

0   800 1600 2400 3200 4000 4800 5600 feet
0   400   800   1200   1600 meters

N

Restored Somerset Place is a highlight of this hike.

The cool thing about this double hike is that it incorporates both the natural beauty and the history of Phelps Lake. From the parking area near the park boat ramp, walk up the road away from the lake and head left, westbound, on the Moccasin Trail to cross Thirty Foot Canal. You will have the lake with adjacent viny hardwood swamps to your left and quiet Lake Shore Road and farmland to your right. At .3 mile, look for the foundations of an old building, then grab a lake view while passing by a break in the swamp forest of sweetgum, sycamore, tupelo, and cypress with wildflowers in spring. At 1.2 miles, look for more lake views near where Mountain Canal Road meets Lake Shore Road to your right. At 2.3 miles, bridge Western Canal, then enter tall woods and leave the roads behind. This is a fine part of the first hike. At 2.7 miles, reach Moccasin Canal. At this point, turn left and gain a lengthy boardwalk cutting through cypress woods toward Phelps Lake. Open onto a deck and Phelps Lake—the Moccasin Overlook. Gaze out across miles of open water. Big Point stands out to your right. From here it is a 2.8-mile backtrack. You can treat this as a standalone hike or continue with the second trail adventure.

After returning to the trailhead, pick up the Lake Shore Trail, which at this point is a boardwalk curving amid swampy maple forest rich with ferns. The boardwalk continues for .4 mile. A ranger here told me it uses enough lumber to build two houses! Be grateful for the chance to hike this gem of a state park track. At .2 mile of the second hike, a spur boardwalk splits right to the park swimming area on Phelps Lake. Stay with the boardwalk of the Lake Shore Trail. At .4 mile the boardwalk ends. Here a spur trail leads left to the park campground (recommended, by the way), but we head right to quickly reach Somerset Place State Historic Site. You can check out the seven original buildings along with the reconstructed structures now or when you return. At .5 mile, resume the trail, leaving the historic site behind.

At .8 mile, pass a spur trail going left to the state park group camp. Then you come to the Bonarva Trail, named for the Pettigrew family estate. Take the path .1 mile out to a fine vista of Phelps Lake after passing through swamp woods. Return to the main track, crossing the Bonarva Canal, and join the Bee Tree Trail. You will come near a ranger residence. At 1.5 miles, take the trail heading away from the lake toward the Pettigrew Cemetery. This wide lane makes for easy hiking, and by 1.9 miles you are at the elevated interment site, raised up because of the wet lakeside soils. Look out on productive farmland. Backtrack southeast on the Bee Tree Trail. Look for old-growth tulip trees hereabouts. At 2.6 miles, cross Bee Tree Canal, then turn right to hike parallel to the canal and reach Bee Tree Overlook at 2.7 miles. Here you can behold the water and not even see the far end of Phelps Lake! Allow yourself time to get back to the trailhead, and perhaps to explore Somerset Place a little more as well.

Mileages		
	0.0	Leave boat ramp trailhead on Moccasin Trail
	2.3	Cross Western Canal
	2.8	Moccasin Overlook
	5.6	Return to boat ramp trailhead
	0.0	Leave boat ramp trailhead on Lake Shore Trail
	0.4	Somerset Place
	1.9	Pettigrew Cemetery
	2.7	Bee Tree Overlook
	4.4	Boat ramp trailhead

45 TAR KILN LOOP
■ Goose Creek State Park

Coastal Goose Creek State Park is the setting for this rewarding loop hike that mixes woods, boardwalks, and even beaches to craft an adventuresome trek. The circuit first treads an extensive wetland boardwalk, then traces foot trails along Goose Creek and the massive Pamlico River, cruising beside beaches before turning into coastal woods along Mallard Creek, passing the site of tar kilns, where naval stores were once produced.

Distance 7.2-mile balloon loop

Hiking time 3.8 hours

Difficulty Moderate

Highlights Tidal waters views, deep woods, wetlands, historic tar kilns

Cautions None

Best seasons Early fall through early summer

Other trail users None

Hours November–February, 8 a.m.–6 p.m.; March–May, September–October, 8 a.m.–8 p.m.; June–August, 8 a.m.–9 p.m.; closed Christmas Day

Trail contact Goose Creek State Park, 2190 Camp Leach Road, Washington, NC 27889, 252-923-2191, www.ncparks.gov/goose-creek-state-park

Finding the trailhead From Washington, NC, head east on US 264 for 9 miles, then turn right on Camp Leach Road (NC 1334). Follow it 2.2 miles to the park. After entering the park, follow Main Road a short distance to the environmental education center, on your left.

GPS trailhead coordinates 35.478058, –76.901933

Have you ever wondered where North Carolina got the nickname *Tar Heel State?* Back in colonial days, the woods of eastern North Carolina became a source of naval stores—tar, pitch, and turpentine—tapped from pine trees and then processed. These products, used to make wooden ships watertight, were why North Carolina became known as the Tar Heel State.

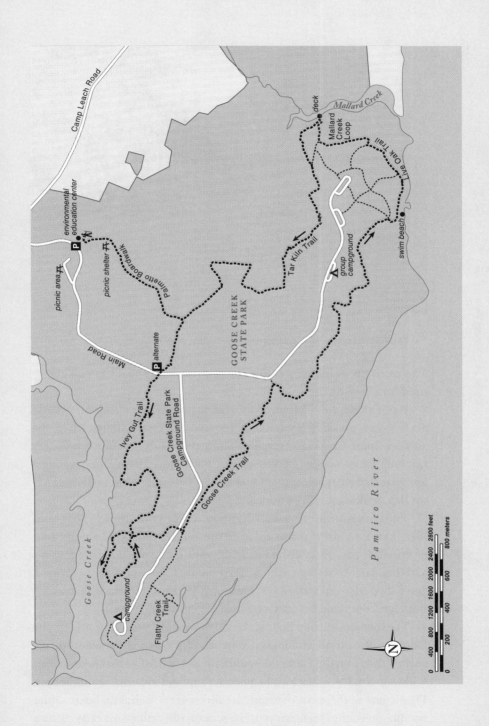

Camp Leach Road

Mallard Creek

deck

Mallard Creek Loop

Live Oak Trail

environmental education center

picnic area

picnic shelter

Palmetto Boardwalk

swim beach

Tar Kiln Trail

GOOSE CREEK STATE PARK

group campground

Main Road

alternate

Ivey Gut Trail

Goose Creek State Park Campground Road

Goose Creek Trail

Goose Creek

campground

Flatty Creek Trail

Pamlico River

0   400   800   1200   1600   2000   2400   2800 feet

0   200   400   600   800 meters

N

This hike takes you by a sand-bordered part of the Pamlico River.

The naval stores industry continued until wooden ships were no longer used for shipping.

Naval stores were garnered in what is now Goose Creek State Park, a 1,672-acre preserve bordered by the massive tidal Pamlico River, the smaller Goose Creek, and smallish Mallard Creek. The peninsula fosters not only piney woods but also upland hardwoods, freshwater swamps, and brackish marshes, transitional areas where environmental ecotones overlap, making it rich in flora and fauna.

The park's environmental education center is where you start your hike, and it's a great place to "bone up" on the ecological significance of this state park, established in 1974, once home to Tuscarora Indians and then later to settlers, who worked the tar kilns, subsistence farmed, and fished adjacent waterways. It was a quiet, slow way of life that seems nostalgic compared to today's hurried, electronic existence.

The hike leaves from behind the environmental center, aiming for the Palmetto Boardwalk in longleaf pine woods. Pass a screened-in picnic shelter, then join the Palmetto Boardwalk at .1 mile. The elevated wooden walkway crosses a blackwater pocosin (upland swamp), southbound. This is one of the most northerly locations of the palmetto bush. Other notable vegetation includes cypress, wax myrtle, and beard cane. Walk a full half-mile on the boardwalk before rejoining terra firma and reaching a trail junction. Here, head right, beginning the actual circuit on the Ivey Gut Trail, while your return trail—the Tar Kiln Trail—leaves left. The wide, well-cared-for pathway runs in the shade of evergreens and some hardwoods such as sweetgum. You may notice blackened trunks of trees in these fire-managed woodlands.

At .9 mile, cross Main Road and near an alternate parking area. Boardwalks span wetter areas. At 1.3 miles, Goose Creek comes into view. This tidal tributary feeds the Pamlico River. Curve away from the waterway, working around a side stream. At 1.8 miles, come to a trail intersection and turn right on a mini-loop of the Ivey Gut Trail, which opens views of Goose Creek again before you complete the mini-loop at 2.4 miles. Resume the main circuit, traveling through woods to cross Campground Road, and reach another trail junction at 2.6 miles. Turn left, eastward, on the Goose Creek Trail. Hike deep, classic coastal woods, crossing boardwalks where seasonal wetlands form. At 3.4 miles, a short spur trail leads left to Main Road. Keep straight here, enjoying the walk in the margin between woods and marshes of the Pamlico River. At 4.0 miles, a spur trail splits left to the park's group campground. This is the first of several intersections in an interconnected network of short nature trails. At 4.4 miles, head right on the wide Live Oak Trail to immediately reach the park swim beach that's accessible only to hikers. The path skirts the beach-bordered shoreline of the Pamlico River, where extensive panoramas of the tidal waterway open beyond the Spanish moss–draped live oaks that shade the sometimes slow and sandy track. At 4.6 miles, the Huckleberry Trail leaves left, while we stay with the Live Oak Trail, eventually turning away from the Pamlico River. At 4.9 miles, turn right onto the Mallard Creek Loop, passing a shortcut to the Huckleberry Trail before reaching an observation deck on intimate Mallard Creek at 5.2 miles. The stream is dwarfed by the Pamlico River.

After leaving the observation deck, you join the Tar Kiln Trail at 5.4 miles. Wind west in thick forest, finding interpretive signage at tar kiln sites where naval stores were made. In places the Tar Kiln Trail uses old roads used by "Tar Heels" to access these pine woods and do their work. Low places harbor seasonal forested swamps, and the Tar Kiln Trail works its way around them. At 6.8 miles, finish the Tar Kiln Trail at the Palmetto Boardwalk. You have completed the loop portion of the hike. Here, enjoy the Palmetto Boardwalk one more time, then return to the environmental education center at 7.4 miles. On this hike you will have completed the majority of the park's 10 miles of hiking trails.

The state park also features fine paddling possibilities on the waterways seen on the hike. I also highly recommend overnighting at the tent campground. The primitive camp is stretched out on a gravel road under pines and oaks. Each widespread campsite features a tent pad, picnic table, lantern post, and fire ring. In the warm season, the swim beach on the Pamlico River lures water lovers. Anglers can catch freshwater and salt species from largemouth bass and bream to flounder and drum. So come here for the hike, then enjoy the additional offerings here at Goose Creek State Park.

Mileages   **0.0** Environmental education center trailhead
0.6 Right on Ivey Gut Trail
2.6 Left on Goose Creek Trail
4.4 Right on Live Oak Trail
5.2 Mallard Creek observation deck
5.4 Tar Kiln Trail
6.4 Palmetto Boardwalk
7.2 Environmental education center trailhead

46   CLIFFS OF THE NEUSE HIKE

Cliffs of the Neuse State Park

Cobble together a fun trek on a scenic protected parcel astride the Neuse River. Take the Lake Trail in deeply sloped woods, circling around Mill Creek to reach the park lake. From there work your way to the banks of the Neuse River at Still Creek, then climb the 90-foot bluffs, which present a fine view of the waterway coursing through woods below. Next, drop to a riverside swamp, then join a sandy track and wooded paths that return you to the trailhead through a variety of ecosystems.

A 90-foot cliff may be no big deal in the North Carolina mountains, but here on the Atlantic Coastal Plain, such a precipice deserves recognition. At this point, the Neuse River flows into steep hills, cutting a bluff in an area that also features clear springs and deep wooded ravines in the

Distance 3.9-mile loop

Hiking time 1.8 hours

Difficulty Easy to moderate

Highlights Park lake, Neuse River, cliff views above Neuse River

Cautions High waters can flood trails near the river

Best seasons Year-round

Other trail users None

Hours November–February, 7 a.m.–6 p.m.; March–April,
     7 a.m.–8 p.m.; May–August, 7 a.m.–9 p.m.; September–
     October, 7 a.m.–8 p.m.; closed Christmas Day

Trail contact Cliffs of the Neuse State Park, 240 Park Entrance
     Road, Seven Springs, NC 28578, 919-778-6234,
     www.ncparks.gov/cliffs-of-the-neuse-state-park

Finding the trailhead From Goldsboro, drive east on US 70 for 5
     miles, to NC 111. Turn right on NC 111 and follow it 9 miles, then
     turn left on Park Entrance Road. Follow Park Entrance Road,
     and shortly you will reach the visitor center on the right.

GPS trailhead coordinates 35.235897, –77.890662

1,000-plus-acre state park. The preserve offers not only hiking but also camping on the hills above the river, as well as swimming, paddling, and fishing on the 11-acre park lake.

You will pass the scenic lake on this hike, where Mill Creek is stilled in a deep valley. Facing the park visitor center, leave right on the Lake Trail, a singletrack foot path curving into very sloped wooded ravine. Beautyberry grows in large numbers along the trail, its purple fruits emerging in early autumn. Songbirds fatten up on the fruit before winter; so do smaller mammals such as possum and raccoon.

Circle around a tributary of Mill Creek, then cut through a gap in the hills. Step over Mill Creek at .7 mile. Keep east to come along the park lake at 1.1 miles. You can see the swim beach, busy in summer. Paddlers can rent boats to ply the waters, but private canoes and kayaks are not allowed. Note the beech trees on the north-facing slope you're walking on.

This park is a place where ecotones of the Piedmont, mountains, and coastal plain blend together, increasing the biodiversity of the region. Atop the hills you may walk in pine, oak, and sweetgum forests of the

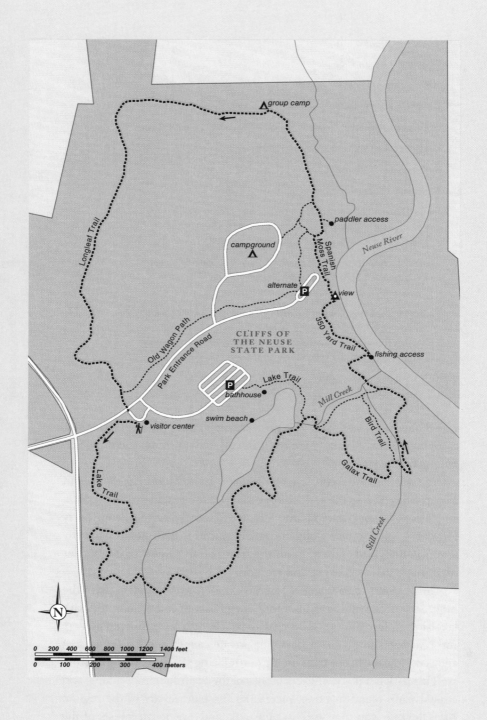

group camp

paddler access

campground

Spanish Moss Trail

Neuse River

alternate

P

view

350 Yard Trail

CLIFFS OF THE NEUSE STATE PARK

Old Wagon Path

Park Entrance Road

fishing access

P

Lake Trail

bathhouse

Mill Creek

swim beach

Bird Trail

Galax Trail

visitor center

Longleaf Trail

Lake Trail

Still Creek

N

0   200 400 600 800 1000 1200 1400 feet
0   100   200   300   400 meters

Standing atop the cliffs of the Neuse.

Piedmont, while down by the Neuse River you can spot live oaks and cypresses. Still other plants include galax and mountain laurel, more commonly seen in the Carolina mountains. Longleaf pine forests recall the sandhills ecosystem and include old-growth longleafs. On the Spanish Moss Trail you will see some sizable bottomland hardwoods.

In other words, you will see a little bit of everything on this fun little hike. At 1.4 miles, head right on the Galax Trail, just before coming to the lake spillway. At 1.6 miles, reach the loop portion of the Galax Trail. Head right here, climbing a wooded hill dividing Mill Creek from Still Creek. Drop to hit the Bird Trail at 1.7 miles. Head right, maximizing the loop, then cross clear and sandy Still Creek, so named for erstwhile moonshining operations in its vale. Continue down Still Creek, then come along the big Neuse River. Meet the Galax Trail, then cross Mill Creek at 2.0 miles. This area can be confusing. Stay right toward the Neuse River, coming to the fishing access on the Neuse at 2.1 miles. Get a close look at the waterway before climbing up to the Cliffs of the Neuse on the 350 Yard Trail, where panoramas await at 2.3 miles. The land drops vertically at the cliffs, and you can look up- and downstream on the Neuse, protected by a wooden fence. (Most visitors admiring the view here will have walked just a few feet from the adjacent parking area.)

Continue the hike, joining the Spanish Moss Trail. Descend along the bluff, passing an arm of the Spanish Moss Trail that exits left. Continue down steps to reach river bottoms and a paddler access trail. Admire big swamp species, including a sweetgum that measures 3 feet in diameter! At 2.6 miles, stay right, toward the group camp, as another leg of the Spanish Moss Trail leaves left. Reach the group camp at 3.0 miles, then join a gated doubletrack sandy road that provides access to the group camp. The walking is easy as you curve south to split left on the Longleaf Trail at 3.5 miles. Here is a relic longleaf pine barren once tapped for naval stores. At 3.8 miles, the Old Wagon Path leaves left. It was used to access the Cliffs of the Neuse before the state park came to be. Finally, cross the park road and reach the park visitor center, concluding the hike at 3.9 miles.

Mileages		
	0.0	Visitor center
	1.1	Park lake
	2.3	View from Cliffs of the Neuse
	3.0	Group camp
	3.9	Visitor center

47 FORT MACON HIKE
Fort Macon State Park

This hike at a coastal island has it all—maritime forests, coastal marshes, beach hiking, and North Carolina history—along a superlative trail. Trek first through coastal maritime forest astride Bogue Sound and then along the Atlantic Ocean beach. After your hike, explore well-preserved and impressive Fort Macon, worth your time for a tour.

This excellent North Carolina state park hike follows the Elliott Coues Nature Trail, except when you are walking along the beach. Named for a doctor who served at Fort Macon, the trail memorializes Elliott Coues's appreciation of the beauty of nature he found while serving here on the

Distance 3.5-mile loop

Hiking time 1.8 hours

Difficulty Moderate

Highlights Live oak forest, Atlantic Ocean
    beachcombing, restored Civil War fort

Cautions None

Best seasons Fall through spring

Other trail users None

Hours October–March, 8 a.m.–6 p.m.; April–May, September,
    8 a.m.–7 p.m.; June–August, 8 a.m.–8 p.m.; closed Christmas Day

Trail contact Fort Macon State Park, 2303 E. Fort Macon Road, Atlantic
    Beach, NC 28512, 252-726-3775, www.ncparks.gov/fort-macon-state-park

Finding the trailhead From the intersection of the Atlantic Beach
    Causeway (linking Atlantic Beach to Morehead City) and NC 58 in
    Atlantic Beach, take NC 58 East for 3 miles to enter Fort Macon
    State Park. Stay with the main park road as it curves around the
    fort and ends in a large parking area north of the visitor center.

GPS trailhead coordinates 34.698174, –76.678787

North Carolina coast back in 1870. Not only was Dr. Coues a physician;
he was also an avid birder. The long and fancy name for that passion is
ornithologist. While serving at the fort, Elliott Coues wrote a birding guide
titled *Key to North American Birds*.

Today you can use the Elliott Coues Nature Trail to sightsee this fine
state park located on Bogue Banks, a barrier island near the town of Beaufort. Start your hike with a visit to the state park visitor center, where you
can learn about the park's history. The nearby ideal harbor that became
Beaufort has been occupied since the English controlled North Carolina.
In those days pirates roamed the Carolina coast, even capturing the town
twice. Defenses were needed, so Fort Hampton (on the site of current
Fort Macon) was finished in 1808. Despite its brick construction, it was
washed into the sea during an 1825 hurricane. A new fort, Fort Macon,
was completed by 1834. Once again Beaufort was protected. The South
occupied Fort Macon early in the Civil War, and the Yankees knew the
fort's importance for shipping goods and supplies here in Beaufort, so
the Union laid siege to Fort Macon. The siege combined with bombing

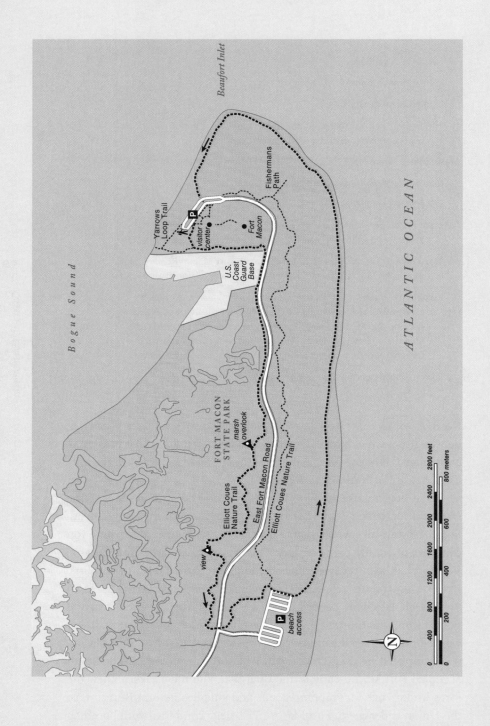

Beaufort Inlet

Bogue Sound

ATLANTIC OCEAN

Fishermans Path

Yarrows Loop Trail

P

visitor center

Fort Macon

U.S. Coast Guard Base

FORT MACON STATE PARK

marsh overlook

Elliott Coues Nature Trail

East Fort Macon Road

Elliott Coues Nature Trail

view

P

beach access

N

0   400   800   1200   1600   2000   2400   2800 feet

0   200   400   600   800 meters

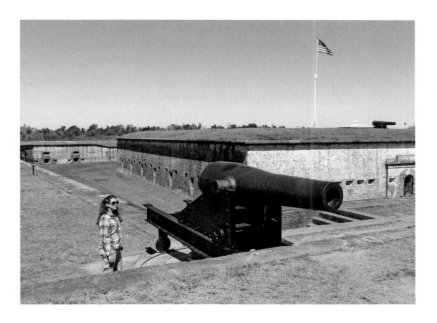

Hiker contemplates the past of Fort Macon.

led to the April 26, 1862, Confederate surrender of the fort. Some Rebels would return to Fort Macon as military prisoners. As decades passed, Fort Macon became obsolete.

This site became North Carolina's second state park (Mount Mitchell was the first) in 1923 after the feds sold Fort Macon to the state for $1. The fort was subsequently restored but was briefly reactivated during World War II. Today the bastion stands as a historical overlay on a superlatively scenic parcel of North Carolina's coast overlooking Beaufort Inlet. You will appreciate the views while touring the fort itself.

And you can hike throughout the 424-acre preserve. With your back to the visitor center entrance, head left to join the signed Elliott Coues Nature Trail and quickly cross a gravel road. At .1 mile, come to an intersection. Turn left as the Yarrow Loop leaves right to make a short circuit. The trail travels along the boundary of the adjacent US Coast Guard base.

At .3 mile, you come to the park access road. The trail turns right. Cruise the grass alongside the park access road in front of the Coast Guard station. At .4 mile, leave the Coast Guard base behind and reenter Fort Macon State Park. Wetlands are crossed on boardwalks in this transitional area where cordgrass marshes give way to twisted live oaks and fragrant green cedars, a transitioning coastal ecosystem rich with birdlife.

At .9 mile you'll come to the marsh pond overlook, a favorable birding location where you might see anything from egrets to herons. At 1.3 miles, after crossing more boardwalks, you'll come to another marsh overlook.

At 1.6 miles, cross the paved park access road. Here a path leads right for the town of Atlantic Beach, but we keep straight with the Elliott Coues Nature Trail under live oaks, then open onto dune scrub brush, revealing big dunes ahead. At 1.8 miles, come to the main beach access parking area near some shaded picnic tables. At this point the Elliott Coues Nature Trail keeps straight, but we split right to a beach access trail heading to the Atlantic Ocean. At 1.9 miles, reach the beach astride the Atlantic. Head east along the sandy shoreline. In the warm season the sands will be populated with beachcombers and relaxers. The American flag flies above Fort Macon.

As you come closer, the guns of Fort Macon rise to the fore. At 3.0 miles, come to a rock jetty extending into Beaufort Inlet. Shackleford Banks, home to wild ponies, stands across Beaufort Inlet. Here the Fisherman's Path heads left to the visitor center parking area. Follow the beach as it curves into Beaufort Inlet, where the waves ease as you turn away from the Atlantic Ocean. By 3.3 miles, the sand beach curves away from Beaufort Inlet. Turn west, now overlooking Bogue Sound on a smaller beach with gentler waves. At 3.5 miles, return to the visitor center parking area after following a designated passage through dunes, completing the hike.

Mileages	0.0	Visitor center
	0.4	Pass Coast Guard base
	1.6	Cross park access road
	1.9	Atlantic Ocean beach
	3.0	Beaufort Inlet
	3.5	Visitor center

48 JONES LAKE LOOP
∎ Jones Lake State Park

Make a glorious circuit around a gorgeous and enigmatic bay lake. Start at the developed part of Jones Lake State Park, enjoying watery vistas, then hike alternating environments from sandy pine uplands to thick waterside swamp woods. Open to more views as you circle around the elliptical lake, looking for wildlife on the water and in the woods. Additional recommended opportunities here include swimming, camping, fishing, and paddling.

Coast and Coastal Plain

Distance 4.4-mile loop

Hiking time 2.2 hours

Difficulty Easy to moderate

Highlights Lake views, Carolina bay lake

Cautions Stay with blazes near service roads

Best seasons September through May

Other trail users None

Hours November–February, 8 a.m.–6 p.m.; March–May, 8 a.m.–8 p.m.; June–August, 8 a.m.–9 p.m.; September–October, 8 a.m.–8 p.m.; closed Christmas Day

Trail contact Jones Lake State Park, 4117 NC 242, Elizabethtown, NC 28337, 910-588-4550, www.ncparks.gov/jones-lake-state-park

Finding the trailhead From Elizabethtown, follow NC 242 north 4 miles to the state park, then turn left into the visitor center.

GPS trailhead coordinates 34.6827, –78.5954

The bay lakes dotting the coastal plain of North Carolina are one of nature's mysteries. Their origin has never been pinned down, but their value has been recognized by North Carolinians since 1911, when the state legislature declared the bay lakes of 500 acres or more in Bladen, Columbus, and Cumberland Counties to be "property of the state for the

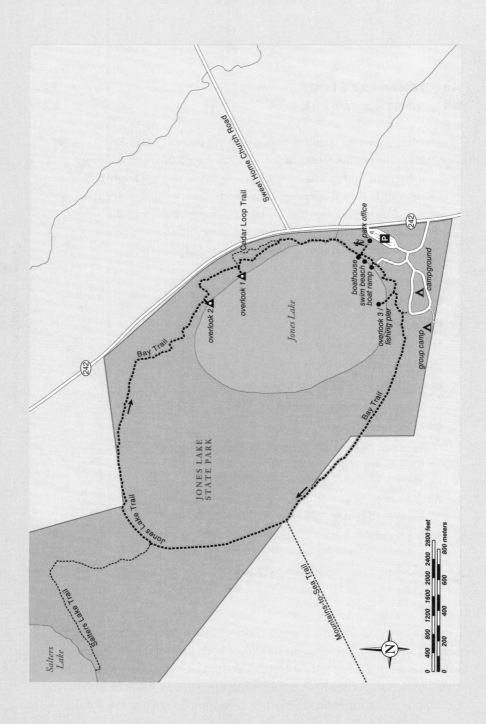

Sweet Home Church Road

Cedar Loop Trail

park office

242

boathouse
swim beach
boat ramp

overlook 1

overlook 2

Bay Trail

Jones Lake

campground

overlook 3
fishing pier

242

JONES LAKE
STATE PARK

group camp

Bay Trail

Jones Lake Trail

Mountains-to-Sea Trail

Salters Lake Trail

Salters
Lake

N

400   800   1200   1600   2000   2400   2800 feet
0
0   200   400   600   800 meters

The park fishing pier provides stellar looks at Jones Lake.

use and benefit of all people." They later passed a law extending the state ownership to bay lakes of 50 acres or more.

The privately held lands around Jones Lake were worn out from over-farming cotton as well as overlogging. The area was purchased by the federal government and restored by the Resettlement Administration, part of a greater federal public works program designed to employ people during the Great Depression. Jones Lake State Park was opened in 1939 as North Carolina's first state park for Black residents. Like all other state parks, it was later desegregated.

Since that time, visitors have been coming to this highly recommended park. Consider combining your visit with other park activities. The campground in particular is a relaxing destination. And the hike is a guaranteed winner. After checking out the visitor center, head out the back door and walk down the concrete path toward Jones Lake, with the swim beach to your left, open among partly wooded shoreline. Head left toward the picnic shelter and boat ramp, and officially pick up the Bay Trail across the boat ramp access road. Here, enter diverse pocosin woods of red bay, fern, fetterbush, and other thickety vegetation underneath a forest of loblolly pines, Atlantic white cedars, and cypresses. Quickly reach Overlook 3 and gaze out on tannin-darkened, tree-bordered 224-acre Jones Lake.

Continue down the trail. Interestingly, this part of the route is also a segment of North Carolina's cross-state master path, the Mountains-to-Sea Trail. At .3 mile a worthwhile spur goes right out to the fishing dock. Perch are the species most often caught, but the acidic, nutrient-poor waters make for only fair fishing. Resuming the Bay Trail, pass a spur left to the park campground at .5 mile. Boardwalks cover wet areas. At .7 mile, the Bay Trail joins a wide service road. The walking is easy on the sandy doubletrack. At 1.1 miles, the trail splits away from the service road, narrowing and running the fringe between pine and swamp woods. You are now hiking away from the open-water part of Jones Lake. Rejoin the service road just before reaching an intersection at 1.6 miles. Here the Mountains-to-Sea Trail leaves left on a doubletrack, while the Bay Trail keeps straight on the service road.

At 2.2 miles, the signed Salters Lake Trail leaves left. Named for Revolutionary War hero Sallie Salters, the lake is 1 mile distant from the intersection, thus a visit to that remote 315-acre bay lake will add 2 miles round-trip to your hike. The Bay Trail continues on the service road in sandy woods and scrub oaks. Leave the service road at 2.3 miles, now on pure hiking trail, in moister woods of cypress and other trees, once again demonstrating that just a little bit of elevation change can result in large vegetation changes. You are in bona fide swamp woods that may prove sloppy after rains.

At 3.4 miles, return to the lake's edge and reach Overlook 2. Here, gaze southward along the remote shores toward the developed part of the park. Continue along the shore and come to the Cedar Loop Trail and a spur to Overlook 1 at 3.7 miles. Follow the spur and relish another panorama of this coastal plain treasure. Keep south along the shore, crossing the outflow of Jones Lake at 4.2 miles. Jones Lake is fed only by rainwater and averages just 8 feet in depth. This outflow feeds into Turnbull Creek, which in turn feeds the Cape Fear River. Soon emerge in the picturesque picnic grounds and reach the boathouse again, completing the hike at 4.4 miles.

49 LAKE WACCAMAW LOOP
Lake Waccamaw State Park

This fun hike at Lake Waccamaw State Park rolls through regal pines to travel along the scenic shore of big Lake Waccamaw, ringed in cypress, visiting overlooks and docks with stellar views before returning via an inland route in sandy woods of pine and oak, where more ecosystems of this richly floraled state park rise to the fore.

Some people think hiking in eastern North Carolina is nothing but easy trekking. This adventure at Lake Waccamaw, though, has it challenges. For starters, our main path on this hike—the Lakeshore Trail—is riddled with roots and dotted with cypress knees. Both can be tripping hazards, so you need to watch your feet and not be too distracted by the gorgeous views of Lake Waccamaw. Furthermore, sandy trails can prove slow going, but who's in a hurry when you have a shoreline North Carolina state park with a rich habitat that first attracted aboriginal North Carolinians?

Early Americans saw the agricultural potential of the lands around Lake Waccamaw. Later, much of the old-growth cypress was timbered for shingles and other wood products. Lake Waccamaw State Park was established in 1976 and since then has been expanded to its current size of 2,176 acres.

The state park was formed to protect another of the peculiar Carolina bay lakes. The heart of their range is found here in eastern North Carolina. And Lake Waccamaw is one of the biggest, covering 9,000-plus surface acres ringing 14 miles of shoreline. Furthermore, the waters here are open; other bay lakes are filled with vegetation. Being fed by springs and having limestone bluffs that naturally neutralize the normally highly

Coast and Coastal Plain

Distance 4.5-mile balloon loop

Hiking time 2.3 hours

Difficulty Moderate

Highlights Lake views, varied ecosystems

Cautions Confusing sand roads in places

Best seasons Early fall through early summer

Other trail users None

Hours December–February, 7 a.m.–7 p.m.; March–April, October, 7 a.m.–9 p.m.; May–September, 7 a.m.–10 p.m.; November, 7 a.m.–8 p.m.; closed Christmas Day

Trail contact Lake Waccamaw State Park, 1866 State Park Drive, Lake Waccamaw, NC 28450, 910-646-4748, www.ncparks.gov/lake-waccamaw-state-park

Finding the trailhead From the junction of NC 211 and US 74 / US 76 near Bolton, take US 74W / US 76W for 4.6 miles, then turn left on Old Lake Road and follow it for 1.4 miles to turn left on Lakeshore Drive. Follow Lakeshore Drive for .6 mile, then turn right on Bella Coola Road and follow it for 2.6 miles to turn left into Lake Waccamaw State Park. Drive just a short distance farther, then turn right into the visitor center parking area.

GPS trailhead coordinates 34.278721, –78.465487

acidic bay lakes leaves Lake Waccamaw a biologically rich body of water. Fish abound, including species such as the Waccamaw killifish, not known to exist anywhere else on earth. Even though Lake Waccamaw is dammed to keep the lake up, the body of water retains its natural splendor and is the headwaters of the biologically significant 140-mile Waccamaw River.

The hike's beginning can be confusing, as many interlaced nature trails lead to and fro. As you face the park visitor center, walk around the left-hand side of the building, then join an asphalt track aiming for Lake Waccamaw. Watch out and stay left as the Overlook Trail splits right. You've got it made when you join the Lakeshore Trail and a boardwalk bisecting a wetland forest of willow, bay, and maple. Look for a covered shelter built into the boardwalk.

At .3 mile, come to a trail junction and another covered shelter. Walk

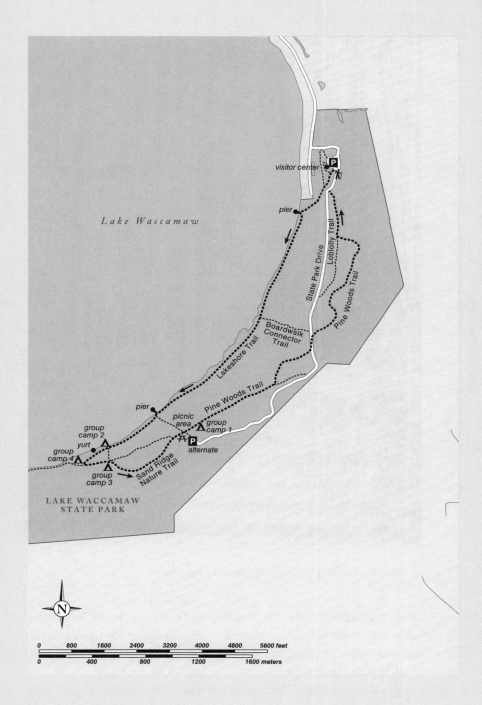

Lake Waccamaw

visitor center

pier

State Park Drive

Loblolly Trail

Pine Woods Trail

Boardwalk
Connector
Trail

Lakeshore Trail

Pine Woods Trail

pier

picnic
area

group
camp 1

group
camp 2

yurt

alternate

group
camp 4

group
camp 3

Sand Ridge
Nature Trail

LAKE WACCAMAW
STATE PARK

N

| 0 | 800 | 1600 | 2400 | 3200 | 4000 | 4800 | 5600 feet |

| 0 | 400 | 800 | 1200 | 1600 meters |

Enjoy this easy part of the Lake Waccamaw Loop hike.

beneath the shelter and out to an overlook of Lake Waccamaw. The waters open wide to the horizon, while the curved shoreline stretches into the distance. After enjoying the vista, backtrack and rejoin the Lakeshore Trail, heading southwest, as waves lap against the shoreline.

You are now free of the trail tangle around the visitor center. Enjoy cruising parallel to the water divided from the lake by cypress, bay, and willow trees rising in thick ranks under a superstory of loblolly pines. In wetter places the Lakeshore Trail drifts back from the shore where upland hardwoods such as oaks and sweetgums are more prevalent. In still other locales, plank boardwalks get you across sloppy spots.

At .9 mile, come to a trail intersection. Here the Boardwalk Connector Trail leaves left for State Park Drive. Keep straight on the Lakeshore Trail, still running parallel to the shoreline, as its name implies. At 1.6 miles, reach a trailside picnic area complete with a picnic shelter. This popular locale is more easily accessed by a boardwalk extending from the terminus of State Park Drive. Take a walk on the wooden pier that stretches well into the waters of Lake Waccamaw. It is no wonder this is a popular spot, where you can walk above the bay lake, feeling and seeing the breeze rippling the waters, and gaining an appreciation of the lake's size.

Resume the Lakeshore Trail, still heading southwest. Stay with the blazes, as old sand roads and user-created trails may cause some confusion. Stay on your toes. At 2.0 miles, the Lakeshore Trail cuts through Group Camp 2, then through Group Camp 5, with its trailside yurt. Stay along the shore, then you'll come to Group Camp 4. Here is where you turn away from Lake Waccamaw, joining a northeast-bound doubletrack that seems more like a road than like a hiking path.

At 2.2 miles, find Group Campsite 3. Continue northeast, and then, just ahead, turn right, leaving the doubletrack and joining the narrower Sand Ridge Nature Trail. Turkey oaks and pines rise above ferns aplenty. Curve along the edge of a landward swamp in an area the park is restoring to longleaf pine habitat. Scan the wetter margins for insectivores such as Venus flytrap and pitcher plant, two more examples of interesting flora at this North Carolina state park.

At 2.6 miles, approach the auto-accessible park picnic area as the Sand Ridge Nature Trail ends. This area can be confusing, too. Head right, toward the picnic area restrooms. Cut across the picnic area and look for the signed Pine Woods Trail. Once you're on the correct trail, you will walk beside Group Camp 1. Not surprisingly, the path leads through evergreens rising above sandy forest floor. At 3.1 miles, a side trail follows an old sand road to State Park Drive. Stay with the Pine Woods Trail as it reaches State Park Drive at 3.4 miles. Here, follow the road north, and then, at 3.5 miles, split right with the Pine Woods Trail as the Boardwalk Connector Trail leaves left for Lake Waccamaw. The walking is easy and glorious amid the swaying pines, then you turn right on meeting the Loblolly Trail at 4.1 miles. More easy woodland strolling brings you back to cross State Park Drive one last time before you reach the visitor center at 4.5 miles, completing the biologically diverse hike at Lake Waccamaw State Park.

<table>
<tr><td>Mileages</td><td>0.0</td><td>Visitor center trailhead</td></tr>
<tr><td></td><td>0.9</td><td>Boardwalk Connector Trail leaves left</td></tr>
<tr><td></td><td>1.6</td><td>Pier</td></tr>
<tr><td></td><td>2.2</td><td>Right on Sand Ridge Nature Trail</td></tr>
<tr><td></td><td>2.6</td><td>Auto-accessible picnic area</td></tr>
<tr><td></td><td>4.1</td><td>Right on Loblolly Trail</td></tr>
<tr><td></td><td>4.5</td><td>Visitor center trailhead</td></tr>
</table>

50 CAROLINA BEACH HIKE
▇ Carolina Beach State Park

This superlative coastal hike makes the grade and will leave you wondering what the other offerings are at the first-rate Carolina Beach State Park near Wilmington. Hike along the tidal Cape Fear River and its pocket beaches before coming to a marsh overlook. Then climb lofty and historic Sugarloaf Dune and savor the view. From there, trek sandy wooded hills before tracing the Flytrap Trail, home to carnivorous flora such as the Venus flytrap and pitcher plants, en route to the trailhead.

Carolina Beach State Park is one of North Carolina's finest coastal preserves. Not only does it feature a tremendous trail system that we explore on this hike, but it also presents quality camping, paddling (the park offers on-site kayak rentals), fishing for marine species, and picnicking. Naturally speaking, the state park is in the heart of the range for that attention-grabbing carnivorous plant known as the Venus flytrap.

And we can experience this park's varied ecosystem on this hike that uses a portion of the preserve's 9 miles of trails, which roll along coastal marshes, quaint beaches, tall dunes, and freshwater ponds. Although this is a coastal preserve, it is surprisingly hilly. Another thing: Bring a trail map to help you navigate the many trail intersections on this park tour of a hike. From the south corner of the marina parking area at a trail signboard, pick up the Sugarloaf Trail, heading right, southwest, under oaks, cedar, wax myrtle, and loblolly pines. You can spot the Cape Fear

Distance 5.6-mile loop

Hiking time 3.1 hours

Difficulty Moderate

Highlights Beaches, huge dunes, views, coastal woods

Cautions Lots of possible sun exposure

Best seasons Early fall through late spring

Other trail users None

Hours December–January, 7 a.m.–6 p.m.; February, 7 a.m.–7 p.m.;
    March–April, 7 a.m.–9 p.m.; May–September, 7 a.m.–10 p.m.; October,
    7 a.m.–9 p.m.; November, 7 a.m.–7 p.m.; closed Christmas Day

Trail contact Carolina Beach State Park, 1010 State Park Road, Carolina Beach,
    NC 28428, 910-458-8206, www.ncparks.gov/carolina-beach-state-park

Finding the trailhead From Wilmington, drive south on US 421
    for 15 miles, crossing the Intracoastal Waterway. Turn right
    on Dow Road past the Intracoastal Waterway, and shortly you
    will reach the park, on your right. After turning right, follow
    the main park road, which dead-ends at the park marina. The
    trailhead is in the south corner of the marina parking area.

GPS trailhead coordinates 34.049033, –77.919131

River through the woods and marsh to your right. Scrub live oaks take over as you near the water. At .2 mile, come along a pocket beach astride the Cape Fear River. Ahead, curve away from the beach to cross a marsh by bridge, entering freshwater wetlands, just one of many quick habitat transitions you will experience on this adventure.

At .4 mile, come to the first of many trail intersections. Turn right here, staying with the Sugarloaf Trail as the Swamp Trail keeps straight. Hike through piney woods. Note the blackened trunks of the evergreens, indicating prescribed fire management. At .6 mile, reach another trail intersection. Here, turn right onto the strangely named Oak Toe Trail. The woods thin out as you head toward the Cape Fear River. Sand and grasses are well represented. At .9 mile, the Oak Toe Trail ends at a perch overlooking the Cape Fear River. After letting the view soak in, backtrack .3 mile to turn right on the Sugarloaf Trail.

Now you are heading for the hills around Sugarloaf Dune. At 1.7 miles, come to the top of Sugarloaf Dune. Grab a historic view to the

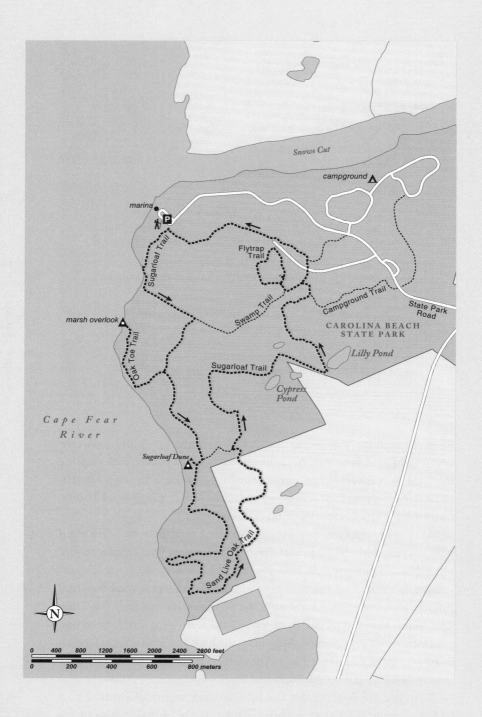

Snows Cut

campground ⛺

marina ●
🅿

Sugarloaf Trail

Flytrap
Trail

Campground Trail

State Park Road

CAROLINA BEACH
STATE PARK

marsh overlook ⛺

Oak Toe Trail

Swamp Trail

Lilly Pond

Sugarloaf Trail

Cypress
Pond

*Cape Fear
River*

Sugarloaf Dune ⛺

Sand Live Oak Trail

N

0	400	800	1200	1600	2000	2400	2800 feet		

0   200   400   600   800 meters

Carnivorous vegetation like these pitcher plants are found at Carolina Beach State Park.

west, as tourists have been doing here for a century. The dune has been used as a marker by mariners in this part of coastal North Carolina since the 1700s. Now, begin dune walking on the Sand Live Oak Trail, rolling over wooded sands running roughly along the Cape Fear River. Begin looping around a wetland before reentering sandy forest rich with short turkey oaks and taller longleaf pines. Stay with the trail blazes from here on out, as old roads can lead you astray from the correct path. In places you will hike atop open, blinding white sand.

At 3.4 miles, turn right after once again meeting the Sugarloaf Trail. Continue walking through less hilly piney woods to come near Cypress Pond. This is one of the park's limesink ponds, sinkholes formed where limestone dissolved, creating a depression that fills with water. Interestingly, Cypress Pond is bordered by dwarf cypress trees, growing less robustly due to the nutrient-poor soils characteristic of the preserve. More limesink ponds lie ahead. Though the Venus flytrap is the star of the show here, two carnivorous plants can be found around these ponds. Bladderwort, known for its yellow flowers growing a few inches above the surface of the pond, uses small bladders to ensnare tiny invertebrate pond creatures after the bladderwort's trigger hairs are set off. Sundews also grow along the edges of these ponds. The nectar-like lure entices insects; the bugs get trapped by the plant's sticky leaves, and then its hairs wrap around them. All of these carnivorous plants are gaining essential food to survive these poor soils.

At 4.1 miles, turn left at Lilly Pond as an old road keeps straight. True to its name, the pond is rich with water lilies. At 4.5 miles, meet a leg of the Campground Trail. Turn left here, then meet the Swamp Trail and turn left on it, only to immediately come to the Flytrap Trail and stay right, making a clockwise circuit. The path takes you near the parking area of the Flytrap Trail, where park visitors make a short walk to see this unusual plant and other carnivores, such as the pitcher plant.

At 5.1 miles, come to the Swamp Trail again after looping the Flytrap Trail. Follow it northeast, passing the Campground Trail again, then cross the paved Flytrap Trail parking area access road. At 5.2 miles you will reunite with the Sugarloaf Trail one last time. Here, enter taller rich woods, passing a leg of the Campground Trail to bisect a coastal freshwater swamp via boardwalk, experiencing yet another habitat before returning to the trailhead at 5.6 miles.

Mileages		
	0.0	Marina parking area
	0.9	Oak Toe Trail viewing platform
	1.7	Top of Sugarloaf Dune
	4.1	Lilly Pond
	5.6	Marina parking area

51 THE HERMIT HIKE
■ Fort Fisher State Recreation Area

This unusual historic hike at Fort Fisher State Recreation Area near Wilmington leads you to the home of Robert Harrill, a squatter who lived in a World War II bunker before passing away. You will follow the Basin Trail to an overlook of the Cape Fear River. After backtracking, turn out to a wide-open Atlantic Ocean beach, walking the sandy shore.

Distance 3.0-mile out-and-back

Hiking time 1.5 hours

Difficulty Easy

Highlights Hermit home, views, Atlantic Ocean, adjacent Civil War Museum

Cautions Excessive sun possible

Best seasons Fall through spring

Other trail users None

Hours December–February, 8 a.m.–6 p.m.; March and October, 8 a.m.–7 p.m.; April–May, September, 8 a.m.–8 p.m.; June–August: 8 a.m.–9 p.m.; closed Christmas Day

Trail contact Fort Fisher State Recreation Area, 1000 Loggerhead Road, Kure Beach, NC 28449, 910-458-5798, www.ncparks.gov/fort-fisher-state-recreation-area

Finding the trailhead From the intersection of US 421 and NC 132 on the south side of Wilmington, take US 421 South and travel for 6.6 miles, then turn right onto Dow Road. Follow it for 4 miles to turn right onto Fort Fisher Boulevard (still US 421) in Kure Beach. Follow Fort Fisher Boulevard for 2.3 miles, then turn left onto Loggerhead Road and stay with it for .2 mile to reach the state recreation area visitor center on your left.

GPS trailhead coordinates 33.964444, –77.922599

Most visitors coming to Fort Fisher State Recreation have ocean-based activities on their mind rather than hiking. But they are missing out, especially when they could hike to the home of a curious hermit and enjoy some oceanside trekking out here on the Cape Fear Peninsula near Wilmington. Enhance your hike with a visit to the North Carolina Aquarium as well as the Civil War Museum, both on site.

Fort Fisher, strategically located at the southern tip of Cape Fear where the Cape Fear River enters the Atlantic Ocean, was built by the Confederates in 1861 to defend the port of Wilmington, an important link in their military supply chain, as well as an export center where the South sold goods to British smugglers. As the war carried on, Wilmington grew in importance to Johnny Reb, while other southern harbors fell to the Union, making everything from food to uniforms more difficult to obtain. But well-constructed Fort Fisher held on till January 1865, when Union forces on land and sea took the bastion. Robert E. Lee's Army of Northern Virginia then lost its last supply depot, hastening the war's end.

Fort Fisher remained a military installation, and during World War II Fort Fisher became a training ground and firing range. It was then that the concrete bunker where future hermit Robert E. Harrill lived was constructed. From 1955 to 1972 Mr. Harrill—better known as the Fort Fisher Hermit—resided here. Rumored to be an escapee from a mental institution, Harrill was born and raised in the western part of the state, near Morganton. How he got here is a mystery, but once he set up he stayed for good, returning even after he was forcibly removed. As time went on, coastal tourists came to visit the recluse, who played his role of sage to the hilt, a would-be wise man gratefully accepting alms from pilgrims visiting his home/bunker. Harrill also lived off the land and sea, growing vegetables as well as harvesting oysters, clams, and fish.

Not all visitors happily signed the hermit's guest book. Some came to harass and argue with him. Yet at one time he was one of the biggest tourist attractions along the coast near Wilmington, thus it was hard to call him a true hermit. And in 1972, Harrill was found deceased in his bunker. Although his death certificate says he died of a heart attack, his death has remained something of a mystery, keeping his legend alive. And a half century later, his story lives on.

On this hike you can see the location where the hermit carried on. Begin this hike by leaving south from the worth-a-visit park visitor center on the Basin Trail, crossing a four-wheel-drive beach access road. The hiking trail then enters low, windswept cedar, oak, and yaupon forest. At .1 mile, bridge a small waterway as a spur trail goes left to an Atlantic Ocean beach. Remember this spot, as you will return to it later. Continue south, staying in forest astride wetlands. At .2 mile, cross another canal as

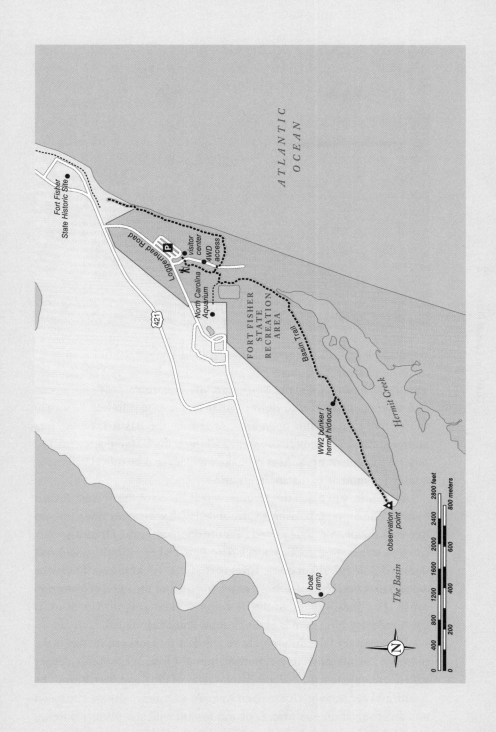

ATLANTIC OCEAN

Fort Fisher State Historic Site

Loggerhead Road

P

visitor center

4WD access

North Carolina Aquarium

421

FORT FISHER STATE RECREATION AREA

Basin Trail

WW2 bunker / hermit hideout

Hermit Creek

observation point

The Basin

boat ramp

N

0   400   800   1200   1600   2000   2400   2800 feet

0   200   400   600   800 meters

Walking the beach on a cold, blustery early spring day.

a spur trail leads right to the North Carolina Aquarium. Leave the woods and enter open sands with views of Atlantic dunes to your left. Be watchful for trail signs in this open area. At .4 mile the Basin Trail reenters scattered trees. The slow, loose sand walking is over. Marsh stretches out beyond the line of trees. At .5 mile, join an elevated boardwalk allowing quality panoramas of distant lands and waters.

At .8 mile, you reach the seventeen-year home of the hermit, Robert Harrill. The concrete bunker is surrounded with vegetation today, but you can walk inside. A plaque placed near the doorway by the Hermit Society in 1995 states, "Robert E. Harrill 'The Fort Fisher Hermit' called this deserted WW II bunker home from 1956–1972. He attracted thousands who shared his views of society, government, and the need of 'common sense.' His body was found the morning of June 4, 1972. His death is unsolved (yet). His grave is at the Federal Point Cemetery."

The interior of the dim bunker seems dark and forlorn, yet this is the place the hermit called home. Beyond here the hike keeps south, deeper into the marsh, toward Federal Point. Vistas of the Cape Fear River, The Basin, and the Atlantic Ocean open wide. At 1.1 miles, come to The Basin and an observation platform. Look out toward wild and protected Zekes Island due south, the Cape Fear River to your right, and the Atlantic to your left. In the warm season you are likely to see boaters and anglers plying the waters.

From here, backtrack a mile, passing the North Carolina Aquarium, and at 2.1 miles, hike east to a pedestrian beach access, cutting across a four-wheel-drive beach access on a loose, sandy track. After reaching the beach, turn left, north, along the Atlantic Ocean, passing an access to the visitor center. Fort Fisher features 5 miles of Atlantic Beach within its boundaries. Note: The beaches here are also open to vehicles. North-bound walkers will pass through a popular warm-season beach-lounging area before coming to the north end of the state recreation area at 2.6 miles, marked by a jetty. If you want to continue hiking, it is a simple matter to pick up the .5-mile asphalt path and keep north through Fort Fisher State Historic Site, where you have an opportunity to visit the Civil War Museum. Otherwise, backtrack to the visitor center, completing the hike at 3.0 miles.

Mileages		
	0.0	Visitor center trailhead
	0.5	Boardwalk
	0.8	World War II bunker / hermit home
	1.1	Observation platform
	2.1	Beach access trail
	2.6	North end of park
	3.0	Visitor center trailhead

Index

About the Author

Johnny Molloy is a writer and adventurer based in Johnson City, Tennessee. A backpacking trip in Great Smoky Mountains National Park ignited his passion for the outdoors. That first foray led him to spend more than 4,000 nights backpacking, canoe camping, and tent camping throughout North America over the past four decades.

Friends enjoyed his outdoor adventure stories; one even suggested he write a book. He pursued his friend's idea and soon parlayed his love of the outdoors into an occupation. The results of his efforts are over eighty books and guides, including *Hiking North Carolina's National Forests* and *Backpacking Virginia* for UNC Press. His other writings include how-to outdoor guides and hiking, camping, and paddling guidebooks covering all or parts of twenty-seven states.

Though primarily involved with book publications, Molloy also writes for various magazines and websites. He continues writing and traveling extensively throughout the United States, endeavoring in a variety of outdoor pursuits.

Johnny is an active member of his local church and Gideons International. His indoor interests include reading, American history, and University of Tennessee sports. For the latest on Johnny's adventures, please visit www.johnnymolloy.com.

Other **Southern Gateways Guides** you might enjoy

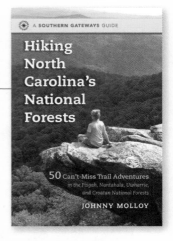

Hiking North Carolina's National Forests
50 Can't-Miss Trail Adventures in the Pisgah, Nantahala, Uwharrie, and Croatan National Forests

JOHNNY MOLLOY

Hiking all four national forests in North Carolina, from the mountains to the sea

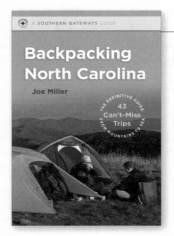

Backpacking North Carolina
The Definitive Guide to 43 Can't-Miss Trips from Mountains to Sea

JOE MILLER

From classic mountain trails to little-known gems of the Piedmont and coastal regions

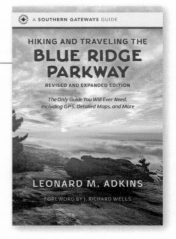

Hiking and Traveling the Blue Ridge Parkway, Revised and Expanded Edition
The Only Guide You Will Ever Need, Including GPS, Detailed Maps, and More

LEONARD M. ADKINS

All you need to know about the Blue Ridge Parkway

Available at bookstores, by phone at **1-800-848-6224**, or on the web at **www.uncpress.org**